WORLD LITERATURE AND DISSENT

World Literature and Dissent reconsiders the role of dissent in contemporary global literature. Bringing together scholars of world and postcolonial literatures, the contributors explore the aesthetics of resistance through concepts including the epistemology of ignorance, the rhetoric of innocence, the subversion of paying attention, and the radical potential of everydayness.

Addressing a broad range of examples, from the Maghrebian humanist Ibn Khaldūn to India's Facebook poets, and examining writers such as Langston Hughes, Ben Okri, Sara Uribe, and Merle Collins, this highly relevant book reframes the field of world literature in relation to dissenting politics and aesthetics. It asks the urgent question: how might critical practice cultivate radical thought, further social justice, and value human expression?

Lorna Burns is Lecturer in Postcolonial Literatures at the University of St Andrews.

Katie Muth is Teaching Fellow in American Literature at Durham University.

WORLD LITERATURE AND DISSENT

Edited by Lorna Burns and Katie Muth

Routledge
Taylor & Francis Group

LONDON AND NEW YORK

First published 2019
by Routledge
2 Park Square, Milton Park, Abingdon, Oxon OX14 4RN

and by Routledge
52 Vanderbilt Avenue, New York, NY 10017

Routledge is an imprint of the Taylor & Francis Group, an informa business

British Library Cataloguing-in-Publication Data
A catalogue record for this book is available from the British Library

Library of Congress Cataloging-in-Publication Data
Names: Muth, Katie, editor. | Burns, Lorna, editor.
Title: World literature and dissent / edited by Katie Muth and Lorna Burns.
Description: New York, NY : Routledge, 2019. | Includes bibliographical references and index.
Identifiers: LCCN 2019007869| ISBN 9781138561854 (hardback : alk. paper) | ISBN 9781138561861 (pbk. : alk. paper) | ISBN 9780203710302 (ebook)
Subjects: LCSH: Social conflict in literature. | Dissenters in literature. | Postcolonialism in literature. | Equality in literature. | Social justice in literature. | Aesthetics, Modern. | Literature, Modern–21st century–History and criticism.
Classification: LCC PN56.S65 W667 2019 | DDC 809/.933581–dc23
LC record available at https://lccn.loc.gov/2019007869

ISBN: 978-1-138-56185-4 (hbk)
ISBN: 978-1-138-56186-1 (pbk)
ISBN: 978-0-203-71030-2 (ebk)

Typeset in Bembo
by Taylor & Francis Books

CONTENTS

PART II
Dissident literatures 101

ACKNOWLEDGEMENTS

This collection has its roots in a symposium organised by the editors at the University of St Andrews, 16–17 June 2016. We would like to warmly thank the School of English for their generous financial support, which allowed us to bring together scholars from across Europe, the US and the UK, and to begin to probe the issue of world literature and dissent. We would like to thank all participants and delegates who contributed to that event, especially Anna Bernard, Timothy Brennan, Sharae Deckard, David Farrier, Djelal Kadir, Oisín Keohane, Nick Lawrence, Dominic Smith, Mads Rosendahl Thomsen, Galin Tihanov, and Robert Young.

We would like to extend our sincerest thanks to the editorial team at Routledge, whose patience and enthusiasm for this project has been unwavering. To that end, we would like to acknowledge the support of Polly Dodson and Zoë Meyer. Finally, we extend our sincerest thanks to all who have contributed essays to this volume.

CONTRIBUTORS

Timothy Brennan is Professor of Comparative Literature, Cultural Studies, and English at the University of Minnesota. He is the author of *Borrowed Light: Vico, Hegel and the Colonies* (Stanford University Press 2014), *Secular Devotion: Afro-Latin Music and Imperial Jazz* (Verso 2008), *Wars of Position: The Cultural Politics of Left and Right* (Columbia University Press 2006), *Empire in Different Colors* (Revolver 2007), *At Home in the World: Cosmopolitanism Now* (Harvard University Press 1997), and *Salman Rushdie and the Third World: Myths of the Nation* (Macmillan 1989).

Lorna Burns is Lecturer in Postcolonial Literatures in the School of English at the University of St Andrews. Her most recent monograph is *Postcolonialism After World Literature: Relation, Equality, Dissent* (Bloomsbury 2019), and she is the author of *Contemporary Caribbean Writing and Deleuze: Literature Between Postcolonialism and Post-continental Philosophy* (Continuum 2012). She is co-editor of *Postcolonial Literatures and Deleuze* (Palgrave 2012), and a special issue of the *Journal of Postcolonial Writing* on the author Wilson Harris. Her work on world literature, postcolonialism, and continental philosophy has appeared in *Angelaki, Deleuze Studies, Journal of Postcolonial Writing, Textual Practice*, and a number of edited collections.

Sharae Deckard is Lecturer in World Literature at University College Dublin. Her monograph *Paradise Discourse, Imperialism and Globalization* was published by Routledge in 2010, and she is a co-author with the Warwick Research Collective of *Combined and Uneven Development: Towards a New Theory of World-Literature* (Liverpool University Press 2015). She has published multiple articles on postcolonial ecocriticism and world-ecology in *Green Letters, Moving Worlds, Interventions*, and various edited collections.

Djelal Kadir is Edwin Erle Sparks Professor Emeritus of Comparative Literature at Pennsylvania State University and a founding president of the International American Studies Association. His books include *Columbus and the Ends of the Earth* (University of California Press 1992), *The Other Writing: Postcolonial Essays in Latin America's Writing Culture* (Purdue University Press 1993), and *Memos From the Besieged City: Lifelines for Cultural Sustainability* (Stanford University Press 2011). He is co-editor with Theo D'Haen and David Damrosch of *The Routledge Companion to World Literature* (Routledge 2012), and with David Damrosch *et al.* of the *Longman Anthology of World Literature* (Pearson 2004).

Nick Lawrence is Associate Professor in the Department of English and Comparative Literary Studies at the University of Warwick. His research focuses on American literature and culture from the nineteenth century to the present, especially within an international context; Hawthorne and Whitman; and Marxism. He is co-author with the Warwick Research Collective of *Combined and Uneven Development: Towards a New Theory of World-Literature* (Liverpool University Press 2015).

Katie Muth is Teaching Fellow in American Literature at Durham University. Her research interests include Cold War studies, African American literatures, world literatures, and digital humanities. She is currently completing a monograph, *Day Jobs: Postwar American Fiction and Work*, and has published on French theory in American experimentalism, Thomas Pynchon's technical writing and other nonfiction, midcentury television, and digital methods in literary analysis.

Anindya Raychaudhuri is a Lecturer in English at the School of English, University of St Andrews. His primary research interest is in the cultural representation and collective memory of war and conflict. He is also interested in postcolonial and diasporic identities and cultures. He edited *The Spanish Civil War: Exhuming a Buried Past* (University of Wales Press 2013) and is the author of *Homemaking: Postcolonial Nostalgia and the Construction of a South Asian Diaspora* (Rowman & Littlefield 2018) and *Narrating South Asian Partition: Oral History, Literature, Cinema* (Oxford University Press 2019). In 2016, he was named one of the BBC/Arts and Humanities Research Council New Generation Thinkers.

Ignacio M. Sánchez-Prado is Jarvis Thurston and Mona Van Duyn Professor of the Humanities at Washington University in St Louis. He is the author of *El canon y sus formas: La reinvención de Harold Bloom y sus lecturas hispanoamericanas* (Gobierno del Estado de Puebla 2002), *Poesía para nada* (Educal 2005), *Naciones intelectuales. Las fundaciones de la modernidad literaria mexicana (1917–1959)* (Purdue University Press 2009), *Intermitencias americanistas. Estudios y ensayos escogidos (2004–2010)* (Universidad Nacional Autónoma de México 2012), *Screening Neoliberalism. Mexican Cinema 1988–2012* (Vanderbilt University Press 2014), and *Strategic Occidentalism.*

On Mexican Fiction, The Neoliberal Book Market and the Question of World Literature (Northwestern University Press 2018).

Dominic Smith is Lecturer in Philosophy at the University of Dundee, Scotland. His research interests lie in phenomenology and contemporary European philosophy (Husserl, Heidegger, Wittgenstein, Deleuze), philosophy of art and literature, and philosophy of technology. He has published in each of these areas, in journals including *Angelaki, Deleuze Studies, Philosophy and Technology*, and *Techné*. His latest book, with Bloomsbury, is *Exceptional Technologies: A Continental Philosophy of Technology* (2018).

Mads Rosendahl Thomsen is Professor in Comparative Literature in the School of Communication and Culture at Aarhus University. He is the author of *Mapping World Literature: International Canonization and Transnational Literatures* (Continuum 2008), *The New Human in Literature: Posthuman Visions of Changes in Body, Mind, and Society after 1900* (Bloomsbury 2013), co-editor with Theo D'haen and César Dominguez of *World Literature: A Reader* (Routledge 2012), and co-author, with Stefan Helgesson, of *Literature and the World* (Routledge 2019).

INTRODUCTION

World literature and dissent

Lorna Burns and Katie Muth

Against the territoriality of national literatures and the reification of genres and periods by institutionalised literary studies, Wai Chee Dimock writes of a planetary literature that is 'the enemy of the state' (2001, 175). Texts 'play havoc with territorial sovereignty' (175) and, for Dimock, operate in an anarchic, asynchronic literary universe that unsettles the fiction of structure demanded by publishers and practitioners alike. Her prime example in this case is Osip Mandelstam, who famously said of literature under Stalin, 'Poetry is respected only in this country – people are killed for it' (cited in Mandelstam 1999, 161). Mandelstam would die in the gulag for the poems like 'Stalin Epigram', and the lethal significance of his work demonstrates, in Dimock's view, literature's fundamental extraterritoriality. That extraterritoriality, she writes, is corollary to literature thought as 'an off-center set of vibrations, chaotic and tangential – expanding with the more or less random accretion of signifying moments, emerging at various temporal and spatial removes' (Dimock 2001, 176). World literature, in other words, challenges stateship when it passes spatial, temporal, and linguistic borders. This is literature's worldly effect, its rippling and polyvalent disruption within the web of uneven relations among writers, books, and readers. This is the revolutionary potential inhering in the unaccountable body of world literature today. The essays collected here take their inspiration from that revolutionary potential, asking how dissenting literatures circulate in a global context and how local conceptions of dissent might help us to reframe the study of world literature as a force for justice and equality.

Contending with a global and ungraspable body of literary works that transgress geopolitical boundaries, circulate across diverse media, and in some cases seem even to have been 'born translated' (Walkowitz 2015), scholars and theorists of world literature in the twenty-first century have not widely shared Dimock's enthusiasm for an anarchy of planetary literature. The editors of the literary magazine *n+1*, for example, condemn the study of world literature today as a parody of 'a Davos summit where experts, national delegates, and celebrities discuss, calmly and collegially, between sips of bottled water, the terrific problems of a humanity whose predicament they appear to have escaped' (Editors 2013, n.p.). At the core of the editors' argument is a distinction drawn between two broad literary periods. They celebrate, on the one hand, literature from the Romantic era to the mid-twentieth century (especially anticolonial literature) that expressly challenged established hierarchies of the state. But they decry, on the other hand, the literatures of our contemporary, globalised moment. Today, they claim, the stuff of literature is abstracted and universal. Pried from the local contexts that give them specificity and political power, concepts like free speech, migration, and identity circulate in a market that values their cultural currency but forecloses their disruptive potential.

Indeed, literatures unmoored from local context comprise the very nature of world literature itself in Pascale Casanova's *The World Republic of Letters*. For Casanova (2004), both the translatability distinguishing world texts that wield high literary capital and the artistic autonomy evident in those that have freed themselves from the determining narratives of nation are signs of abstraction and the emptying out of specificity. The world literary texts closest to the core of Casanova's autonomous literary field or republic either facilitate easy translation by virtue of their universality, or redefine literary modernity by virtue of their avant-garde creativity. In either case, entry into the world republic demands distance from the politics of national struggle and, by extension, anticolonial struggle. This outline, however, contrasts starkly with the proclaimed aim of *The World Republic of Letters* to arm writers of the peripheries in their struggle against the cultural imperialism of the centre. The problem with Casanova's account of world literature is well read by Christian Thorne, who argues that her 'title is simply wrong, utterly contravened by her own argument, which describes nothing like a "world *republic* of letters", with whatever faded egalitarian associations that term still has' (Thorne 2013, 60). Rather, Thorne highlights 'a literary world-system, neocolonial in effect, if rarely in intentions: stratified, full of power imbalances, "a world of rivalry, struggle, and inequality"' – in short, an 'empire-not-republic of letters' (60). Casanova's imperious world literary field not only presents us with an expanded, global canon that promises to co-opt every text under the universalising umbrella of world literature, but also instates a theory of world literature that structuralises a divide between text and the world, literature and politics. As signalled above, and as argued by Thorne, in Casanova's hands:

> *world literature* is the name for a certain tendency toward abstraction within the global literary system, the propensity of works aiming for an international readership to make themselves frictionless. [...] Such, in a nutshell, is Casanova's splendid revision of the concept of *Weltliteratur*, which here stops functioning as the name for an (especially tedious) canon and instead makes its rightful contribution to a materialist history of letters.
>
> *(Thorne 2013, 60–1)*

The irony of Casanova's contribution to what Thorne rightly dubs a 'materialist history of letters' should not be lost on us here. Although promising to offer 'a sort of critical weapon in the service of all deprived and dominated writers' (Casanova 2004, 354–5), the empire of world literature envisioned by Casanova imposes a teleology by which literary cultures move in the direction of abstraction, translatability, and universally recognised themes. In order to do so, they must disengage from the local specificity that inspires political action as a form of resistance and dissent. Dominated writers are hostage to the logic that governs the global literary field: the erasure of historicity and particularity as they assimilate the forms and modes that characterise international modernism, and, by extension, a literary-historical teleology that both originates and ends in European abstraction (Joyce and Beckett are the exemplary citizens of Casanova's world republic).

We have here the germs of two competing accounts of world literature. On one hand, world literature's very modes of material circulation – translation, textual migration and editorial shepherding, and so on – determine its disruptive potential. On the other hand, however, those same modes of circulation circumscribe revolutionary promise, guaranteeing that world literature replicates and reinforces existing global power differentials. Of course, this apparent disjunction is false. It is no more the case that all literature which crosses national or linguistic boundaries is subversive than it is the case that no literature which crosses national or linguistic boundaries is subversive. Nonetheless, an implicit assumption underpinning both Dimock's and Casanova's accounts deserves attention. Both accounts presume that literature's material circulation determines its political valence. This assumption is surely true in some sense. The politics of literature does not exist outside of the production and reception of texts. But the relationship between material circumstances of dissemination and the political effects of a given text is not straightforward at all. Rather, that relationship is contingent, mutable, and multiform. Material circumstances that produce politically potent literature for certain readerships might just as easily defang a text for others.

When, for example, in 1929 W. E. B Du Bois published a letter from Rabindranath Tagore in the National Association for the Advancement of Colored People (NAACP) magazine *The Crisis*, he carefully contextualised Tagore's words to appeal to a highly politicised black American readership. Situated beneath an image of the poet by the British photographer E. O. Hoppé and above a commentary by Du Bois, Tagore's letter appeared both in photographic reproduction and type. As Rachel Farebrother has pointed out, through Hoppé's lens, Tagore's image 'is stripped of historical specifics and he is cast as a "sage" who embodies a timeless exoticism' (2012, 615). And Du Bois's commentary itself shapes Tagore's plea in the letter to 'show, each in our own civilization, that which is universal in the heart of the unique' (Du Bois 1929, 333) into a warning against American provincialism, emphasising at the same time its linguistic and cultural illegibility. 'Many of our readers', he writes, 'will peruse these words with a certain puzzlement. Here is a man, who is colored, who writes with practically nothing of what we are learning to call race consciousness' (334). Thus, Tagore's complicated anticolonialism recedes into the background as an unknowable other, while his celebrity in the West as a mystic is deployed in the cause of American antiracist activism. Material circumstances – both of production and of reception – alter the political valences of dissentious literature. But those political valences hardly map their material circumstances in a static or uniform way.

The essays in this volume ask what it would mean to frame the interrogation of world literatures around the volatility and instability of dissent. What can we learn from dissentious texts as they move among and between political, national, cultural, and linguistic contexts? What can dissent teach us about our own critical methods and about our assumptions as scholars? Rather than asking whether there is room for dissent and resistance within the monetised spheres of global publishing, translation, and literary prestige, we ask how dissent might be expressed and how, as literary scholars, we might develop a criticism that learns from international resistance, furthers social justice, and values human expression in all its particularity. While the contemporary study of world literature often attends to circulation, market systems, and cultural capital, the essays collected here reframe the field in relation to dissenting politics and aesthetics. We address, for example, the themes of knowledge work and the epistemology of ignorance, a rhetoric of innocence and enchantment, and the aesthetics of revolution, asking in each case how we might theorise a world literature that cultivates radical thought and that supports uncompromising resistance to the apparatuses of global inequality. Bringing together scholars of world and postcolonial literatures, the volume asks how critical practice in these fields might meaningfully incorporate dissent as a corrective to interpretive habits that erode literature's local potency or that smooth the jagged contours of its unpredictable movement across space and time.

The essays in this volume resist, too, the entrepreneurial impulses that reduce writers to global brands, and texts to mere expressions of national or cultural capital. We are not alone in raising concerns about world literature's despecifying pull and the market pressures that seek to exploit it. Aamir Mufti takes aim against a global publishing market in which Anglophone Indian writers are 'packaged in the world literary system [...] as an instance of pure diversity' even while their educational background and literary success marks them as 'the end product of an epochal historical process of assimilation' (2010, 492). David Damrosch has worried that under world literature's current rejuvenation, historical specificity and difference become something like the '"local color" tipped in to distinguish the lobby of the Jakarta Hilton from that of its Cancún counterpart' (2003, 17). Emily Apter condemns the field for 'flaccid globalisms' whose superficial commitment to alterity does 'little more than to buttress neoliberal "big tent" syllabi' (2013, 7–8). Even Pascale Casanova has associated commercialised world literature with the generic repetition of 'tested aesthetic formulas designed to appeal to the widest possible readership' (2004, 171) – a claim which reveals the inconsistency at the core of *The World Republic.* For all that Casanova rails against the imperialism of the centre and against the currency of standardised literary forms, she quite obviously promotes modernist abstraction and with it the frictionless translatability that grants texts and writers the greatest degree of literary capital. This, then, is one challenge facing contemporary world literary theory: valuing difference against global capital's homogenising forces and the aesthetic standardisation that Erich Auerbach prophesied would be the end of world literature (cf Auerbach 1969, 3), and at the same time setting out the case for a capacious theory that will account for the production, circulation, and reception of an infinitely diverse body of texts.

Casanova's elevation of literary innovation and abstraction to the core of her literary republic eschews the radicalism implicit in the challenge noted above because, simply put, rather than theorising the relationality of text and world, and through that process opening both up to potential deterritorialisations (in Dimock's sense and in Deleuze's), her theoretical framework entrenches their dualism and firmly relegates literature's dissident capacity to the aesthetic sphere alone. Indeed for Casanova, as for the editors of *n+1*, politics as resistance is expressly tied to the nation and to nationalist struggle. Literature which enters into this domain will be national literature, and national literatures employ 'the most conservative narratives, novelistic, and poetical forms' (Casanova 2004, 199). In Casanova's world republic, only world literatures display the requisite depoliticisation and purity for entry into that rarefied domain. Unlike the literatures of local resistance, world literatures are works in which 'the almost complete disappearance of popular or national themes [marks] the appearance of "pure" writing – texts that, freed from the obligation to help to develop a particular national identity, have no social or political "function"' (199–200). Behind such arguments is a view of revolutionary politics as that which is expressly concerned with the reordering of a given social hierarchy rather than with its radical transformation: like national literatures, nationalist politics, even in its most revolutionary articulation, will be the vehicle for readymade ideologies and predetermined aims. Indeed, this is precisely where Casanova challenges the notion of politics embedded in Deleuze and Guattari's minor literature. The philosophers' reading of Kafka is wrongheaded, Casanova claims, because 'they hold that Kafka was political, but only in a prophetic way; he spoke of politics, but only for the future, as if he foresaw and described events to come' (Casanova 2004, 204). For Casanova, politics can only address 'the burning political questions of [one's own] time' (204) and will always fail to imagine a community yet to come. And yet certain historical circumstances necessitate a politics of the future. For example, the literature of decolonisation, which the editors of *n+1* celebrate as the politically vigorous precursor to today's tepid postcolonialism, can be lauded as such because authors, such as the 'outraged' Rushdie of *Midnight's Children*, sought to 'radically reorder [...] the nation state' (Editors 2013, n.p.). However, as anticolonialist theorists such as Albert Memmi noted long ago, the alienation caused by colonisation cannot be overcome by the mere reordering of colonial society. Memmi calls for the 'complete disappearance of colonization – including the period of revolt' (2003, 185). Or, consider Frantz Fanon's anticipation of a 'new humanity' based on 'a fundamentally different set of relations between men' (2001, 198) and for which 'we must work out new concepts, and try to set afoot a new man' (255). Both suggest that decolonisation is a stage to be surpassed in the creation of a new society, one in which the binarism of coloniser and colonised, however those two sides are arranged, is overcome. In short, the emergence of a properly postcolonial society (cf Burns 2015). It is in this sense that postcolonialism as a concept gestures toward what Immanuel Wallerstein dubs 'utopistics' (2000, 285). Such a revolutionary project is conceived not as a reordering of the present but as a leap into the unknown, since when '[w]e design our utopias in terms of what we know […] [w]e act in the end, and at best, as prisoners of our present reality who permit ourselves to daydream' (285).

In the context of postcolonial studies, the drive towards a politics of the future, rather than reordering of the (colonial) present or return to a more authentic (precolonial) past, is necessitated by the experience of colonisation. Indeed, as Neil Lazarus has argued in the context of decolonisation across Africa, nationalist struggle could only have been a politics of the future since there was no original, precolonial culture to which the African *subject* (a construct of colonialism) could default postindependence. Decolonisation 'calls for a fundamental transformation rather than a mere restructuring of the prevailing social order' (Lazarus 1999, 79). This is postcolonialism's 'utopistic' project: a politics that is no mere reordering of social hierarchies, but a new arrangement. Casanova obscures this transformative drive and all the potential it holds in her dismissal of minor literature, but that drive is essential to Deleuze and Guattari's formulation of the term. The politics of dissent by their account starts with throwing a white-hot light on the specific circumstances in which we find ourselves in order to reveal that which escapes codification in the present. Minor politics, like minor literature, can witness 'a fundamental transformation rather than a mere restructuring of the prevailing social order' because it is privileged to an alterity that makes dissent a radical act of re*creating* and not just refiguring the present.

On two counts, then, world literature demands politically acute concepts of alterity and of potentiality. First, to save it from the standardisation predicted by Auerbach. Second, to redeem it from the endless reshuffling of extant social hierarchies. But the now dominant materialist theories of world literature cannot accommodate radical novelty. Rather, they describe how world literatures, by virtue of their dependence on circulation, markets, and prestige, replicate the world from which they come. For David Damrosch, world literature obtains its particular distinction by its ability to move beyond its originating national territory through circuits of global readerships, publishing, and translations. For Casanova, as we have seen, the exchange and accumulation of cultural capital forms the whole of the literary world. For Franco Moretti, world literature is 'one literary system (of interrelated literatures); but a system which is […] profoundly unequal' (Moretti 2013, 46). Recently this model has been taken up by the Warwick Research Collective, who coin the term 'world-literature' to denote '*the literature of the world-system*' (WReC 2015, 8, emphasis in the original). This world-critical manifesto sets out a methodology in which the literary text displays the 'registration of modernity under the sign of combined and uneven development' (17). Literature of the world-system reveals the structures of global capitalism, and the task of critique is to bring to light that 'literary "registration"', a task that accordingly 'does not (necessarily) involve criticality or dissent' (20). Evident in these materialist approaches to contemporary world literature is the influence of Frederic Jameson, or at least those aspects of Jameson's symptomatic method which have been questioned by critics like Stephen Best and Sharon Marcus, or Rita Felski. In *The Limits of Critique*, Felski argues that the 'critical mood' (2015, 20) or 'stance' (132) common to the practice of symptomatic reading amounts to a 'digging down' (53), in which the critic makes the text reveal its subtextual complicity with – or subversion of – differential power, capitalist ideology, gender normativity, or what have you. Channelling Ricoeur and Latour, she advocates deprioritising the 'hermeneutics of suspicion' and privileging instead an attitude that treats texts like non-human actors, deprioritising '*the "de" prefix*' and privileging instead '*the "re" prefix: its ability to recontextualize, reconfigure, or recharge perception*' (17, emphasis in original). Best and Marcus likewise question symptomatic reading, advocating instead for 'surface reading', which attends to 'what is evident, perceptible, apprehensible in texts; what is neither hidden nor hiding' (2009, 9). 'A surface', they insist, 'is what insists on being looked *at* rather than what we must train ourselves to see *through*' (9, emphasis in original). Symptomatic reading, in both accounts, not only makes the literary text a secondary phenomenon of the more fundamental reality of global capitalism, but, as Felski cautions, prefigures the work of criticism as a process of discovering precisely what we expect: careful literary analysis will reveal the hidden structures of an economy to which the text is wholly blind. Few of the contributors gathered in this collection would consider themselves to be 'postcritical', indeed we suggest that there is good reason to demand more of 'surface reading'. Nonetheless, the authors gathered here, by injecting the concept of dissent into world literary theory, upend the question of whether texts are mere epiphenomena of the capital systems that produce them. By looking head-on at dissent, we don't seek out subversion in margins or subtexts but, rather, look for challenge and protest in texts themselves. Further, we engage critical practices that learn from dissent and that open space for revolutionary novelty.

In our view, world literature need not be global in the pejorative sense; it can also be internationalist. Instead of focusing on circulation, market systems, and cultural capital, the essays collected here ask how theorising world literature in light of dissenting politics and aesthetics might cultivate radical thought and support uncompromising resistance to the apparatuses of global inequality. With this key aim in mind, *World Literature and Dissent*, adopts a two-part structure that first interrogates how dissent could inform the theoretical frameworks by which we approach world literature. Second, we describe some lessons learned from dissenting literatures themselves. Part One, 'Dissent (in theory)', sets out the theoretical dimensions of dissent in its historical and contemporary articulations as the basis for a reformulated understanding of world literature. Contributors address the epistemology of ignorance and the rhetoric of innocence, the biopolitics of protest, the commodification of attention, the disruption of literary reflexivity. Approaching the subject of dissent from philosophical or theoretical perspectives, these essays posit various dissident aesthetics as curative to economisation and illiberal politics.

Djelal Kadir opens our wide-ranging interrogation of dissent, asking what critical and literary discourse might teach us about resisting the wilful ignorance and strategic disinformation that increasingly dominate the history of the present. Through the exemplum of the Know-Nothing Party in the nineteenth-century United States, Kadir traces how 'programmed ignorance' works as a political tool to advance and obscure hegemonic ambitions. Indeed, Kadir points out, the current rise of agnotology, or the science of ignorance, merely codifies 'a long and tortured record of antecedents entwined with the history of hegemony and colonial empire'. Arguing that we now live under a planetary resurgence of such imperialist impulses, Kadir warns against the co-option of dissent under the mantle of epistemological management. In so doing, he forcefully demonstrates the power of literary historiography to unveil the imbrication of 'spin' with material violence, disenfranchisement, and hegemonic expansion. In reconstructing a history of manufactured ignorance, Kadir makes a powerful case for the value, and indeed the necessity, of critique.

Katie Muth explores the volatility of dissent as a political force. While writers associated with dissent accrue cultural prestige in world literary circulation, writers associated with propitiation walk a fine line between rarefied autonomy and cultural diplomacy. While the autonomous author lays claim to aesthetic virtue, the cultural diplomat plays the hand of the state, subverting art to someone else's geopolitical aims. Looking at two cases of alleged state compromise – Mo Yan's conciliatory statements about censorship in the People's Republic of China and Langston Hughes's capitulation to Joseph McCarthy's Senate Permanent Subcommittee on Investigations – Muth argues that looking for dissent in literature often entails recovering the traces of its erasure. Dissent, in other words, is evental and relational. But this is good news for students of world literatures, whose work it is to detail the complex web of translations, elisions, paratexts, and other supplements attendant on any work of literature in global circulation.

Expanding the literary-philosophical enquiry of Part One, Dominic Smith confronts the possibilities for dissent in within the 'total noise' of contemporary globalisation. Smith's essay exploits the economic grammar inherent in the concept of paying attention in a context where the accumulation or loss of capital can be a measure of (in)visibility and (in)audibility. Like unpaid labour, silence is the necessary but unrecognised condition for such accumulations, but it does not register within the economic grammar of capitalist modernity. The dissident task facing critical theory and philosophy, then, is one that compels us to listen to what is rendered silent or obscured in a globalising world of digital communication, social media, and mass information.

For Smith, silence enables a subversive politics in the face of the total noise of global capitalism; in Lorna Burns's essay 'Rhetoric of innocence or literary dissent? Franco Moretti, world-systems theory and the case of magical realism', gaps, absences, and alterity offer a parallel gateway to an aesthetics of dissent. In this essay, Burns stages this theoretical-philosophical investigation as postcolonial riposte to world literature theory, most notably that of Franco Moretti. Although known best for his theory of a world literary system that is one and unequal, Moretti's earlier work condemns literature as a rhetoric of innocence aimed at securing our consent to the prevailing hegemony. Magical realism, Moretti argues in *Modern Epic*, is as complicit in this deception as its Western counterparts. Interrogating the Kantian and Marxist basis of Moretti's account of literature, Burns proposes an alternative understanding of literature's disruptive and dissident potential. Through the example of magical realism, she argues that alternatives to the Kantian separation of noumenon and phenomenon preserve the relation between text and world, representation and reality, and as such maintain the potential of literature to impact on, critique, and resist the hegemonies operative in the world.

Part One concludes with a turn to a figure notably absent from contemporary debates in world literature scholarship: the fourteenth-century Maghrebian scholar Ibn Khaldūn. As Timothy Brennan's contribution to this collection, 'Khaldunia: The literary politics of radical Arabic humanism', relates, Ibn Khaldūn was the author of the first modern historical sociology and an early advocate of the necessity of a global approach to the study of civilisations. The *Muqaddimah*, Brennan argues, Ibn reveals Khaldūn as an Arab humanist whose place alongside Giambattista Vico and Erich Auerbach in the evolution of comparative philology offers scholars of world literature an alternative to the depersonalising, desubjectifying abstractions of Franco Moretti, Pascale Casanova, and David Damrosch. Identifying Ibn Khaldūn as a forbearer of Marxism and anticolonialism, opposed to the destruction of indigenous cultures and author of the first theory of labour value, Brennan's article sheds light on the humanism and nascent cosmopolitanism of an overlooked figure in the history of modern world letters.

Aesthetic representations of revolution, as well as the revolutionary force of aesthetics itself, prompt the essays collected in Part Two, 'Dissident literatures', to extend the theoretical framework developed in the collection's early chapters. Focusing on diverse literary figurations of resistance, dissidence, and revolution from across the Caribbean, China, India, Latin America, and the USA, Part Two addresses the dissident potential of contemporary world literatures. Here, authors unpack, for example, the literary activism of established and amateur Indian poets using social media as a counterweight to the ideology of Hindutva, the dissident possibilities inherent in the everyday, the 'negative enchantment' of contemporary magical realism, the necropolitcs of Mexican 'anti-world literature', and the revolutionary ecological rhetoric of Caribbean writing. These pieces creatively and concretely unfold dissident literary criticisms.

Part Two opens with an exploration of the everyday as the potential seed of dissident action through the poetry of revolutionary struggle in Nick Lawrence's essay 'Everyday dissent: Colonised lifeworlds in postwar poetry'. For Lawrence, everyday activities such as walking and shopping, when refracted through a literary logic, can become a potential source of dissent. Drawing on Henri Lefebvre's sociological study of the everyday as well as the anticolonial poetry of Aimé

Césaire, Frank O'Hara, Jeremy Cronin, Reina María Rodríguez, and Kirill Medvedev, Lawrence proposes the everyday as a contested site, both subject to the logic of capitalist modernity and a potential source of resistance to that logic.

For Lawrence, the revolutionary and poetic value of the everyday lies in its capacity to confront capitalist modernity from within its governing logic; Anindya Raychaudhuri takes forward this notion of immanent resistance in his reading of protest poetry on social media in Indian and diasporic communities. In this piece, Raychaudhuri traces the emergence of a new literary community of dissent through the circulation and translation of poems via Facebook and WhatsApp. This form of literary circulation, Raychaudhuri argues, challenges the secure attribution of authorship and refigures the poet–reader relation as a non-hierarchical, cocreative practice of reading, sharing, and translating. This poetry, while nonetheless tied to tech corporations and globalised capital, presents a counter-discourse to the anti-Muslim rhetoric of the Hindu right.

Putting pressure on the utopian promise of world literature as a means to sublate the trauma of the capitalist world system, Ignacio M. Sánchez Prado poses the concept of 'anti-world literature' as a powerful response, from Mexican writers in particular, to the theoretical gaps and aporias in contemporary theorisations of world literature. Building on Cristina Rivera Garza's concept of 'necrowriting' and Sayak Valencia's notion of 'gore capitalism', Sánchez Prado explores a Mexican necropolitics that challenges world literary frameworks informed by systems theory and by Heideggerian thought. Writers like Sara Uribe and Julián Herbert, he argues, radically undercut the idea that the lived world is a form of resistance politics. In so doing, Sánchez Prado impels us to rethink our assumptions about literature's relation to geopolitics, economic inequality, and cultural capital.

Returning our critical discussion to the revolution as the literary figuration of dissident and resistance, Sharae Deckard brings together the work of Amitav Ghosh, Lindsey Collen, and Merle Collins to consider the aesthetic figuration of political (and ecological) revolution in postcolonial and world literatures. Drawing on the shared symbolism of the typhoon, the cyclone, and the hurricane as a metaphorical representation of revolution in Ghosh's *The River of Smoke*, Collen's *There is a Tide* and *Mutiny*, and Collins's 'Tout Moun Ka Pléwé (Everybody Bawling)', Deckard argues that world literature scholarship bears the responsibility not merely of critiquing capitalism but of disclosing subaltern histories of repression and resistance. These novels, then, do not simply reflect or register dissent understood as frustration against existing political structures, but offer the imaginative resources for the creation of insurgent possibilities and alternative, postcapitalist futures.

Part Two concludes with 'Negative enchantment' by Mads Rosendahl Thomsen, which explores trauma as a recurring motif in contemporary world literature and as a means to understand, through its literary inscription, the fragmentation or 'disenchantment' of the modern world. By reference to Roberto Bolaño's *2666*, Ben Okri's *Starbook*, and Mo Yan's *Shifu, You'll Do Anything for a Laugh*, Thomsen discusses the literary response to the trauma and incomprehensible violence of world history, and argues that its resistance lies in literature's capacity to imagine paradoxical connectivity and precarious coherence as a respite to the grand, universal narratives of modernity.

By shifting the frame on world literature as a field, the essays collected in *World Literature and Dissent* offer fresh perspectives on the aesthetics of politics and the politics of aesthetics. They intervene in a set of debates too often distanced from contemporary questions of global justice and, increasingly, caught up in descriptive historicisms that stand removed from affective, moral, and ethical interests. Contrary to the tendency toward taxonomy and description, scholars of world literature, we argue, felicitously positioned to converse across borders both national and disciplinary, can and must be dissidents.

Works cited

Apter, Emily. 2013. *Against World Literature: On the Politics of Untranslatability*. London: Verso.

Auerbach, Erich. 1969. 'Philology and Weltliteratur'. Trans. Marie Said and Edward Said. *The Centennial Review* 13(1): 1–17.

Best, Stephen and Sharon Marcus. 2009. 'Surface Reading: An Introduction'. *Representations* 108(1): 1–21.

Burns, Lorna. 2015. *Contemporary Caribbean Writing and Deleuze: Literature Between Postcolonialism and Post-Continental Philosophy*. London: Continuum.

Casanova, Pascale. 2004. *The World Republic of Letters*. Trans. M. B. DeBevoise. Cambridge, MA: Harvard University Press.

Damrosch, David. 2003. *What is World Literature?* Princeton and Oxford: Princeton University Press.

Dimock, Wai Chee. 2001. 'Literature for the Planet'. *PMLA* 116(1): 173–188.

Du Bois, W. E. B. 1929. 'A Message to the American Negro from Rabindranath Tagore'. *The Crisis* (October): 333–334.

Editors. 2013. 'World Lite: What is Global Literature?'. *n+1* 17. Available at: https://nplusonemag.com/issue-17/the-intellectual-situation/world-lite/ (Accessed 15 March 2018).

Fanon, Frantz. 2001. *The Wretched of the Earth*. Trans. Constance Farrington. London: Penguin Classics.

Farebrother, Rachel. 2012. 'The Lesson Which India is Today Teaching the World: Nationalism and Internationalism in *The Crisis*, 1910–1934'. *Journal of American Studies* 46(3): 603–623.

Felski, Rita. 2015. *The Limits of Critique*. Chicago and London: University of Chicago Press.

Jameson, Fredric. 2002. *The Political Unconscious: Narrative as a Socially Symbolic Act*. London and New York: Routledge.

Lazarus, Neil. 1999. *Nationalism and Cultural Practice in the Postcolonial World*. Cambridge: Cambridge University Press.

Mandelstam, Nadezhda. 1999. *Hope Against Hope: A Memoir*. Trans. Max Hayward. New York: Modern Library.

Memmi, Albert. 2003. *The Colonizer and the Colonized*. Trans. Howard Greenfeld. London: Earthscan.

Moretti, Franco. 2013. *Distant Reading*. London: Verso.

Mufti, Aamir R. 2010. 'Orientalism and the Institution of World Literatures'. *Critical Inquiry* 36(3): 458–493.

Thorne, Christian. 2013. 'The Sea Is Not a Place: Or, Putting the World Back into World Literature'. *boundary 2* 40(2): 53–79.

Walkowitz, Rebecca. 2015. *Born Translated: The Contemporary Novel in an Age of World Literature*. New York: Columbia University Press.

Wallerstein, Immanuel. 2000. *The Essential Wallerstein*. New York: The New Press.

WReC. 2015. *Combined and Uneven Development: Towards a New Theory of World-Literature*. Warwick Research Collective. Liverpool: Liverpool University Press.

PART I
Dissent (in theory)

1

DISSENT IN THE REIGN OF IGNORANCE, OR PARSING THE EPISTEMOLOGY OF EMPIRE

Djelal Kadir

Wilful ignorance is a powerful enablement – so I was taught by Harold Bloom, a most able agonist in the gladiatorial arena of poetic discernment and my first poetry teacher in an ordinary place in New Haven, Connecticut, some time in the last century. By the beginning of the current century, I found ample confirmation of that insight in the realpolitik of the world, a substantiation that corroborated for me the worldliness of literature as world literature and the transferability of critical comprehension into political awareness. The distance between wilful ignorance and belligerent ignorance, I have come to realise, can be scant and easily traversed. And whereas poets create worlds by an act of will, historically politicians and those for whom they rule define the world for convenience by bellicose acts of expediency directed through self-serving management of the intricate ratio between knowledge and ignorance, a process glibly encoded in public discourse as 'spin'.

The efficacy of managing knowledge to purpose becomes foregrounded in periods of hegemonic ascendancy when the world to be ruled is ruled with greatest efficacy as the world that is to be known. The declaration of 'critical languages' and the rubric of 'area studies', the institutional framework for academic pedagogy and scholarly discourse on the world throughout most of the twentieth century and into the twenty-first, is a compelling instance of this connection between knowledge management and the pursuit of worldly mandate. This is the historically repeated confirmation that yokes epistemology to empire and links knowledge management with colonisation and hegemonic occupation. Optimally, the hegemon comes to realise, what is not known becomes just as important as, if not even more crucial than, what is known. As with the paradox of negative theology, where faith is predicated on what cannot be known, the doxa of imperial epistemology rests on what must be kept from being known, that is, on what perforce must be strategically ignored. Hegemony's understanding of the potential of ignorance, in other words, makes the production, management, and sanctioning of ignorance of paramount importance.

And the ratio between the level of accountability and the credibility index of those who do the managing of knowledge and the purveying of ignorance can be quite stark, even if conveniently dismissed by the governing operatives and their media apparatus. As the latest polls by TruePublica and Ipsos MORI, who have been conducting surveys of the British public since 1983, demonstrates, what they call the 'Veracity Index' for 2015 was 22% for government ministries and 21% for government officials and politicians (Vanbergen 2016). Given the disparity between government action and government accountability to the public, it should not be surprising that 78% to 79% of the people in the UK think that their government and politicians lie to them all the time. The results of any such poll in the USA, if indeed they should be allowed to become public, are not likely to be any better. Trading on ignorance, or 'manufacturing consent', as the Gramscian title of a 1988 treatise by Edward S. Herman and Noam Chomsky would have it, then, is the trademark of the modern imperial era, and no more so than now, when media are consolidated into monopolistic corporations, monolithic ideologies, and univocal echo chambers. Edward Bernays, Sigmund Freud's nephew and the man who in the twentieth century legitimated propaganda under the name of 'public relations', lived long enough, over a hundred years, 104 to be exact (1891–1995), to see what he termed 'the engineering of consent' rule the world. Any theorisation and pedagogy that would countenance and aim to ethically contest hegemony, colonisation, and the predations of imperial extraction cannot do so without taking the measure of engineered ignorance and its paramount potential when purposively instrumentalised. In our task of searching, diagnosing, managing, and purveying knowledge, then, we cannot overlook the fact that the possibilities, virtual and actual, of ignorance may well be infinitely greater and pragmatically more potent than any knowledge curriculum or discursive formation, whether theoretical, practical, or aesthetic, if indeed any such differentiation could be sustained.

It should not be surprising, then, that the vehemence with which programmatic ignorance has been instrumentalised as hegemonic and neocolonial stratagem in the first decades of the twenty-first century has spawned a specialism and field of research called *agnotology*, literally the science of ignorance, most suggestively explained in a couple books from the past decade, one by specialists in philosophy and the other by experts in the history of science. The first is a collective volume of essays edited by two philosophers, Shannon Sullivan and Nancy Tuana, *Race and Epistemologies of Ignorance* (2007). The other, a collection of essays by various specialists in the history of science and the public interest, is edited by Robert N. Proctor and Londa Schiebinger, *Agnotology: The Making and Unmaking of Ignorance* (2008). Neither volume draws the connection between epistemology and hegemony, despite the fact that their areas of investigation are intricately enmeshed with colonialism and imperial history. The first is focused on the question of race, while the latter is trained on the management of information dealing with product safety by the tobacco industry. The appearance of both volumes in an epoch of hegemonic control of information and the programmatic production of ignorance, what is known as the era of 'spin', 'branding', and 'marketing', may not be altogether fortuitous. George Orwell might well see the emergence of this discursive phenomenon as a manifest symptom of what is elided in public discourse, including, alas, in the protocols of university governance, namely, the doublespeak of a neocolonial, imperial era that reigns by purposive occlusion, disinformation, and the manipulation of knowledge for management and imperial expediency. The corrosive role of the media in the entropy of public discourse and the vitiation of any possibility for truth in the first two-and-a-half decades of the twenty-first century echoes the beginning of the previous century, but incisive analyses such as Upton Sinclair's 1919 book *The Brass Check* that exposed those orchestrated catastrophes in the service of capital and its hegemony always seem to have a penchant for getting waylaid somewhere in the warehouse section of the library. The waning of analytical critique in our own scholarly discourse, a lamentable development blithely hectored by certain literary critics (Felski 2015), may not be altogether unrelated to this symptomatology, but it should serve as occasion to countenance, once again, certain ethical imperatives that should be categorical for our profession, despite the structural impediments in our university governance and the institutionalised lassitude of our intellectual discourses.

The paradox in finding ourselves living simultaneously with the most advanced state of global communication tele-technologies along with the super-valuation of ignorance production and management should be no less compelling for our own labours in critical thought and analyses of patterned language, poetic or prosaic, than it is for philosophers and historians of science. Especially since the paradoxical convergence of these phenomena are integral to narratives of literary production in such twenty-first-century works as William Gibson's 2003 novel suggestively titled *Pattern Recognition* and Umberto Eco's last novel, *Numero Zero* (2015).

Wakefulness to the proscriptions that circumscribe and condition knowledge, critique, and the juxtaposition of discursive performance and linguistic structure has been integral to critical thought and pedagogy in the Western tradition since time immemorial. We are instructed from the earliest stages of our formation that an unexamined life is not worth living. This imperative may have never been as critical as it is at this moment, when examining and interrogation are hijacked and reframed as the monopoly of the state and the sanctioned violence of its industrial scale security apparatuses, from whose perpetual scrutiny none of us are immune. Under these circumstances, it may well be imperative to spectralise that venerable philosophical injunction and ask, as well, is an unlived life worth examining?

This crucial juncture in our life world where the imperatives of critical reflection, analytical critique, and the pragmatics of precarious existence intersect is the pivotal moment of dissent and of ethical self-assessment. Inasmuch as dissent comes at a cost, it may well be a test of the courage of our commitment as to whether we are capable of meeting the demands of an ethical imperative we signed on to when we committed ourselves to profess as professors of knowledge and to critically interrogate the known, the knowable, and the possibilities – felicitous, fateful, or nefarious – of the unknown. The alternative to rising to the occasion and meeting this responsibility could well risk implosion into that warped sanity Emily Dickinson, a most knowing poet of world literature's dissenters, called 'assent', namely, a capitulation, willy-nilly, to what is given as it is given. That given, or datum, in our outsized age of hyperbole and hyperpuissance comes in the plural and on an inordinate scale, that is, as 'mega-data'. The degree of any success in our discernment, limning, and conveyance of knowledge may well be the degree to which we succeed in interrupting the engineered proliferation of ignorance and its elaborate web that ceaselessly seeks to circumscribe what can be known and how it may be known. Given the ubiquity and global insidiousness in the capabilities of current informatics and tele-technologies, the ramifications of knowledge circumscription and epistemic management of knowability are immense, as is the profitability in the capitalisation and control of those capabilities. Hence, the economic and political incentives and Darwinian, not to say Hobbsian, competition for governing their functionality. The unprecedented shift toward privatisation of the commonweal and monetisation of public resources that convert the state and its governing apparatuses into franchise and enforcer on behalf of capital lie at the heart of this materialistic Darwinism, a materiality we certainly cannot afford to overlook, especially as it proliferates in our institutions, pitifully flimsy and mean as the material stakes of that proliferation might be.

We should not be surprised, then, by the fact that the twenty-first century is ushered in by a momentous lesson in hegemonic epistemology, delivered by the mouthpiece of the most powerful, certainly the best funded, government agency on the planet – the Secretary of Defense of the United States of America, Mr Donald Rumsfeld. At a news briefing from the Department of Defense on February 12, 2002, in response to a reporter's question on preparations for the imminent invasion of Iraq, on the lack of evidence on weapons of mass destruction and on the spuriousness of claims regarding the Iraqi government's supply of such weapons to terrorists, Mr Rumsfeld gave a reply that is now indelibly etched in the annals of hegemonic epistemology and the expedient management of ignorance and obfuscation as instruments of sanctioned violence. Here is the voice of empire's epistemic reason: 'Reports that say that something hasn't happened are always interesting to me, because as we know, there are known knowns; there are things we know we know. We also know there are known unknowns; that is to say we know there are some things we do not know. But there are also unknown unknowns – the ones we don't know we don't know. And if one looks throughout the history of our country and other free countries, it is the latter category that tend to be the difficult ones.' The page with the transcript of this news briefing has since been taken down from the Department of Defense website (www.defense.gov), thus demonstrating yet another twist in the management of knowability, of knowns, unknowns, and what is foreclosed as possibility for being knowable.

Foot soldier and mouthpiece of the New World Order that had recently been decreed by George Bush the Elder, Rumsfeld was engaged in the verbal legerdemain Orwell called doublespeak on behalf of the impending imperial act of aggression with which George Bush the Younger ushered in the new century and the new millennium, thus setting the stage for a self-declared and still enduring perpetual war. Rumsfeld's centurial, millenarian, and apocalyptic rhetoric that echoed the evangelical zeal of the born-again Younger Bush, was, in fact, a mimetic iteration, as most self-convinced novelty is prone to be, of a poem by D. H. Lawrence from the previous century and another war that was to have ended all wars, a poem resonant with apocalyptic echoes that date to the visions of John of Patmos in the last chapter, Revelations, of the Christian New Testament. Lawrence's poem carries the Johannine title of 'New Heaven and Earth', and serves as a reminder to students and scholars of world literature of the worldliness of literature and the poesis, or making of the world as mimetic iteration of literature. For some this might be a startling reversal, a spectralisation, as the ghostly critical idiom would have it, of the commonplace understanding of the relationship between world and literary representation. Poems like Lawrence's, in other words, trouble that reductive view of the existence of literature as manifest symptom of the world in which it is embedded, on the one hand, or of literary production as promissory note of a perpetually anticipated imminent futurity, on the other. Lawrence's poem is neither. It is at once an ambivalent diagnosis of a historical moment living through the ravages of World War I and an ambiguously keen reflection on visionaries and prognostications of the future. Critical discourse, in its deluded self-perception as midwife of these processes, perennially oscillates between the bipolar obsession of 'New Heaven and Earth'. That obsession dates, in the case of the mimetic symptomatologists, from antiquity and Plato's *Republic* to modern sociologists and their *World Republic of Letters* (Casanova 2004). In the case of the apocalyptic tradition of the Latin vulgate's 'nondum', or 'not yet', it extends from John of Patmos to contemporary postcolonial brokers who wager on the futures of history's commodity market and the expected yield of historical outcome as the imminent ideal community. Lawrence's troublesome poem critically dramatises an anxious prosopopoeia of such visionary schemes, whether these be visions of scientific historians who prophesy the past, or of inspired sociologists who prospect in the potential equities of the future. The poem, written in 1917, is on the long side and echoes Lawrence's reflections on America and American literature at a time when he was seriously considering emigrating to the United States, with his ambivalence at that prospect in full bloom. Here is Lawrence's judgment of the place through his analysis of James Fenimore Cooper's equivocal patriotism and his five *Leatherstocking* novels. Lawrence noted:

> it is easier to love America passionately, when you look at it through the wrong end of the telescope, across the Atlantic water, as Cooper did so often, than when you are right there. When you are actually *in* America, America hurts, because it has a powerful disintegrative influence upon the white psyche. [...] America is tense with latent violence and resistance
>
> *(Lawrence 1971, 56)*

In the twenty-first century, the history of the present demonstrates, that violence is far from being simply 'latent', and there no longer is a 'wrong end of the telescope' since modern technologies have collapsed space and distance and, even when one might not be *in* America, America is ubiquitously wherever anyone happens to be in the rest of the world. The poem's New World, then, is the coming of 'a madman in rapture', as the text would have it. And Lawrence's is certainly not the Salvationist second coming of Kipling's hortatory poem of 1899 'The White Man's Burden', so meaningful to Theodore Roosevelt, more about which presently. Lawrence's prosopopoeia is a primal eschatology that displaces the primacy of all who came before, an emphatic exacerbation of Thomas Jefferson's and Ralph Waldo Emerson's disquietude about American primacy and secondariness. Neither Jefferson, nor Emerson, by the way, figures in the collection of essays on American literature Lawrence was also writing at the time. Here is the key passage from part VI of the eight-part poem:

> Cortes, Pisarro, Columbus, Cabot, they are noth-
> ing, nothing!
> I am the first comer!
> I am the discoverer!
> I have found the other world!
>
> The unknown, the unknown
> [...] Ha, I was a blaze leaping up!
> I was a tiger bursting into sunlight.
> I was greedy, I was mad for the unknown
>
> I, new-risen, resurrected, starved from the tomb
> Starved from a life of devouring always myself
> Now here was I, new-awakened, with my hand stretching out
> And touching the unknown, the real unknown
> The unknown unknown!
>
> *(Lawrence 1994, 10)*

How knowingly Mr Rumsfeld might have been echoing Lawrence's poem may have to remain one of those known unknowns in the annals of agnotology. What we do know, however, is the correlation we recognise between the poetic persona dramatised in Lawrence's poem and the historical person of the political operative as crazed state apparatchik mad with power and the pathology of what at the time was decreed as the defining teleology of national policy, which endures still as axiomatic tenet of US realpolitik in all its righteousness, namely, 'full spectrum dominance' – key doctrine and de facto governing principle of a thoroughly militarised international and domestic agenda. That visionary doctrine goes by the official title of 'Joint Vision 2020', and its script dates from 30 May 2000 (U.S. Department of Defense 2000). The translation of that doctrine from declared agenda into global action is now self-evident; its baneful worldly consequences around the globe speak for themselves. In the case of Lawrence's poem, a critical interpretation as part of the larger context of Lawrence's oeuvre comes from a scholar of theology and psychiatry by the name of John McDargh in a book chapter titled 'Desire, Domination, and the Life and Death of the Soul':

> In his long poem, "New Heaven and New Earth" [*sic*] Lawrence [...] in harrowing imagery [...] evokes the psychic hell of a kind of narcissistic implosion, the condition of someone whose defenses against the risks of mutuality and relationship have sealed him into self-sufficiency and splendid isolation. The poem suggests as well what happens when ideology of domination, as reified and politically realized in the masculine cultures of science and technology, runs to its desperate limits.
>
> *(McDargh 1995, 227)*

The harrowing world dramatised by D. H. Lawrence, and so aptly characterised by McDargh, will find its objective correlative, as T. S. Eliot would have it, in the world made by Mr Rumsfeld and his neocolonial neocon cadres, just as his echolaliac doublespeak reverberates with the revenant ravings of Lawrence's poem. The gender-inflected conclusion of Professor McDargh on 'what happens when the ideology of domination, as reified and politically realised in the *masculine* cultures of science and technology, runs to its desperate limits' (emphasis mine), however, has become mooted somewhat in its gender specificity by the historic achievements of women such as former Secretary of State Madeleine Albright, who considered perfectly justified the death of half a million Iraqi children as a result of her sanctions policy preparatory for the 'shock-and-awe' operation against that country in 2003; by the diligence of current Assistant Secretary of State for European and Eurasian Affairs Victoria Nuland, fondly referred to as the 'cookie lady of Maidan Square' with her 'successful' seven-billion-dollar cookie jar for the destabilisation of and regime change in the Ukraine; and by the farrago of former Secretary of State and failed presidential aspirant Hillary Clinton, whose 'we-came-we-saw-he-died' mission in Libya, as she succinctly described it, resulted in the sadistic murder of Muammar Gaddafi under her boastful supervision, along with the dystopian consequences of her Caesarean operation. Clearly, the 'ideology of domination' and its pathologies prove to be an equal opportunity enterprise when it comes to gender. And what we need not forget, of course, is the historical fact that the first age of globalisation and empire began with the invasion, conquest, and colonisation of what was dubbed, also in the language of John of Patmos and the Book of Revelation, the New World, and occurred under the aegis of her Majesty Queen Isabella of Castile, of 'tanto monta, monta tanto' fame, as recounted in a book in the annus mirabilis of 1992 titled *Columbus and the Ends of the Earth: Europe's Prophetic Rhetoric as Conquering Ideology* (Kadir 1992).

Isabella of Castile set the precedent for the intricacies of agnotology as imperial instrument in the American New World, transferring the modus operandi of epistemological management of the knowable from the Old World to the New. Alerted in 1492 by the Latin philologist and first grammarian of the Spanish language, Antonio de Nebrija, that language and empire are inextricably symbiotic, the Queen had to decide which among possible languages would be the most efficacious for her godly enterprise. Naturally, she opted for God's favoured idiom at the time, which was so designated not by the philologist Nebrija, who, as a philologist, clearly knew better, but by her ascetic confessor and royal counsellor Francisco Jiménez de Cisneros. In the annals of epistemology and the management of knowledge, the significance of Jiménez de Cisneros could possibly be matched only by the third-century Chinese emperor Qin Shi Huang, who, in 213 BC is said to have burnt all the books, except the books of medicine, agriculture, forestry, and divination, and buried alive 400 scholars after they were individually interrogated and, consistent with the perennial history of our guild, ended by accusing each other. Qin arrived at his decision to cleanse history and its memory at the instance of his court chancellor Li Si, a key role the twice-regent for the Spanish monarchy Jiménez de Cisneros played in Isabella's decision to cleanse the newly conquered Moorish territories of all languages and cultures that were not Catholic, including, as the legend of numerology would have it, all of the books of the Moorish kingdom of Granada, some 5000 volumes of secular and Quranic text, except those in medicine, and cast out some 400 scholars, in addition to expelling all the Jews, and setting the wheels in motion for extirpation of all Muslims from Spain within a century. Cisneros was also the *eminence gris* behind the appointment of Torquemada as the head of the Spanish Inquisition and, even more importantly for the American New World, he served as model for Fray Diego de Landa, also a Franciscan, who began his ecclesiastical career in the same monastery as Cisneros, and who left his mark in the annals of history by burning thousands of Maya codices during his holy mission in Mexico which began in 1549. Landa is no less known as an avid member of the Inquisition who introduced a number of innovative technics in enhanced interrogation, still in official use in the American New World from Guantanamo to Chicago. In 1571, in recognition for his historic achievements, Diego de Landa was named bishop of the Yucatan. Thus, the history of the American New World is founded in the intricacies of epistemic management and the innovative acts of enhanced interrogation for the extraction of the knowable and shaping of the unknown, enduring legacies that encircle the American Hemisphere and now circumnavigate the globe.

While still a fairly new field, then, at least in having belatedly acquired a name, *agnotology*, or the science of ignorance, has a long and tortured record of antecedents entwined with the history of hegemony and colonial empire. One thing is consistent in this venerable entanglement of agnotology and imperial dominion, and that is the perennial and, by now, predictable consistency with which programmed ignorance surges with the eruption of imperial impulses. The burning of books and the burying of book people, dead or alive, literally or figuratively, and the foregrounding of purposeful ignorance as epistemic governing principle, have become predictable concomitants of imperial ambition. We witness this phenomenon in the invasion and occupation of such places as Baghdad by the ransacking hordes from the east in 1258 and by the ransacking hordes from the west in 2003. We are witness to it still in any number of baneful locations under siege and continuing occupation, most notably from the shores of the eastern Mediterranean to the mountain passes of central Asia.

The most recent manifestation of this baleful convergence has certain historical precedents in the particular history of the current war-obsessed hegemon hell-bent on invasion, extractive colonisation, and what it terms 'full spectrum dominance'. The mid-nineteenth-century decade between 1845 and 1855 in the history of the USA stands as a textbook example of the convergence of imperial impulse, wilful ignorance, and world literature, a fateful triangle that becomes illustrative of the fate of dissent and also serves as precedent-setting template for wars of choice as instrument of capital and the securing of competing vested interests, economic and territorial, all behind the ideological screen of national consolidation. In terms of agnotology, this period in American history is witness to the most overt declaration of wilful ignorance as political project, with all the pathologies of solipsistic invagination, xenophobia, and belligerence that John McDargh diagnosed in the poetic dramatisation by D. H. Lawrence in 'New Heaven and Earth', already cited: 'psychic hell of a kind of narcissistic implosion, the condition of someone whose defenses against the risks of mutuality and relationship [...] [that seal one] into self-sufficiency and splendid isolation [...] what happens when ideology of domination, [i]s reified and politically realized' (McDargh 1995, 227). The realisation of what McDargh diagnosed occurs in the national psyche and the political party that stands as stark synecdoche for the nation at that time. This is the self-declared Know-Nothing Party that emerged in New York in 1843, was officially named the American Republican Party in 1845, was renamed the American Party in 1855, and would be dissolved in 1860, only to resurface periodically, in key elements of its political agenda and psychic symptoms, most recently in the spectacle of the Republican and Democratic Parties and their televised presidential 'debates' that in saner times might have proved a national embarrassment. But the political reality in the country at this moment mirrors starkly the conditions that brought the Know-Nothing Party to the fore, and contemporary public discourse resonates as echo of that 'nativist' precedent. Not unlike the amnesiac elision of the first Americans in the current declaration of 'America first', in referring to itself as 'native American' the Know-Nothing Party betrayed its racist agenda on various fronts, certainly in its erasure of the true Natives, the indigenous people of the country who had been forcibly expelled from their native territory in the previous decade under the presidency of Andrew Jackson, an ignominious chapter in ethnic cleansing for the benefit of white European settlers that culminated in the Trail of Tears between 1836 and 1839. The party's xenophobic anti-immigration hysteria, principally against Irish and German Catholics, but, no less significantly, though US historians tend to overlook this element, against the Mexican population that the war on Mexico and the appropriation of half its territory suddenly made part of the USA, should sound very familiar to anyone listening to the current political discourse, especially on the topic of immigration and what are significantly referred to as 'illegal aliens' and, more euphemistically, as 'illegal immigrants'. The literary response to this pivotal decade in American history is succinctly analyzed in a recent treatise by Jaime Javier Rodríguez (2010) titled *The Literatures of the U.S.–Mexican War: Narrative, Time, and Identity.*

The potato famine in Ireland starting in 1845 led to a surge of Irish immigration; and the revolutions of 1848, particularly the March 13 revolution in Vienna that spread across the German states, brought a sudden increase in German, mainly German Catholic immigration, all of which was perceived by the white Protestant Americans as an economic, religious, and ethno-racial threat. The Know–Nothing Party could not very well round up immigrants and dump them across the newly redrawn Mexican border behind a wall, as is the ambition and current practice of the US government. They proposed, instead, that all civil service and teaching positions be reserved strictly for white Protestants, and the waiting period for application to become a naturalised US citizen be extended to 21 years. Though the newly arrived and newly conquered non-wasp peoples were not referred to as 'illegal aliens', they were treated no differently from those so designated today. The emergence of the Know–Nothing Party was not a spontaneous event, but the manifest symptom of a hegemonic mainstream political culture that was on a war footing and a relentless push for territorial invasion, occupation, and settlement, with the self-legitimating sanction of divine providence, fully righteous in the pursuit of turning an 'ideology of domination [into] reified and politically realized' conquest, to cite McDargh (1995, 227) once more. The year 1845 was the year in which John O'Sullivan gave the new administration of James K. Polk the war cry of 'Manifest Destiny' in *The United States Magazine and Democratic Review,* and the Polk administration promptly set out to turn it from political declaration into geographical reality. The following year, 1846, would witness America's first war of choice, the war on Mexico launched in May and couched as pre-emptive action, in anticipation of the rhetoric that accompanies the more recent series of wars of choice that usher in the twenty-first century. A month later, on June 24, 1846, to be exact, the US settlers in California proclaimed their settlements an independent republic, which promptly requested to be, and was, annexed, as was the territory of New Mexico. 1848, the year of revolutions in Europe, was the year of the Treaty of Guadalupe Hidalgo through which the USA appropriated half of Mexico's territory, from Kansas to California. It was also the year in which, *mirabile dictu*, gold was struck in the newly acquired territories, prompting the California Gold Rush that ensued. In a lecture at the Concord Lyceum titled 'The Rights and Duties of the Individual in Relation to Government', better known by its subsequent published title as 'Civil Disobedience', Henry David Thoreau pronounced his dissent and refusal to pay his taxes in protest against slavery and the war on Mexico. The Know–Nothing Party took a different view. Its declared primary concern was how to contain the Catholic Mexicans within the former Mexican territories even while appropriating their land, and to demonise the hungry horde of Irish Catholics and German Catholic political refugees who managed to cross the Atlantic. Viewed as a party of dissenters within a fractured national consensus, as the Civil War that was less than five years away would demonstrate, the dissent of the Know–Nothing Party was, in fact, in accord with the overarching consensus of a society bent on war, territorial expansion, and the harnessing of natural resources as capitalisable booty to which imperial right-eousness feels perennially entitled, a conviction that comes when narcissistic solip-sism, as in the xenophobic 'nativism' of the dissenting party, is catalyzed by the ideology of domination and the boon of conquest. When the phenomenon of *agnotology* is embodied in the self-declared curtailment of epistemology – that is, when strategically cultivated ignorance becomes a booster for imperial ends and suspends the knowability of anything except as object for or as instrument of conquest and colonisation – dissent too can be instrumentalised into a catalyst for imperial hegemony. By 1860, the Know-Nothing Party was disbanded, ceding the agonic arena to the patriotic gore and economic opportunism of the Civil War and its aftermath. The Civil War and the predatory Darwinism of the Reconstruction era, history demonstrates, were fundamentally a contest between alternative eco-nomic systems of capitalisation – the slave-based plantation economy and the sla-vish exploitation of labour by the second industrial revolution. In contention, then, was the mode of use and maximal exploitation of the newly conquered territory and the economic potential of its human geography. That internecine agon honed the instinct and desire for domination beyond the achieved continental frontier that had finally reached its providential destiny from sea to shining sea. Barely a generation after that bloodletting, yet another war of choice, called the Spanish American War, proved an inevitability, as did the reach across the Pacific into the Philippines which ushered in the twentieth century, dubbed the American century, and the new era of globalisation with enhanced modes of extractive colonialism on a planetary scale.

The centurial transition, like the trans-oceanic imperial adventure across the Pacific, occurred quite naturally, starting with the heeding of a February 1899 exhortation by the British imperial poet Rudyard Kipling entitled 'The White Man's Burden: The United States and the Philippine Islands', published in *McClure's Magazine*, in which Kipling urged Washington to pick up the imperial mantle from London with what he called, without irony, 'the savage wars of peace' (Kipling 1899, stanza 3, line 2). The soon-to-be Vice-President, and shortly after President, Theodor Roosevelt was moved enough to copy the poem and send it to Senator Henry Cabot Lodge with a note that reveals his acumen as poetry critic and his imperial enthusiasm. Kipling's, Roosevelt remarked in his note, was 'rather poor poetry, but good sense from the expansion point of view' (cf Foster and McChesney 2003). To my knowledge, Mr Roosevelt does not say anything about the writings of Mark Twain and the philosopher William James, two leading figures of the Anti-Imperialist League whose views challenged Kipling's and Roosevelt's imperial logic. And, so, by April of 1898, the USA would declare war on Spain, acquiring dominion over Cuba, Puerto Rico, Guam, and the Philippines, a prelude to what would become the American Twentieth Century. That transition is consolidated with Roosevelt's 1904 'Corollary' to the 1823 Monroe Doctrine. 'Roosevelt's Corollary', as it is known, would reassert geo-political hegemony over the Western Hemisphere, a reiteration that discursively anticipated the mid-twentieth-century carving up of the globe between east and west into spheres of influence during the Cold War.

When D. H. Lawrence was composing his poem 'New Heaven and Earth', in 1917, he had also begun writing his book of essays titled *Studies in Classic American Literature* which would be completed and published in 1923. Those essays would prove determinative in the historiography of American literature and its canon formation grounded in the controversial history of non-conformism and the intricate fortunes of dissent. Lawrence undertook the composition of his poem and of the essays under difficult circumstance. Hounded by the British authorities that questioned his political loyalties during World War I, he became the target of the Defence of the Realm Act (DORA). He would set out on an intercontinental itinerary that passed through the New World and ended, a decade later, in the French city of Vance, where, in 1930, he succumbed to tuberculosis. His only book of literary criticism, however, would prove a touchstone for nineteenth-century American literary history and for what would become the corpus of what he termed 'classic American literature'. Despite Lawrence's unorthodox insight and idiosyncratic language, his wry diagnoses proved determinative in the cultural criticism of such seminal figures as F. O. Matthiessen and his 1941 treatise that defined the American canon, *American Renaissance: Art and Expression in the Age of Emerson and Whitman*; and Leslie Fiedler, a student of Matthiessen's Harvard graduate seminar on American poetry and author of *Love and Death in the American Novel* (1960). Both scholars of a dissensual vintage with Marxist ideological leanings and an early critical interest in the homoerotic strains of American masculinity, their legacy from a tumultuous historical period at mid-twentieth century has proved formative of the American canon and its critical discourse. Lawrence's 1923 volume and William Carlos Williams's book of essays *In the American Grain* two years later would foreground the insurgent discourse of American literary historiography whose grain, or defining attribute, is being against the grain, as the ironies of Williams's iconoclastic sketches of America's iconic figures illustrate. Thus, a convergence of these dissenting critical voices with a number of literary figures such as James Fenimore Cooper, Edgar Allan Poe, and Herman Melville, all variously at variance with their own historical time, has engendered the core of a national canon still dissonant with the pathologies of domination and incorrigible bellicosity that characterise the society from which it has emerged. The irony of this historical dissonance was not lost on Lawrence or on certain literary historians who appreciated his wry, at times sardonic, critical insight.

Lawrence's book on American literature has certain American antecedents, particularly, in the irony and iconoclasm of James Russell Lowell, a demotic poet who voiced his critique of war-crazed America at the mid-nineteenth century through the persona and colloquial voice of Hosea Biglow. *The Biglow Papers,* a satirical critique of war published in the bellicose year of 1848, with a second series in the course of the Civil War in 1862, questioned, in vernacular verse, the social and political anxieties that made the Know-Nothing Party possible. As wartime critique, Lowell's *Biglow Papers* could be read as the American version of Lucan's

Pharsalia, the Roman anti-epic on the first-century civil war between Julius Caesar and the Roman Senate, a work that led to its dissident author's becoming a suspect in the Pisonian Conspiracy of 65 AD and to being sentenced by Nero to commit suicide along with his uncle, the Stoic philosopher Seneca. Lowell and his contemporaries knew Lucan's *Pharsalia* well enough for the Confederate War Memorial at Arlington National Cemetery to have a line from it engraved in its base, '*Victrix causa deis placuit sed victa Catoni*' – 'The victorious cause pleased the gods, but the vanquished pleased Cato'. It is a consolatory dictum in tribute to the honour of the losing side, with Cato being the noble Stoic and the sole redeemable hero of a world gone mad with internecine cruelty and depraved blood lust. So, if there should be an American prototype for Lawrence's *Studies in Classic American Literature*, it would have to be Lowell and, specifically, Lowell's *A Fable for Critics, or A Glance at A Few of Our Literary Progenies from the Tub of Diogenes,* also from 1848. Only, Lowell's *jeu d'esprit* takes on a darker cast in Lawrence, even though the two coincide, more often than not, in their assessment of the writers they sketch. Where they do coincide most meaningfully is in the question of epistemology, of knowing and being. Their portrayal of Richard Henry Dana, Jr. and his 1840 sea voyage narrative, *Two Years Before the Mast,* is especially telling in this regard (Amestoy 2015). One could justly speculate that the very appearance of Dana in Lawrence's book might well be due to Lowell's poetic sketch of this would-be-poet, a portrait that focuses on doing, being, and knowing, terms that Lawrence writes with capital letters when discussing Dana: 'KNOWING and BEING are opposite, antagonistic states. The more you know, exactly, the less you *are.* The more you *are,* in being, the less you know. [...] This is the great cross of man, his dualism. The blood-self, and the nerve-brain self. [...] The goal is know how not-to-know' (Lawrence 1971, 121). And this, precisely, is the knowledge that eluded the Know-Nothing Party of Lowell's time, as Lowell well knew. In concluding his sketch, Lawrence notes:

> Dana's small book is a very great book: contains a great extreme of knowledge, knowledge of the great element.
>
> And after all, we have to know all before we can know that knowing is nothing.
>
> Imaginatively, we have to know all: even the elemental waters. And know and know on, until knowledge suddenly shrivels and we know that forever we don't know.
>
> Then there is a sort of peace, and we can start afresh, knowing we don't know.
>
> *(Lawrence 1971, 138)*

I do not know that Lawrence knew the 1440 treatise by Nicholas of Cusa, *De Docta Ignorantia.* But it would be safe to wager that the Latin student Lowell did. For those interested in the minutiae, chapter three of *Memos from the Besieged City,* 'Of Learned Ignorance: Nicholas of Cusa and Cardinal Spaces of Culture' (Kadir

2011), is devoted to the German-Italian cardinal's epistemology. The elemental knowing that Lawrence attributes to Dana is in contrast to the ideological knowledge of his contemporaries, whether the utopian transcendentalists, the isolationist and phobic Know-Nothings, or the disciples of 'Saviourism', as Lawrence refers to them, that is, those perennial Salvationists who take on Kipling's 'White Men's Burden' for whom knowledge and its management are integral to their imperial calculus. 'Saviourism is a despicable thing', Lawrence (1971, 127) declares unequivocally. One can only imagine what his judgment would be of today's 'humanitarian interventionists' who maximise the return on their soteriological calculus that invariably turns out to be catalyzed with political cynicism and predatory rapaciousness.

Acknowledgement

A preliminary, abbreviated version of this essay appeared as 'Agnotology and the Know-Nothing Party: Then and Now' in *Review of International American Studies, RIAS,* 10: 1 2017: 117–29.

Works cited

Amestoy, Jeffrey L. 2015. *Slavish Shore: The Odyssey of Richard Henry Dana.* Cambridge, MA: Harvard University Press.

Bernays, Edward L. 1947. 'The Engineering of Consent'. *Annals of the American Academy of Political and Social Science* 250 (March): 113.

Bernays, Edward L. and Howard Walden Cutler. 1955. *The Engineering of Consent.* Norman, OK: University of Oklahoma Press.

Casanova, Pascale. 2004. *The World Republic of Letters.* Trans. M. B. DeBevoise. Cambridge: Harvard University Press.

Eco, Umberto. 2015. *Numero Zero.* Trans. Richard Dixon. New York: Houghton Mifflin Harcourt.

Felski, Rita. 2015. *The Limits of Critique.* Chicago: University of Chicago Press.

Fiedler, Leslie. 1960. *Love and Death in the American Novel.* New York: Criterion Books.

Foster, John Bellamy and Robert W. McChesney. 2003. 'Kipling, the "White Man's Burden", and U. S. Imperialism'. *Monthly Review* 1 November. Available at: https://monthlyreview.org/2003/11/01/kipling-the-white-mans-burden-and-u-s-imperialism/ (Accessed 13 August 2018).

Herman, Edward S. and Noam Chomsky. 1988. *Manufacturing Consent: The Political Economy of the Mass Media.* New York: Pantheon Books.

Gibson, William. 2003. *Pattern Recognition.* New York: G. P. Putnam's Sons.

Kadir, Djelal. 1992. *Columbus and the Ends of the Earth: Europe's Prophetic Rhetoric as Conquering Ideology.* Berkeley, CA: University of California Press.

Kadir, Djelal. 2011. 'Of Learned Ignorance: Nicholas of Cusa and Cardinal Spaces of Culture' in Djelal Kadir, *Memos from the Besieged City.* 64–83. Stanford: Stanford University Press.

Kipling, Rudyard. 1899. 'The White Man's Burden: The United States and the Philippine Islands'. *McClure's Magazine* 12(4). Available at: http://www.unz.org/Pub/McClures-1899feb-00290 (Accessed 27 July 2018).

Lawrence, D. H. 1971 [1923]. *Studies in Classical American Literature*. New York: Thomas Seltzer, Inc. Rprt. Harmondsworth: Penguin Books.

Lawrence, D. H. 1994. '*New Heaven and Earth*'. *The Complete Poems of D. H. Lawrence*. Introduction and Notes, David Ellis. Ware, UK: Wordsworth Editions/Cumberland House.

Lowell, James Russel. 2014 [1848]. *A Fable for Critics, or A Glance at A Few of Our Literary Progenies from the Tub of Diogenes*. Berkeley: University of California Libraries, Rprt. Miami, FL: HardPress Publishing. Kindle Edition.

Matthiessen, F. O. 1941. *American Renaissance: Art and Expression in the Age of Emerson and Whitman*. Oxford: Oxford University Press.

McDargh, John. 1995. 'Desire, Domination, and the Life and Death of the Soul' in Richard K. Fenn and Donald Capps, eds, *On Losing the Soul: Essays in the Social Psychology of Religion*. 213–230. Albany, NY: State University of New York Press.

O'Sullivan, John Thomas. 1845. 'Annexation'. *The United States Magazine and Democratic Review* 17(1): 5–10.

Proctor, Robert N. and Londa Schiebinger, eds. 2008. *Agnotology: The Making and Unmaking of Ignorance*. Stanford, CA: Stanford University Press.

Rodríguez, Jaime Javier. 2010. *The Literatures of the U.S.–Mexican War: Narrative, Time, and Identity*. Austin, TX: University of Texas Press.

Sinclair, Upton. 1919. *The Brass Check: A Study of American Journalism*. Pasadena, CA: self-published. Rprt. London: FB&c Ltd. Dalton House, 2015.

Sullivan, Shannon, Nancy Tuana, eds. 2007. *Race and Epistemologies of Ignorance*. Albany, NY: State University of New York Press.

Thoreau, Henry David. 1848. 'Resistance to Civil Government, or Civil Disobedience'. Available at: http://archive.vcu.edu/english/engweb/transcendentalism/authors/thoreau/civil/ (Accessed 27 July 2018).

U.S. Department of Defense. 2000. *Joint Vision 2020*. Washington, DC: U.S. Department of Defense. [No longer available online.] http://www.defense.gov/news/newsarticle.aspx?id=45289.

Vanbergen, Graham. 2016. 'British Public Being Sold Down the River in Democracy Deception'. *Information Clearing House* 16 February. Available at: http://www.informationclearinghouse.info/article44234.htm (Accessed 5 March 2019).

Williams, William Carlos. 2004 [1925]. *In the American Grain*. Rprt. New York: New Directions.

2

THE PROBLEM OF DISSENT

Katie Muth

What is literary dissent? And how do we know it when we see it? Instances of political dissent seem easier to locate. We might think of iconic images like 'Tank Man' in Tiananmen Square, civil rights marchers with arms linked on the Edmund Pettus Bridge, a hundred thousand anti-Mubarak demonstrators in Tahrir Square, or Edward Crawford throwing a tear gas canister in Ferguson, Missouri. These images document bodily resistance. The unidentified subject of Jeff Widener's 'Tank Man', for example, wields power not through the mechanisms of participatory government or political speech but, rather, by positioning his body against the wordless technologies of military suppression.

Political protest in these instances is a form of Rancièrian *dissensus* in that it 'redistributes the sensible' without recourse to shared political argumentation and representation (Rancière 2015). In this vein, we might think of the Occupy movement as a particularly distilled form of Rancièrian protest, since it made very few positive demands but rather resisted the neoliberal order by physically repurposing urban spaces (Bassett 2014, Rancière 2017). Giorgio Agamben frames a similar sort of resistance – 'Tank Man' is a particular point of reference, in fact – when in *The Coming Community* he identifies a political agent 'whatever singularity', whom he calls 'unnameable' or 'the being-in-language of the non-linguistic' (Agamben 1993, 76). 'Whatever singularity' becomes, then, an early formulation of what he would later theorise as bare life and a foundational concept for his framing of utopian potentiality (Agamben 1998, 1999). The appeal of Rancière's *dissensus* or Agamben's 'whatever singularity' is that each allows us to think a politics outside the representational frameworks that govern public discourse, to inject genuine novelty into the political realm. Arguably, each describes a conduit not just between radical political thought and real-world praxis but also between radical art and politics. This chapter asks what such concepts of dissent can offer the study of world literature.

The essay will unfold around two cases. The first, the case of Mo Yan's Nobel Prize, demonstrates how certain ideas about political dissent become entangled with literary and cultural value. Mo Yan's refusal to stand against state censorship or to defend the jailed dissident Liu Xiaobo blighted his laurels for some and reduced the question of his work's literary value to a question of its political valence. The problem of Mo Yan's unwillingness to speak explicitly against the alleged human rights abuses of the People's Republic of China (PRC) became a source of consensus among American and European critics who find him unworthy of prestige by reason of bad politics. But Mo Yan's defenders suggest that we should see a subtle form of critique embedded in his elliptical narration. The concepts of *dissensus* and 'whatever singularity' potentially frame Mo Yan's work in more nuanced relation to Western notions of dissent.

Such a reading doesn't fully satisfy, however, and a second case study from American literature makes clear at least one reason why. In the 1940s and 1950s, Langston Hughes programmatically scrubbed socialist sentiment from his body of poetic work. That socialist sentiment constituted an integral component of his anti-lynching rhetoric in the 1930s, and it earned him state surveillance, a hefty FBI file, and eventually a Congressional hearing. By the time his *Selected Poems* appeared in 1957, nary a socialist verse was among them, and by 1966 he was the face of the state-sponsored delegation to the First World Festival of Negro Arts in Dakar, Senegal. The Hughes who became a representative of black American writing on the global stage was not a socialist poet but, rather, the enduring Hughes of 'The Negro Speaks of Rivers' (1921) and *Montage of a Dream Deferred* (1951). By encouraging Hughes to suppress his own verse, the State Department and the FBI played a key role in crafting the global literary legacy of Langston Hughes.

The humanist ethos Langston Hughes cultivated in distancing himself from his radical writing jibes remarkably well with Mo Yan's coyly apolitical rhetoric. But when we recover the history of state aggression against African American writers in the context of civil rights and global anticolonial struggle, what's left unspoken in Hughes's canonical poetry becomes meaningful as a site of dissident political potential. In the case of Mo Yan, however, such interstices, self-conscious as they may be, more ambivalently gesture toward a lack or absence. Rancièrian *dissensus* and Agambean potentiality offer compelling models for the analysis of dissent in world literature, but that analysis only works when we are also responsive to the complex structures that circumscribe literary production and circulation. It demands, in other words, that we attend to the structures of consensus.

Parallax and prestige

In 2012, Mo Yan (Guan Moye) became the first Chinese national living in China but not in jail to win a Nobel Prize. He endorsed universality and detachment as key elements of his aesthetic program when he was called to defend his award against those critical of his close relationship with the PRC. 'As a member of society', Mo Yan said in Stockholm, 'a novelist is entitled to his own stance and viewpoint; but when he is writing he must take a humanistic stance, and write accordingly. Only then can literature not just originate in events, but transcend them, not just show concern for politics but be greater than politics' (Mo Yan 2012a, n.p.). Disavowing the political entanglements of the PRC and its complicated relationship to the West, Mo Yan walked a fine line to maintain his good standing with the Communist Party while appeasing the liberal democratic gatekeepers to the higher echelons of Western literary prestige. Espousing a globally legible humanist aesthetic, he highlighted the particularity of his narratives: they come from personal experience, his own and that of the people around him. And by virtue of that personal element – what Ximen Donkey in *Life and Death Are Wearing Me Out* (2008) would call 'a valuable window on history' – Mo Yan laid claim to the Swedish Academy's criterion that laureates demonstrate 'uncompromising "integrity" in the depiction of the human predicament' (Mo Yan 2008, 82; Espmark 1999, n.p.).

In spite of its universalist rhetoric, the Academy has tended since the mid-1980s or so to celebrate writers who can stand as representatives of regional or national locales (Brouillette 2014). Indeed, James English notes the tendency of the Nobel committee to privilege writers who represent non-European nations, diasporic communities, and postcolonial sites and, especially, to privilege those writers as a way of signalling the 'emergence' of those communities on the world-literary stage (English 2008). 'These writers *represented* not just particular local (or diasporic) literary communities,' he writes, 'but the highly selective emergence of those communities, or certain of their aspects, into the global articulation of world literature' (304, emphasis in original). English underscores the multiple valences of 'representation' at work in such awards – given to writers like Wole Soyinka, Naguib Mahfouz, Octavio Paz, Derek Walcott, Toni Morrison, V. S. Naipaul, and Gao Xingjian. On the one hand, they are called to represent the experiences of, in the case of Toni Morrison, for example, black women in America. On the other hand, they are called to represent the inclusion of the communities for whom they are imagined to speak not just in the canon of world literature but, indeed, in the realm of the 'human predicament'. In Mo Yan's award, European cultural gatekeepers recognised mainland China as a site of globally legible human experience (Lovell 2002, 2006; Roberts 2011). Indeed, Chinese authorities concurred. In a letter to the Chinese Writers Association, the state-run arts council in which Mo Yan holds an honorary position, Politburo member Li Changchun wrote that Mo Yan's Nobel was 'not only an embodiment of the flourishing progress of Chinese literature but also an embodiment of the continuing rise in the overall strength of our state and its international influence' (cited in Link 2012, n.p.).

In coming to stand for China's full inclusion in contemporary world literature and its increased power in the world, Mo Yan also came to stand for Western democracies' acceptance of the PRC's openly acknowledged state censorship, its alleged labour abuses, maltreatment of dissidents, religious persecution, anti-LGBTQ+ discrimination, and other human rights violations. In other words, representing China's arrival also meant representing China's international reputation at large. Mo Yan's refusal to distance himself from the Communist Party of

China met with widespread critique. Fellow laureate Herta Müller called his win a 'catastrophe', and Salman Rushdie compared him to apparatchik writer Mikhail Sholokhov, a 'patsy of the regime' (Daley 2012, n.p.; Associated Press 2012, n.p.). Even Perry Link – ultimately somewhat sympathetic to the difficulties faced by writers working 'inside the system' – wondered quite publicly whether Mo Yan deserved his new global prestige (Link 2012, n.p.).

Link cited as problematic Mo Yan's ready participation in the state-mandated boycott of Dai Qing and Bei Ling at the 2009 Frankfurt Book Fair, his nonchalant adoption of neutral and evasive language in response to politically loaded questions from the press, his prominent contribution to the seventieth anniversary celebration of Mao's 1942 'Talks at the Yan'an Forum on Literature and Art', and especially his refusal to speak straightforwardly on behalf of jailed dissident Liu Xiaobo. The last is the most telling because Mo Yan's statement on Liu, Link argues, evidences the hand of the state. Specifically, Link finds in Mo Yan's apparently generous well-wishing the remnants of censorship and dictation: 'I now hope', Mo Yan said in 2012, 'that [Liu] can get his freedom as soon as possible – get his freedom in good health as soon as possible – and then be able to study his politics and study his social systems as he likes' (cited in Link 2012, n.p.). Describing the tendency of state officials to visit with persons likely to be interviewed by Western media and how the trope 'seeking medical care' has come to euphemise expulsion from the PRC, Link speculates that Mo Yan's emphasis on Liu's health was perhaps a way for Chinese officials to prepare the West to grant the Lius asylum upon the conclusion of Liu Xiaobo's 11-year sentence (Liu died under guard in 2017). The whole statement, Link suggests, may be nothing more than a complex 'word-game' designed to maximise Mo Yan's positive image in the West without sacrificing his political standing at home. Mo Yan, in other words, may have come to represent China in another sense: as a cultural ambassador.

The suspicion that Chinese authorities might be speaking through Mo Yan – that his novels and stories might reflect state interests and commitments – has influenced the reception of his work in English. At issue here is whether we should see Mo Yan as a free writer, and this question becomes a question of dissidence. In his omnibus review in the *New York Review of Books*, Link uses Mo Yan's hedging statement on Liu Xiaobo to articulate the difference between party politicos and pro-democracy dissidents. Even as he claims not to judge those who work within the Chinese regime, he valorizes Liu's 'highly unusual' choices about how to relate to the PRC. 'It would be wrong', Link concedes, 'for spectators like you and me, who enjoy the comfort of distance, to demand that Mo Yan risk all and be another Liu Xiaobo. But it would be even more wrong to mistake the clear difference between the two' (Link 2012, n.p.). Link is more generous than some of Mo Yan's interlocutors, to be sure. Still, he reminds us not to confuse Mo Yan's political ambiguity with political dissent. Worse than failing to understand the pressures writers face under the PRC, Link says, would be to imagine that the 2012 Nobel winner is a champion of liberal progressivism. Implicit in this commentary is the possibility that the Swedish Academy made a mistake in handing Mo Yan the coveted award, that they misjudged the politics and, hence, mischaracterised the literary value of his work. Nikil Saval put it more bluntly in the *London Review of Books*: 'this time the Nobel's literature–politics mix came out all wrong. [...] Mo Yan's dissident reputation in the West, it turned out, was false' (Saval 2013, n.p.).

Mo Yan's political compromise, Saval argues in his review of *Change* (2012), *Sandalwood Death* (2013), and *POW!* (2012), three works that appeared in English around the time of the prize, corrupts his literary aesthetics. For Saval, Mo Yan's vision of 'species regression', a phrase snapped up from the opening of *Red Sorghum* (1992), is symptomatic of the author's politically retrograde tendencies (Saval 2013, n.p.). 'The Nobel is in hand, and the Party is behind him. The good life is his. Mo Yan is in no danger of going hungry, or of becoming anything other than a child', Saval writes. Saval then extends this *ad hominem* into the aesthetics of the body of work as a whole. Of narrator Jintong's inability to wean in *Big Breasts and Wide Hips* (2004), Saval writes that Mo Yan's metaphor of 'arrested development, intended to be a stand-in for a whole nation's immaturity', evidences instead the author's personal lack of sophistication. What he calls Mo Yan's 'breast obsession' unfolds in a tedium of repetition, 'pages of breasts' appearing in increasingly fantastic but empty rhetorical figures. If, in *The Republic of Wine* (2000), gluttony is meant to satirise a corrupt bureaucracy or even 'the decadence of an entire society', Saval finds that the novel's theme infects its form, which 'exudes a fatness, exhaustion and decay'. The formal tics and excesses then stand as evidence in a political indictment, both of Mo Yan and of the PRC. 'To see him as a political writer you have to interpret his novels' derangement,' Saval concludes. 'His China is indeed a terrifying place'. But Saval finds Mo Yan complicit in that terror.

Saval echoes the refrains of John Updike's earlier *New Yorker* review of *Big Breasts and Wide Hips* when he finds in Mo Yan's 'breast obsession' evidence of government influence, though Updike finds suppressed liberalism where Saval finds propitiation. Updike describes Mo Yan's allegory for the 'dilution of the Chinese character' in this way: 'It's a rare page that fails to mention breasts: they smell of sulfur and lamb; nipples are likened to dates, cherries, and button mushrooms [...]. Amid so much slapstick mayhem and mammary lewdness, this moral risks being lost' (Updike 2005, n.p.). Once again, Jintong's boob obsession distracts us from what matters, and slapstick 'extravagancies' incapacitate the author's more serious aims. Like Saval, Updike questions the efficacy of satire when ribald picaresque and bawdry threaten to overtake moral argument. Unlike Saval, however, Updike supposes this failure must be a result of state censorship, celebrating Mo Yan's 'spirit' and making him an example in the argument for freer speech in China. Updike paints Mo Yan as a liberal – indeed *too* liberal – champion ruthlessly edited and fated 'to operate on the edge of official constraints'. Quoting Howard Goldblatt's preface to the novel, Updike cites the 'ire' with which mainland critics responded to the original Chinese publication of *Big Breasts and Wide Hips* (*Feng ru fei tun*, 1996) as the reason Mo Yan's novel of 'nearly half a million words' has suffered 'trimming and rearrangement right up to this translation'. With Goldblatt, he notes the author's participation in the censorship of his own novel, and like

Saval, he pits stylistic excess against moral argument, but Updike seems to assume beneath all this a basically liberal sensibility. 'Free spirits in China', he warns, 'are still short of enjoying free speech.'

How is it that more-or-less the same evidence leads to conflicting assessments of Mo Yan's political character? Is he a propagandist or a victim of government suppression? Part of the issue to hand has to do with how we judge literary dissent. For critics like Saval – who would go on to rail in *n+1* against 'Global Lit' as an extension of neoliberal economics – a writer practices dissent by participating in an 'internationalist literary project [...] of *opposition* to prevailing tastes, ways of writing, and politics' (Editors 2013, n.p., emphasis in original). Implicit in Saval's critique of Mo Yan is the conflation of radical art and radical politics. The relation between the two, however, demands a more thorough unpacking, a theoretical framework for connecting oppositional literary form with dissident political content.

Dissent and literature

The purpose of this section is to describe the relation between aesthetic form and political content by looking at the post-Marxist philosophy of Giorgio Agamben and Jacques Rancière. However else they might differ, Agamben and Rancière put the politics of dissent at the heart of theory. Following Gilles Deleuze, both writers take Herman Melville's 'Bartleby the Scrivener' as an emblem of dissent's democratic promise. Agamben's Bartleby aligns with the earlier formulation in *The Coming Community* of 'whatever singularity' as a messianic figure of potentiality or contingency. Rancière's Bartleby, on the other hand, instantiates what he will call 'a gap in the sensible itself', or politics as *dissensus* (Rancière 2015, 46). In each case, the potential of art to break with past regimes of representation mirrors, or in stronger formulations literally enacts, a more abstract potential to break with extant political regimes. Literature's revolutionary potential, both theorists contend, inheres in the rupture of dissent specifically because dissent (or *dissensus*) fundamentally refuses the prevailing rules of public discourse. Bartlebyesque dissent is opposition in its purest form.

The central conceit in which I'm interested originates with Gilles Deleuze's reading of Melville in 'Bartleby ou la formule' (1993), where Deleuze describes Melville's scrivener as 'the doctor of a sick America, the *Medicine Man*, the new Christ or the brother to us all' (Deleuze 1998, 90). The messianic Bartleby represents for Deleuze the possibility of a democratic community of becoming, or as he puts it in the essay, Bartleby is an instantiation of 'pragmatism as an attempt to transform the world, to think a new world or new man insofar as they *create themselves*' (86, emphasis in original). Melville's contribution to the project of democratic becoming, further, is tied directly to two things: Bartleby's famous utterance 'I would prefer not to', and writing itself as part of a 'collective enunciation' that 'preserves the rights of a people to come' (90). In other words, Bartleby's distinctive refusal of his employer's demands – his dissent, we might say – literalises literature's potential to disrupt the workings of power, of capital, and of the law as such. The essay's influence, and in particular its influence in thinking about resistance and dissent, has been widespread. Agamben and Rancière develop its suggestive argument about the relation between political dissent and aesthetics, and both address Deleuze's Bartleby essay directly.

In 'Bartleby, or On Contingency', originally published alongside an Italian translation of Deleuze's essay, Giorgio Agamben further develops Bartleby's messianic interpretation (Agamben and Deleuze 1993). '[I]f Bartleby is a new Messiah,' he writes, 'he comes not, like Jesus, to redeem what was, but to save what was not' (Agamben 1999, 270). Agamben's Bartleby is not just a messenger of becoming but, even more powerfully, a messenger of potentiality, or the possibility of not becoming. Bartleby's utterance, in inhabiting the 'zone of indistinction between yes and no' (Deleuze's phrase), also opens a zone of indeterminacy 'between the potential to be (or do) and the potential not to be (or do)' (255). Agamben finds in Bartleby's 'I would prefer not to' a political agent who escapes the traps and constraints of political discourse as it actually exists, creating a space for novelty and for a democratic community of equals. Further, Bartleby's enunciation inaugurates a form of being beyond the conscriptions of citizenship, identity, or subjecthood. In Bartleby, Agamben writes, '*pathos* is purified of all *doxa*, all subjective appearance, and becomes the pure announcement of appearance, the intimation of Being without any predicate. In this light, Bartleby's formula shows its full sense' (257). Bartleby's utterance, then, should be read as an expression of Being thought as pure potentiality, which is the state of suspension between making or doing (actualisation) and not making or doing (impossibility).

The essay on Bartleby grows out of a brief fragment in *La comunità che viene* (1990), a book inviting us to imagine a human social arrangement that counters the state of exception endemic, in Agamben's view, to contemporary life. In this text, Agamben seeks a revolutionary 'new planetary humanity' that will 'enter into a community without presuppositions and without subjects' (Agamben 1993, 65). Agamben argues in *Homo sacer. Il potere sovrano e la nuda vita* (1995) that the postwar discourse on human rights establishes the 'originary figure of the inscription of natural life in the juridico-political order of the nation-state' (Agamben 1998, 127). In other words, the modern nation-state subsumes bare life (*zoē*) into political life (*bios*), thus encoding into the core of its make-up the sovereign exception and its biopolitical corollary (cf McLoughlin 2016). In *The Coming Community*, bare life takes the form 'whatever being', or 'the figure of pure singularity' (Agamben 1993, 67). Though it's beyond the scope of this essay to describe all the philosophical (non-)attributes of 'whatever singularity', two things matter to the present discussion of dissent and literature. First, whatever singularity is a figure whose power and promise lies in 'the totality of its possibilities' (67). Second, in thinking whatever singularity, Agamben seems to have struck on the relation between Bartleby and political potentiality, or the relations among dissent, language, and utopianism. Agamben writes:

> The perfect act of writing comes not from a power to write, but from an impotence that turns back on itself and in this way comes to itself as a pure act

(which Aristotle calls intellect). [...] Bartleby, a scribe who does not simply cease writing but 'prefers not to', is the extreme image of this angel that writes nothing but its potentiality to not-write.

(Agamben 1993, 37)

In this earlier and much pithier formulation, Bartleby inhabits the ethos of 'whatever singularity' not just by his choice, but by the way in which his dissenting language – 'I prefer not to' – disrupts the linguistic order which would inscribe him into the law, its constitutive state, and the economic apparatuses of contemporary capital. Thus, Bartleby's formula characterises the utopian potential of what would become, in a less hopeful series of diagnoses, Agamben's most well-known figure, *homo sacer*. The key element to take away from this discussion is that Agamben's figures for potentiality must not settle into positive descriptive identities. Bartleby's 'I would prefer not to' and *The Coming Community*'s 'whatever singularity' speak to the fundamental problem of voicing radical dissent in a context where the very languages of reference and representation must be challenged. One further figure of comparison deserves attention here. That figure is the protester at Tiananmen Square, whom Agamben calls 'a herald from Beijing' (85). Specifically, Agamben points out that the 1989 protests were significant for the 'relative absence of determinate contents in their demands' (85). The Tiananmen demonstrators, then, and the PRC's violent massacre of those demonstrators, illustrate for Agamben how contemporary political struggle 'will no longer be a struggle for the conquest or control of the State, but a struggle between the State and the non-State (humanity)' (85). In Tiananmen, we see the political counterpart to Bartleby's formula.

Jacques Rancière might disagree with Agamben on biopolitics and sovereignty – and he certainly eschews the nihilism bearing down on even the most optimistic propositions in *The Coming Community* and *Potentialities* – but dissent, or a particular form of it, comprises the foundation of his intertwined philosophies of politics and aesthetics as well. Rancière provides an alternative theory of how formal rupture might produce social change, a vision of politics in the present rather than a vision of utopia deferred. According to Rancière, 'the essence of politics is *dissensus*' (Rancière 2015, 46). The argument depends on Rancière's conception of a specific 'distribution of the sensible' without 'gap or supplement', which he calls the 'police' (44). In order to understand what's meant by *dissensus* in this context, we have to first understand what's meant by the 'distribution of the sensible', by 'police', and by *demos*, or the people. For Rancière, the *demos* 'can be identified neither with the race of those who recognise each other has having the same beginning or birth, nor with a part or sum of the parts, of the population' (41). Like Agamben's 'whatever singularity', the people cannot be identified with a descriptive predicate or set of predicates. We are not talking about a subject or citizen, or a set thereof. Rather, 'the people is the supplement that disjoins the population from itself' (41). In other words, the people in and of itself is a disruptive concept, one that exceeds agreed-upon understandings of the state or the body politic. Rancière frames this supplement in relation to democracy itself, which he differentiates from any democratic state or voting populace. 'The "all" of the community named by democracy,' he writes, 'is an empty, supplementary part that separates the community out from the sum of the parts of the social body' (41). Democracy, then, is characterized as both a supplement and a community, and it cannot be reduced to the 'sum of the parts' of any actually existing group of persons, subjects, or citizens.

The sum of the parts of a community, or an actually existing political body, is governed by the 'police', not to be confused with either the *polis* or literal law enforcement bodies, though certainly both puns inflect Rancière's meaning. He writes that 'the police is not a social function but a symbolic constitution of the social' (44). And here is one of the ways Rancière differs from Agamben. Where Agamben finds in the state, or that which is opposed to 'whatever singularity' (humanity), the power to literally subjugate, Rancière finds instead a 'symbolic constitution' which renders the *demos* illegible. He elaborates this way:

> The essence of the police lies in a partition of the sensible that is characterized by the absence of void and of supplement: society here is made up of groups tied to specific modes of doing, to places in which these occupations are exercised, and to modes of being corresponding to these occupations and these places.
>
> *(Rancière 2015, 44)*

So similarly to Agamben in *The Coming Community* and 'Bartleby, or On Contingency', Rancière is interested in a community or *demos* that exceeds predicated ways of describing people or codified social formations like parties or states. But while for Agamben literal state violence transforms potentiality into the annihilation of *homo sacer*, for Rancière what subjugates the *demos* is a system of representation in which society is categorized (we might say 'predicated') according to three things: occupation, place, and being. 'Modes of being' depends on both occupations and place. 'Places in which these occupations are exercised' depends on occupation. The first predicate here is 'modes of doing', or occupation, and the play on 'occupation' as activity, as literal space, and as performance or ethos invites us to move between and among aesthetic and political realms.

Dissensus, then, disrupts social categorization and makes the *demos* visible. Rancière calls it 'the demonstration (*manifestation*) of a gap in the sensible itself' (46). Like 'occupation', 'demonstration' carries multiple meanings, as does its French original, *manifestation*. The notion of demonstrating as explaining or showing something is not adequate to Rancière's meaning. Rather, we need the notion, too, of political protest. Rancière writes:

> Political demonstration makes visible that which had no reason to be seen; it places one world in another – for instance, the world where the factory is a public space in that where it is considered private, the world where workers

speak, and speak about the community, in that where their voices are mere cries expressing pain.

(Rancière 2015, 46)

Political protest in this formulation doesn't just argue a point or contest a precedent. It is not litigious. Rather, political protest depends on the disorganization of space and, indeed, of the multiple orders of occupation set out by the 'police', or the distribution of the sensible which denies the *demos*. That is why Rancière's *dissensus* exceeds the kind of political disagreement with which we are most familiar. It is not a disagreement about particular propositions, the terms of which are generally part of a shared way of understanding the world. Rather, *dissensus* is a disagreement about the very ways in which we understand the possibilities of being, using, and doing at the most fundamental level.

We can easily imagine importing Bartleby's 'I would prefer not to' into Rancière's conceptual frame. The disruption of his employer's demands enacted by Bartleby's formula is tantamount to a disruption of the sensible; it opens a space for originality, for politics, and perhaps even for the *demos*. Thus, Rancière writes that the formula 'disorganizes life' and 'erodes the attorney's reasonable organization of work and life' (Rancière 2004, 146). The formula's power to disrupt extends beyond the relationship between Bartleby and his employer. 'It shatters', Rancière has it, 'not just the hierarchies of a world but also what supports them: the connections between causes and effects we expect from that world' (146–7). So we seem to have here the germ of a potential connection between politics and aesthetics, for Bartleby's enunciation not only leads to 'catastrophe' within the regime of the story, but destroys the 'causal order' that rules the 'world of representation' itself (147). Rancière concludes that Bartleby's formula 'could summarize the very notion of literary originality' (147). Bartleby's 'I would prefer not to', in other words, both disorganises a political regime – that in which his employer orders both work and place (occupation) – and inaugurates a new aesthetic regime in that it breaks from *mimesis* to *aesthesis*. What can this kind of rupture tell us about reading dissent in world literature? Specifically, what promise do *dissensus* and potentiality hold for our understanding of a politically ambiguous figure like Mo Yan?

Mo Yan's defenders find in the elisions, circumlocutions, displacements, and obsessive-compulsive figuration of his fiction a subtle subversion of the PRC's official narratives. Charles Laughlin, for example, in responding to Perry Link's critique, argues that Mo Yan's black humour should be read through the lens of trauma insofar as 'any artistic approach to historical trauma is inflected or refracted' (Laughlin 2012, n.p.). For Laughlin, Mo Yan's oblique handling of traumatic history 'shows orthodox politics to be profane in the face of humanity'. Sabina Knight finds in *Life and Death Are Wearing Me Out* the displacement of political risk from 'a human mouth' into the mouths of animals (Knight 2014, 97). Ximen Donkey bears witness to the torture of communist cadres, Ximen Ox the catastrophic effects of forced land collectivisation. In each case, the suffering of the people and the political critique that accompanies acknowledging that suffering can only be expressed through the figures of non-human animals. Chengzhou He identifies in Mo Yan's careful performance of 'rural Chineseness' – a performance that draws on animal fable, local opera, and other folk traditions – 'a counterdiscourse to resist, revise, and supplement, if not subvert, the dominant grand discourse of modern China' (He 2014, 78). Here, the earthiness of Mo Yan's figures and formal echoes, along with the melancholic pathos or narcissistic hedonism of many characters, challenges (one might even say disrupts) official government narratives of progress, modernity, and growth. Finally, Alexa Huang and Angelica Duran point directly to Guan Moye's choice of pen name – 'Mo Yan' translates literally to 'Don't Talk' or 'Don't Speak' – as a 'critical tool' that underscores the effects of his comedic displacements 'to speak the unspeakable in writings which reimagine political history' (Huang and Duran 2014, 155). Each of these is suggestive in light of the previous discussion on *dissensus* and potentiality.

I'll show how with examples from *Life and Death Are Wearing Me Out*, which spans the second half of the twentieth century and tells the story of Mo Yan's own Northeast Gaomi Township through the eyes, mostly, of the benevolent landlord Ximen Nao. At the hands of underground Communist Party branch member Hong Taiyue, Ximen Nao has been executed during Mao's first wave of land reforms near the end of the civil war. The novel then unfolds in five books that follow Ximen through a series of animal reincarnations in which he witnesses early land reform, the Great Leap Forward, the Cultural Revolution, Mao's death, Deng Xiaoping's economic reforms, and so on, until he finally comes back in human form at the turn of the millennium. Can we see the displacement of political risk in each successive incarnation – the evasion of clear argumentation with respect to key events in the Mao era and Reform period – as a 'redistribution of the sensible'? Do *Life and Death*'s narrative refractions (to borrow Laughlin's phrasing) unsettle the 'orthodox politics' of official Chinese history by inhabiting a liminal space between speaking and not speaking? And is the novel self-conscious about the political potency of its evasions?

Life and Death almost compulsively calls attention to the inability of Ximen Nao as animal to speak, even as Ximen narrates much of the winding narrative we are reading. 'My story begins on January 1, 1950', Ximen begins, before jumping back two years to tell how he was fried in boiling oil in the 'bowels of hell' and sent back to earth as a donkey (Mo Yan 2008, 3, 4). His 'cruel torture' in Lord Yama's Audience Hall is designed to force a confession, which Ximen refuses (3). 'I am innocent,' he insists, 'and I ask to be sent back so I can ask those people to their face what I was guilty of' (3). But, of course Ximen Nao is sent back to Earth as a non-human animal who cannot speak. As Ximen Nao finds himself in the body of Ximen Donkey, he tells us that his 'throat felt exactly the way it had when the two blue-faced demons had throttled me', drawing a line of comparison between his rebirth as an animal and torture in the afterlife (13). Likewise, the landlord compares Lord Yama's interrogation to his own execution at the hands of Mao's peasant rebels. Ximen Nao 'could say nothing in [his own] defense' before Hong

Taiyue shot him in the head (23). Hong Taiyue, on the other hand, is verbose: 'If you want to accuse someone, you'll never run out of words. We'll make sure you die convinced of your crimes' (23–4). Ximen Nao's mute presence as Ximen Donkey – unrepentant, unconvinced, and undead – can be said to disrupt Hong's regime of representation and law. 'Hong Taiyue', he thinks, 'your words meant nothing, you did not make good on your promise' (24). But of course Ximen Donkey can no more demonstrate his defiance of Hong than he can enquire about his own guilt. Ximen Donkey inhabits a liminal space, articulating (to readers) his inability to voice public argument within the scene he describes.

Indeed, the schema of Ximen Donkey's mute verbosity encapsulates in minia-ture one of the novel's broader strategies. Ximen Donkey is slaughtered and eaten during the famine of 1959–61, and by the end of the novel, after he's been rein-carnated as an ox, a pig, a dog, and a monkey, he comes back at the stroke of the millennium as Lan Qiansui, a 'big-headed child' with an 'extraordinary gift for language', who at the age of five 'spread[s] his arms like a storyteller, and embark[s] upon the narration of a long tale' (109, 540). That 'long tale' is the one we've been reading. But Lan Qiansui is not *Life and Death*'s only narrator. Ox's story, for example, is narrated by Lan Jiefang, the son of an independent farmer, as if told to Lan Qiansui himself. 'During my years as an Ox', Lan Qiansui says to Jiefang, 'I stuck to you like a shadow, and you are well versed in the things that happened to me, so there's no point in my repeating them, is there?' (109). But in key moments, Lan Qiansui interjects in Jiefang's story. When, for example, Jiefang's father Lan Lian is nearly blinded by the Red Guard, Lan Qiansui breaks in: 'Another accomplishment of the Great Cultural Revolution!' he says 'coldly' (165). Is this interjection meant to critique? Is it an expression of dissent or commentary on the moral status of Mao Zedong Thought? It's not clear. A bit later in the episode, once Lan Lian's eyes are washed and bandaged, a 'strange sound' emerges from the ox's shed – 'somewhere between a cry, a laugh, and a sigh [...]. Tell me, were you crying or laughing or sighing?' (171). Lan Qiansui won't say. 'Go on with your story, Big-head Lan Qiansui said icily. Don't ask me that' (172). Lan Qiansui dismisses the reading of meaning into Ox's cry. 'Maybe I made that strange sound because I had a clump of grass caught in my throat', he says. 'But you've taken a simple matter and turned it inside out, deliberately complicating it in your jumbled narration' (172). Again, the novel seems both to speak and not speak, to give voice to critique and to deflect that critique. That deflection, further, seems self-conscious, an effect of metafictional technique that calls attention to itself while withholding final interpretation.

If we are reading formally for *dissensus* or potentiality, these elements of *Life and Death* are evocative. In fact, the very debate over the novel's political content seems to underscore a point which both Agamben and Rancière make in their readings of Bartleby. Agamben highlights how Bartleby's absolute contingency stymies the lawyer by refusing his fundamental categories of argument (and, indeed, of being). 'The categories of the man of law have no power over Bartleby', Agamben writes, and so, when the lawyer tries to understand Bartleby's behaviour, he is always 'off the mark' (Agamben 1999, 254, 269). Rancière is even more straightforward. Bartleby's formula 'shatters not just the hierarchies of a world but also what supports them' (Rancière 2004, 146). Arguably, then, these instances of politically undecidable non-speech within speech similarly disrupt our interpretive frameworks and send us into a flurry of confusion about how, precisely, to read them. And in fact, the many very public debates about Mo Yan's Nobel suggest that this is at least in part precisely what's happening in the Western reception of his work in English translation. For the gaps of *Life and Death*'s self-reflexive insistence on not speaking while speaking mirror yet another set of gaps, which live in the interstices of any translated work and which are particularly fraught, given the ideological traces of Cold War binarism latent in at least some practitioners of twenty-first-century Western literary criticism (cf Klein 2016). For Western readers especially, Mo Yan's refusal to engage politics directly in his fiction creates an effect which looks very much like a gap in the sensible, or an instance of genuine politics.

This is problematic for two reasons. First, if dissent is visible only in the interstices of what's said, if it's merely disruptive, then dissent can never have positive content. Second, if interstices like the ones in Mo Yan's work constitute dissent, then we would have to say that any work exhibiting such interstices is dissenting. Read this way, dissent seems to be both nowhere and everywhere. Is our definition somehow wrong or insufficient? Does Bartleby not model something useful? Is there some other philosophically consistent principle we might apply to distinguish Mo Yan's elisions from protestors facing violent suppression at the hands of the state? A second case helps to clarify something missing from our account so far. That supplement will help to explain the uneasy relation between art and life in the context of dissent. It will also, I hope, suggest why Bartlebyesque dissent might be useful for the reading of world literatures.

Art and the state

The second case involves Langston Hughes's erasure of socialist sentiment from his body of work. Hughes's interest in Soviet socialism in the 1930s, his harassment by the Christian right in the 1940s, his subsequent surveillance under J. Edgar Hoover's FBI, and his eventual interrogation by the Senate Permanent Subcommittee on Investigations of the Committee on Government Operations in 1953 are all well-known to scholars (Berry 1983, Dawahare 1998, Maxwell 1999, Maxwell 2015, Rampersad 2002, Scott 2006, Chinitz 2013). Well documented, too, is Hughes's emergence in the late 1950s and early 1960s as a cultural ambassador to Africa, as well as his life-long engagement with left-leaning writers in Latin America and the Caribbean; his early travels there, in Africa, and in the U.S.S.R.; and his sympathy with the anticolonial movements across Africa (Rampersad 2002, Baldwin 2002, Kim 2007, Dworkin 2012, Kutzinski 2012). Despite those political *bona fides* – or perhaps because of them – Hughes is sometimes discussed as a writer who compromised his politics under pressure from patrons, publishers, and the state. In his later work and life, he emphasises, like Mo Yan, the autonomy of art from politics, the fallacy of reducing imaginative writing to an author's beliefs, and the futility of believing you can identify those beliefs in the first place. 'I've always taken pride in my lack of ideology', Mo Yan writes, 'especially when I am writing' (Mo Yan 2012b, 386). When asked before Joseph McCarthy's Senate Permanent Sub-committee on Investigations of the Committee on Government Operations in 1953 whether he shared the revolutionary sentiment expressed in 'Ballads of Lenin' (1933), Hughes replied bluntly, 'That is a poem. One can not state one believes every word of a poem' (U.S. Congress 1953b, 978). Hughes and Mo Yan share a sense that political ideology can never be reduced to poetics and that, conversely, poetics can never be reduced to political ideology. While we can only guess as to the relation between this sentiment and Mo Yan's actual interactions with Chinese officials, however, we have concrete evidence in the case of Hughes. In what follows, I will look closely at Hughes's closed-door Executive Session Congressional testimony as it relates to his more conciliatory public testimony. What will emerge is a legitimate disagreement over politics and poetry, or, in other words, dissent.

Hughes's televised testimony before Senator McCarthy, chief counsel Roy Cohn, consultant G. David Schine, and McCarthy's Senate Subcommittee has been a source of some embarrassment. Faith Berry considered Hughes's performance nothing less than a 'capitulation', 'complete, from beginning to end' (Berry 1983, 319). Arnold Rampersad lamented that Hughes 'had given in to brutish strength', and though he celebrates the 'rhetorical *tour de force*' with which Hughes rebutted Cohn's attempts to elicit a clear refutation of socialist sentiment, he judges that 'triumph' to have cost 'a victory of the spirit' (Rampersad 2002, 2:218–19). Hughes's 'dignity', Rampersad decided, 'had been largely passive' (219). Indeed, Hughes's public testimony reads as placid, especially in comparison with figures like Dashiell Hammett, who invoked his Fifth Amendment rights rather than answer McCarthy's interrogation; or Paul Robeson, who went further and lectured the House Un-American Activities Committee on civil rights and the legacies of slavery. Hughes, on the other hand, admits that 'there was such a period' when he 'believed in a Soviet form of government' (U.S. Congress 1953b, 74). Asked whether those of his books placed in United States Department Information Program in overseas libraries 'did largely follow the Communist line', Hughes answered that 'some of these books very largely followed at times some aspects of the Communist line, reflecting my sympathy with them' (79). He was 'surprised' to find his books placed in State Department libraries, and when McCarthy asks if 'those books should be on our shelves throughout the world, with the apparent stamp of approval of the United States Government', Hughes responded in clear terms: 'I would certainly say "No"' (79). Most damningly, McCarthy extracted from Hughes an endorsement of the Committee's abuses of power. 'We have had so much screaming by certain elements of the press that witnesses have been misused', he said. 'Do you feel that you were in any way mistreated by the staff or by the committee?' (83). Despite the fact that his subpoena demanded he appear in Washington on almost no notice, and that his reasonable request for a week to prepare and make travel arrangements was rejected, he tells the American public that he was 'agreeably sur-prised at the courtesy and friendliness with which [he] was received' (Rampersad 2002, 2:210; U.S. Congress 1953b, 83). He even goes so far as to thank Senator Dirksen and 'the young men who had to interrogate me, of course, had to interrogate me' (83). McCarthy reportedly winked (Rampersad 2002, 2:218).

The Executive Session testimony, declassified in 2003, tells a different story, however, one in which Hughes's refusal definitively to answer these same questions produces the kind of Bartlebyesque disruption we might well associ-ate with a genuine politics of dissent. Three examples demonstrate what Ran-cière might call a fundamental disagreement in terms, or what Agamben might call the opening of radical contingency. For example, when Cohn asks 'Have you ever believed in communism', Hughes replies 'Sir, I would have to know what you mean by communism to answer that truthfully' (U.S. Congress 1953a, 976). This seems like a basic evasive strategy. But a second exchange suggests a more fundamental disagreement in terms:

> Mr. COHN. Mr. Hughes, is it not a fact now that this poem here did repre-sent your views and it could only mean one thing, that the "Ballads to Lenin" [*sic*] did represent your views? You have told us that all of these things did, that you have been a consistent supporter of Communist movements and you have been a consistent and undeviating follower of the Communist party line up through and including recent times. Is that not a fact?
>
> (*U.S. Congress 1953a, 983*)

Cohn's simple 'Is that a fact' belies the fact that his 'question' has set a trap in which acquiescence on one point implies acquiescence on a multitude of accusations. Namely, he has wrapped up the claims (a) that 'Ballads of Lenin' represented Hughes's genuine political beliefs; (b) that the poem does not carry more than one meaning; (c) that Hughes has 'consistently' supported Com-munist movements; (d) that he has supported the 'Communist party line up through and including recent times'; and (e) that he has previously confirmed (a) through (d). Hughes asks him to break the question into its components. Cohn parries thus:

> Mr. COHN. Surely. I personally do not think it is necessary. You say you do not understand the question?
> Mr. HUGHES. No, sir, I do not say I do not understand the question. It is not a question. It is a series of questions.
>
> (*U.S. Congress 1953a, 983*)

Hughes understands Cohn perfectly well, but he refuses the terms of Cohn's interrogative strategy. When Cohn begins to break down the series, Hughes responds with variations of 'I would have to know what you mean by commun-ism', and Cohn abandons the line. In each case, Hughes doesn't outright refuse to respond, but he couches his evasions so as to further expose a gap between his own viewpoint and his interrogators'.

Hughes's insistence on exposing the gap between his worldview and the committee's becomes perhaps most evident in a third example, when he begins to provide a detailed autobiography in lieu of explicating 'One More "S" in the U.S.A.' (1934). Like Melville's lawyer, the senators and counsel are flustered. Cohn tries to cut short Hughes's 'exegesis' by conceding what he believes to be its fundamental point:

> Mr. COHN. I do not want to interrupt you. I do want to say this. I want to save time here. I want to concede very fully that you encounter oppression and denial of civil rights. Let us assume that, because I assume that will be the substance of what you are about to say. To save us time, what we are interested in determining for our purpose is this: Was the solution to which you turned that of the Soviet form of government?
>
> Mr. HUGHES. Sir, you said you would permit me to give a full explanation.
>
> Mr. COHN. I was wondering if we could not save a little time because I want to concede the background which you wrote it from was the background you wanted to describe.
>
> Mr. HUGHES. I would much rather preserve my reputation and freedom than to save time.
>
> *(U.S. Congress 1953a, 986)*

Cohn's strategy is to agree that black Americans 'encounter oppression and the denial of civil rights', but then to get Hughes to admit that he found a 'solution' in Communism. When this doesn't work, he tries to collapse 'the background which you wrote it from' and 'the background you wanted to describe' into context. Hughes will not submit, insisting that this so-called 'background' is, rather, 'a full interpretation' of the poem (986). He then continues for nearly 1400 more words before Senator Dirksen finally cuts him off. 'Do you think we need more emotional background to tell what you meant by USSA?' Dirksen asks (989). 'I think you do, sir. Because critical work goes out of a very deep background', Hughes replies (989). Cohn responds that Hughes is 'missing the point completely'. And here the full impasse comes into view. Hughes demands that 'One More "S" in the U.S.A.' can only be understood as a response to racial segregation, open discrimination, and wealth inequality in Jim Crow America. The committee considers these details frivolous, mitigating details at best. The assumption, however, that racial segregation is 'background' entails an assumption of shared autonomy that Hughes will not grant. The 'background' he provides by way of interpretation is not context for self-expression; it is inextricably imbricated in the self. Hughes and his interrogators disagree not just about the terms of argument, but about the terms of the *demos*.

This mode of dissent is not fully available within the poetry or prose in isolation. Hughes's dissenting politics become visible in interstices of a literal encounter with the state which sought to (and some would argue did) suppress his work. But what emerges here is of twofold significance. First, Hughes's refusal to agree to the state's terms of interrogation opens a space for revolutionary politics. It does not do so by explicitly claiming socialist sentiment, for to espouse socialism would be to agree to the terms of the state. Rather, in disputing those very terms and in asserting, obliquely and demonstratively, the presence of an experience and a *demos* the state denies, Hughes in fact *reasserts* the revolutionary hope of poems like 'A New Song', which called for interracial unity and solidarity. 'I speak in the name of black millions / awakening to action', Hughes wrote in 1933, 'Revolt! Arise! / The Black / And White World / Shall be one! / The Worker's World!' (Hughes 1994, 170, 171–2). In 'A New Song', as in many poems of this period, Hughes finds in socialist solidarity a response to white supremacy, which he frames according to labour and self-possession:

> Bitter was the day
> When I bowed my back
> Beneath the slaver's whip.
>
> That day is past.
> [...]
> I know full well now
> Only my own hands,
> Dark as earth,
> Can make my earth-dark body free.
> O, thieves, exploiters, killers,
> No longer shall you say
> With arrogant eyes and scornful lips:
> "You are my servant,
> Black man—
> I, the free!"
>
> That day is past—
> *(Hughes 1994, 170–1)*

Notably, this poem echoes, structurally, one of Hughes's most famous early poems 'I, Too', in which the 'darker brother' sent to eat in the kitchen 'grow[s] strong' and takes his place at the table: 'Nobody'll dare / Say to me / "Eat in the kitchen," / Then' (46). Expanded in 'A New Song', the basic argumentative form of 'I, Too' – its refusal of racist segregation and white terror followed by a claim to power – remains intact in the later more explicitly revolutionary poem. 'A New Song' imports socialist sentiment to bolster Hughes's unceasing demand for black inclusion in the *demos*. But the note of dissent in the later poem derives not only from its internationalist chorus, but also from its persistent insistence on progressive revision of a self-declared democratic nation built on white supremacy. In other words, from exactly the kind of claim Hughes makes in his Executive Session testimony when he disputes the grounds of questioning by inserting an auto-biographical narrative that demonstrates how his work cannot be read independently from the context of institutional American racism. Hughes will revisit 'I, Too' again in 1963's 'We, Too', a poem of solidarity with Congolese nationalists following the assassination of Patrice Lumumba:

> Oh, Congo brother
> With your tribal marks,
> We, too, emerge
> From ageless darks.
> We, too, emit
> A frightening cry
> From body scarred,
> Soul that won't die.
> We encarnadine the sky.
> [...]
> We, too,
> Congo brother,
> Rise with you.
>   *(Hughes 1994, 538)*

The pan-African unity of 'We, Too' echoes the red poems of the 1930s in the lines 'We encarnadine the sky' and 'We, too, / Congo brother, / Rise with you'. It also revises once more the struggle signaled in 'I, Too', claiming common ground for domestic civil rights activists at home and anticolonial activists in Africa. As several critics persuasively have argued, Hughes's late period can and should be read in continuity with his earlier verse, rather than in opposition to a disavowed radicalism following his confrontation with McCarthy (Smethurst 2002, Kim 2007, Dworkin 2012). Reading for the traces of dissent as it was expressed – or, better, demonstrated – in Hughes's confrontation with Dirksen and Cohn gives us yet another way to frame the radical politics of his commitment to social progressivism across the whole of his career. The Bartlebyesque dissent with which he faced direct state confrontation marks not a break with Hughes's earlier socialism but, rather, a line of continuity in which we can read the socialist sentiment as complementary to an on-going commitment to independence and full rights for formerly colonised peoples around the globe, including within the domestic United States.

    The second way in which reading dissent through Hughes's congressional testimony becomes significant is in what it tells us about more abstract question of dissent and literature. The case of Langston Hughes outlined here demonstrates how dissent becomes meaningful in the context of the powers that constrain it. Elision and circumlocution, the politics of which are undecidable in Mo Yan's work, become potent in Langston Hughes's Congressional testimony, and by extension in his work at large. That visibility arises from a direct confrontation between the artist and the state, and from a genuine disagreement about the very terms on which art and, indeed, politics itself should be engaged. Thus we might say that dissent becomes visible only relationally, in the context of systems of production, circumstances of reception, and instances of overt confrontation. A slippery thing, dissent. Moments of disagreement in the Rancièrian sense, or of unspeakable potentiality in the Agambean sense, are not always visible in isolation (as Rancière himself well knows). The political intentions and political effects of art are not coextensive but rather intertwined (Rancière 2015). This is good news for students of world literatures. Reading for dissent as a gap in the sensible or, in Agamben's framing, as 'not a *state* but an *event* of language' opens fertile ground for critics invested in the global circulation of texts (Agamben 2000, 116). The awareness in world literary studies of mediation through cultural and linguistic translation, as well as through sometimes surprising publishing channels, can heighten our facility in tracking and documenting instances of disagreement and dissent. Correspondingly, looking for dissent in world literatures encourages ever more fastidious attention to the material and social circumstances of texts in global circulation. Where there is dissent, Agamben counsels, 'sooner or later, the tanks will appear' (Agamben 1993, 87). Indeed, we can't see 'Tank Man' without them.

Works cited

Agamben, Giorgio. 1993 [1990]. *The Coming Community*. Trans. Michael Hardt. Minneapolis, MN: University of Minnesota Press.

Agamben, Giorgio. 1998 [1995]. *Homo Sacer: Sovereignty and Bare Life*. Trans. Daniel Heller-Roazen. Stanford, CA: Stanford University Press.

Agamben, Giorgio. 1999. *Potentialities: Collected Essays in Philosophy*. Trans. Daniel Heller-Roazen. Stanford, CA: Stanford University Press.

Agamben, Giorgio. 2000. *Means Without End: Notes on Politics*. Trans. Vincenzo Binetti and Cesare Casarino. Minneapolis, MN: University of Minnesota Press.

Agamben, Giorgio, and Gilles Deleuze. 1993. *Bartleby, la formula della creazione*. Macerata, Italy: Quodlibet.

Associated Press. 2012. 'Censorship is a Must, Says China's Nobel Winner'. *The Guardian* 7 December. Available at: https://www.guardian.co.uk/ world/2012/dec/07/mo-yan-censorship-nobel (Accessed 10 August 2018).

Baldwin, Kate A. 2002. *Beyond the Color Line and the Iron Curtain: Reading Encounters between Black and Red, 1922–1963*. Durham, NC: Duke University Press.

Bassett, Keith. 2014. 'Rancière, Politics, and the Occupy Movement'. *Environment and Planning D: Society and Space* 32: 886–901.

Berry, Faith. 1983. *Langston Hughes: Before and Beyond Harlem*. Westport, CT: Lawrence Hill and Company.

Brouillette, Sarah. 2014. 'Literature is Liberalism'. *Jacobin* 15 October. Available at: https:// www.jacobinmag.com/2014/10/literature-is-liberalism/ (Accessed 10 August 2018).

Chan, Shelly W. 2000. 'From Fatherland to Motherland: On Mo Yan's Red Sorghum and Big Breasts and Full Hips'. *World Literature Today* 74(3): 495–500.

Chinitz, David E. 2013. *Which Sin to Bear? Authenticity and Compromise in Langston Hughes*. Oxford, UK: Oxford University Press.

Daley, David. 2012. 'Rushdie: Mo Yan is a "Patsy of the Regime"'. *Salon* 7 December. Available at: https://www.salon.com/2012/12/07/rushdie_mo_yan_is_a_patsy_of_the_regime/ (Accessed 10 August 2018).

Dawahare, Anthony. 1998. 'Langston Hughes's Radical Poetry and the "End of Race"'. *MELUS* 23(3): 21–41.

Deleuze, Gilles. 1998. *Essays Critical and Clinical.* Trans. Daniel W. Smith and Michael A. Greco. London: Verso.

Duran, Angelica and Yuhan Huang, eds. 2014. *Mo Yan in Context: Nobel Laureate and Global Storyteller.* West Lafayette, IN: Purdue University Press.

Dworkin, Ian. 2012. '"Near the Congo": Langston Hughes and the Geopolitics of Internationalist Poetry'. *American Literary History* 24(4): 631–657.

The Editors. 2013. 'World Lite'. *n+1* 17. Available at: https://nplusonemag.com/issue-17/the-intellectual-situation/world-lite/ (Accessed 10 August 2018).

English, James F. 2008. *The Economy of Prestige: Prizes, Awards, and the Circulation of Cultural Value.* Cambridge, MA: Harvard University Press.

Espmark, Kjell. 1999. 'The Nobel Prize in Literature'. Nobelprize.org. Nobel Media AB 2018. Available at: https://www.nobelprize.org/nobel_prizes/themes/literature/espmark/ (Accessed 10 August 2018).

He, Chengzhou. 2014. 'Rural Chineseness, Mo Yan's work, and World Literature' in Duran, Angelica and Yuhan Huang, eds, *Mo Yan in Context: Nobel Laureate and Global Storyteller.* West Lafayette, IN: Purdue University Press, pp. 77–90.

Huang, Alexa, and Angelica Duran. 2014. 'Mo Yan's Work and the Politics of Literary Humor' in Duran, Angelica and Yuhan Huang, eds, *Mo Yan in Context: Nobel Laureate and Global Storyteller.* West Lafayette, IN: Purdue University Press, pp. 153–164.

Huang, Alexander C. Y. 2009. 'Mo Yan as Humorist'. *World Literature Today* 83(4): 32–37.

Hughes, Langston. 1994. *The Collected Poems of Langston Hughes.* Eds. Arnold Rampersad and David Roessel. New York: Vintage.

Hughes, Langston. 1999. *Selected Poems.* New York: Serpent's Tail.

Kim, Daniel Won-gu. 2007. '"We, Too, Rise with You": Recovering Langston Hughes's African (Re)Turn 1954–1960 in *An African Treasury,* the *Chicago Defender,* and *Black Orpheus'. African American Review* 41(3): 419–441.

Klein, Lucas. 2016. 'A Dissonance of Discourses: Literary Theory, Ideology, and Translation in Mo Yan and Chinese Literary Studies'. *Comparative Literature Studies* 53(1): 170–197.

Knight, Sabina. 2013. 'Mo Yan's Delicate Balancing Act'. *The National Interest* 124: 69–80.

Knight, Sabina. 2014. 'The Realpolitik of Mo Yan's Fiction' in Duran, Angelica and Yuhan Huang, eds, *Mo Yan in Context: Nobel Laureate and Global Storyteller.* West Lafayette, IN: Purdue University Press, pp. 93–106.

Kutzinski, Vera M. 2012. *The Worlds of Langston Hughes: Modernism and Translation in the Americas.* Ithaca, NY: Cornell University Press.

Laughlin, Charles. 2012. 'What Mo Yan's Detractors Get Wrong'. *ChinaFile* 11 December. Available at: http://www.chinafile.com/what-mo-yans-detractors-get-wrong (Accessed 10 August 2018).

Link, Perry. 2012. 'Does This Writer Deserve the Prize?' Review of *Red Sorghum, The Garlic Ballads, Big Breasts and Wide Hips,* and *Live and Death Are Wearing Me Out* by Mo Yan. *New York Review of Books* 6 December. Available at: https://www.nybooks.com/articles/archives/2012/dec/06/mo-yan-nobel-prize/ (Accessed 10 August 2018).

Lovell, Julia. 2002. 'Gao Xingjian, the Nobel Prize, and Chinese Intellectuals: Notes on the Aftermath of the Nobel Prize 2000'. *Modern Chinese Literature and Culture* 14(2): 1–50.

Lovell, Julia. 2006. *The Politics of Cultural Capital: China's Quest for a Nobel Prize in Literature.* Honolulu: University of Hawai'i Press.

Maxwell, William J. 1999. *New Negro, Old Left: African American Writing and Communism Between the Wars*. New York: Columbia University Press.

Maxwell, William J. 2015. *F.B. Eyes: How J. Edgar Hoover's Ghostreaders Framed African American Literature*. Princeton, NJ: Princeton University Press.

McLoughlin, Daniel. 2016. 'Post-Marxism and the Politics of Human Rights: Lefort, Badiou, Agamben, Rancière'. *Law Critique* 27: 303–321.

Mo Yan. 2008. *Life and Death Are Wearing Me Out*. Trans. Howard Goldblatt. New York: Arcade.

Mo Yan. 2012a. 'Nobel Lecture: Storytellers'. Nobelprize.org. Nobel Media AB 2018, Available at: https://www.nobelprize.org/prizes/literature/2012/yan/lecture/ (Accessed 10 August 2018).

Mo Yan. 2012b. *POW!* Trans. Howard Goldblatt. London: Seagull.

Ngai, Ling Tun. 1998. 'Anal Anarchy: A Reading of Mo Yan's 'The Plagues of Red Locusts'. *Modern Chinese Literature* 10(1/2): 7–24.

Rampersad, Arnold. 2002. *The Life of Langston Hughes*. 2nd ed. 2 vols. Oxford, UK: Oxford University Press.

Rancière, Jacques. 2004. *The Flesh of Words: The Politics of Writing*. Trans. Charlotte Mandell. Stanford, CA: Stanford University Press.

Rancière, Jacques. 2015. *Dissensus: On Politics and Aesthetics*. Trans. Steven Corcoran. London: Bloomsbury.

Rancière, Jacques. 2017. 'Democracy, Equality, Emancipation in a Changing World'. Paper presented at the International Antiauthoritarian Festival of Babylonia Journal, 27 May, Athens. Available at: https://www.babylonia.gr/2017/06/11/jacques-ranciere-democracy-equality-emancipation-changing-world/ (Accessed 10 August 2018).

Roberts, Gillian. 2011. *Prizing Literature: The Celebration and Circulation of National Culture*. Toronto: University of Toronto Press.

Saval, Nikil. 2013. 'White Happy Doves'. Review of *Change, Sandalwood Death*, and *Pow!* by Mo Yan. *London Review of Books* 29 August. Available at: https://www.lrb.co.uk/v35/n16/nikil-saval/white-happy-doves (Accessed 10 August 2018).

Scott, Jonathan. 2006. *Socialist Joy in the Writing of Langston Hughes*. Columbia, MO: University of Missouri Press.

Smethurst, James. 2002. '"Don't Say Goodbye to the Porkpie Hat": Langston Hughes, the Left, and the Black Arts Movement'. *Callaloo* 25(4): 1–14.

Updike, John. 2005. 'Bitter Bamboo: Two Novels from China'. Review of *My Life as Emperor* by Su Tong and *Big Breasts and Wide Hips* by Mo Yan. *New Yorker* 9 May. Available at: https://www.newyorker.com/magazine/2005/05/09/bitter-bamboo (Accessed 10 August 2018).

U.S. Congress. 1953a. *Executive Sessions of the Senate Permanent Subcommittee on Investigations of the Committee on Government Operations*. Vol. 2. Senate Committee on Government Operations. 83d Cong., 1st sess. Made public January 2003.

U.S. Congress. 1953b. *State Department Information Program – Information Centers. Hearing before the Permanent Subcommittee on Investigations of the Committee on Government Operations. United States Senate*. Senate Committee on Government Operations. 83d Cong., 1st sess., S. Res. 40, March 24, 25, and 26.

Wang, David Der-Wei. 2000. 'The Literary World of Mo Yan'. *World Literature Today* 74(3): 487–494.

3

PAYING ATTENTION

Philosophy as dissenting therapy for the information age

Dominic Smith

Thank you for paying attention. In a world saturated with information, this is a lot to ask and to offer. This chapter's aim, however, is to dissent from these rules. Put simply, I am not asking you to 'pay attention'. Instead, my aim is to point out the contingency of a grammar that, just as it prepares you to pay attention, also prepares you to conceive of attention in crudely economic ways: as a resource, capital, commodity, investment, or deficit.[1]

Consider these words from David Foster Wallace:

> There are, as it happens, intergenre differences that I know and care about as a writer, though these differences are hard to talk about in a way that someone who doesn't try to write both fiction and nonfiction will understand. I'm worried that they'll sound cheesy and melodramatic. Although maybe they won't. Maybe, given the ambient volume of your own life's noise, the main difference will make sense to you. Writing-wise, fiction is scarier, but nonfiction is harder – because nonfiction [is] based in reality, and today's felt reality is overwhelmingly, circuit-blowingly huge and complex. Whereas fiction comes out of nothing. Actually, so wait: the truth is that both genres are scary; both feel like they're executed on tightropes, over abysses – it's the abysses that are different. Fiction's abyss is silence, *nada*. Whereas nonfiction's abyss is Total Noise, the seething static of every particular thing and experience, and one's total freedom of infinite choice about what to choose to attend to and represent and connect, and how, and why, etc.
>
> *(Wallace 2012, 302–3)*

A key question driving this chapter is this: Where does philosophy sit in relation to Wallace's 'intergenre differences'? Is philosophy 'fiction' or 'nonfiction', or something irreducible to either? If philosophy is irreducible, is it 'scarier' or 'harder' than both? Why, if its 'irreducibility' can be posed at all, is philosophy something Wallace, himself a philosophy graduate (Max 2012), sees no difficulty in omitting? Is philosophy something so downright difficult or negligible that it has no obvious role to play in making sense of the abysses that threaten our contemporary 'felt reality'? The first section takes up Wallace's term 'Total Noise' to refer to the predicament of attention in our contemporary Information Age of networks, feedback, social media, search engines, and ubiquitous computing (Castells 2010). I argue that if the capacity to 'pay attention' is in crisis today, this may have to do with issues concerning how the topic is framed. A core problem, I suggest, is that we are inheritors of an engrained crudely economic grammar that frames attention as a resource or form of capital to be paid.

The second section takes up 'silence'. If paying attention is in crisis today, the capacity to be silent emerges as both a threat and an opportunity. It is a threat because it stands to let the loudest and most distracting statements and narratives shape the world's accepted character; it is an opportunity because it allows us to recognise and step outside the terms of the crudely economic grammar. Put simply, what happens when we dissent to the terms of a narrative that frames attention as something to be 'paid'? Can we then also dissent to a view of it as a resource to be mined, leveraged, exploited or exhausted, or as a form of capital to be invested, and that can, correlatively, be subject to deficits, monetised, leveraged, and exploited by marketing? What happens when we start telling other stories about attention, according to different grammars, in terms of a capacity to be 'nourished', 'drawn', 'dedicated', 'demanded', 'defended', 'devoted', 'attracted', or to act in 'harmony', 'dissonance', or 'concert'?

The third section returns to Wallace's 'intergenre differences': 'there are, as it happens, intergenre differences that I know and care about as a writer, though these differences are hard to talk about in a way that someone who doesn't try to write both fiction and nonfiction will understand' (Wallace 2012, 302–3). These remarks can come across as condescending and exclusive, to the point where they risk obscuring Wallace's remarks on the abysses of 'Total Noise' and 'silence'. What is significant about these abysses, I will argue, is that they do not merely threaten the lives of writers; rather, they threaten the 'ambient volume' of everyone connected to the Information Age.

There are, on the reading to be developed in this chapter, two good reasons why philosophy does not feature in Wallace's discussion of 'intergenre differences'. First, philosophy is not a 'genre' at all: it is a practice or 'way of life' (Wittgenstein 2009, 86; Hadot 2001). Specifically, philosophy is a form of critical, creative, and therapeutic practice, dedicated to working through distortions and inconsistencies in the narratives we tell ourselves about the world. Second, this means that philosophy is the type of practice capable of refiguring our understanding of what counts as 'nonfiction' and 'fiction', and of refiguring why these categories matter. Before they are 'genres' for writers and critics, nonfiction and fiction are ways of turning the ambient volume of our lives up and down, and this is why they matter today: because oscillations between 'Total Noise' and 'silence' have perhaps never been greater than in the contemporary 'Information Age'.

Total noise

If the capacity to 'pay attention' is in crisis today, this may have to do with an engrained tendency to conceptualise attention in crudely economic terms. I make the case for this by detecting signs of this tendency across different contexts in this section, including continental philosophy, marketing, cognitive psychology, and philosophy of mind. In *Suspensions of Perception*, Jonathan Crary writes:

> I am interested in how Western modernity since the nineteenth century has demanded that individuals define and shape themselves in terms of a capacity for 'paying attention', that is, for a disengagement from a broader field of attraction, whether visual or auditory, for the sake of isolating or focusing on a reduced number of stimuli. That our lives are so thoroughly a patchwork of such disconnected states is not a 'natural' condition but rather the product of a dense and powerful remaking of human subjectivity in the West over the last 150 years. Nor is it insignificant now at the end of the twentieth century that one of the ways an immense social crisis of subjective disintegration is metaphorically diagnosed is as a deficiency of 'attention'.
>
> *(Crary 2001, 1)*

These remarks indicate that Crary is performing a 'genealogy' of attention, as befits influences drawn from Nietzsche and Foucault (Crary 1990, 2014; Foucault 1991). In this 'masters of suspicion' vein of philosophy, 'genealogy' is the attempt to tell the hidden history of the apparently obvious.

Crary's work has applied genealogy to topics including attention (2001), the changing status of the observer (1990), and sleep (2014). Nevertheless, we might still suspect his handling of attention of being insufficiently genealogical. The problem is this: Crary wants to tell us the hidden history of attention, but, in doing so, he underplays the fact that framing attention in economic terms also has a history. Granted, Crary does appear to highlight certain 'economic' characteristics of the history of attention by using scare quotes for 'paying attention', and by describing 'deficiency' as a 'metaphor'. But such allusions do not amount to an investigation of the hidden history of the economic grammar. They are placeholders for it. Indeed, they might even be interpreted as a kind of 'insurance policy': absent a thoroughgoing investigation into the grammar of paying attention, they seem to indemnify Crary from any criticism that he was unaware of the need for such an investigation. But at least Crary was conscious enough of the economics of attention to get caught up in this problem. In contrast, the 'economics of attention' often seem to be so engrained in everyday language as to go unnoticed.

Consider a few examples from diverse contemporary contexts. In 2004, Patrick Le Lay, chairman of the French television channel TF1, stated:

> There are many ways to speak about TV, but [from] a business perspective, let's be realistic: [...] TF1's job is helping Coca-Cola, for example, sell its

product [...] [I]n order for an advert to be seen, it is necessary for the brain of the viewer to be available. The vocation of our programmes is to render the [viewer's brain] available: [...] to amuse and to relax it in order to prepare it [...], between two adverts. What we sell to Coca-Cola is available human brain time. Nothing is more difficult than obtaining this availability. This is where permanent change is located. We must always look out for popular programs, follow trends, surf on tendencies, in a context in which information is speeding up.

(Le Lay 2004; cf Stiegler 2004; Stiegler and Ars Industrialis 2008)

When Le Lay states 'let's be realistic', is this a throwaway figure of speech or an ontological assertion about the primacy of a 'business perspective', or both? When he states 'between two adverts', what does this say about the status of TF1's programmes, and where do these sit in relation to the marketing narratives employed by companies like Coca-Cola? Why, when referring to what TF1 seeks to 'render available' to these companies, does Le Lay mention the 'brain', not attention? Is this because he considers attention to be too allusive or ethereal, or because he implicitly adopts a crudely 'neurological' grammar that refuses to consider attention as something more comprehensively somatic? To what extent does Le Lay's reference to 'always [looking] out for popular programs' presuppose a hunter's vigilance, and to what extent does that grammar converge with and diverge from neurological and economic grammars? My aim in posing this glut of questions is self-consciously rhetorical: to draw attention to the extent to which a crudely economic grammar acts as their discursive condition. The contention to be developed, in this sense, is this: critical questions like these are only possible because they issue from the same discursive register as Le Lay's comments. That is, they are possible because, syntactically, they 'speak the same language'.

Let's now switch contexts, to cognitive psychology. The aim in doing so is to observe the ways in which the ostensibly everyday grammar of paying attention is *trans-disciplinary*. That is, the aim is to observe the ways in which this grammar gets carried across from contemporary everyday discourse into discrete theoretical contexts and specialisms.[2]

Consider these remarks from Mihalyi Csikszentmihalyi, a thinker famous for conceptualising states of attentional 'flow':

Attention is the medium that makes information appear in consciousness. The human organism is limited to discriminating a maximum of about seven bits – or chunks – of information per unit of time [...]. [T]he duration of such an attentional unit [is estimated] to be on the order of 1/18th per second; in other words, we can become aware of 18 × 7 bits of information, or 126 bits of information, in the space of a second. Thus a person can process at most in the neighbourhood of 7,560 bits of information each minute. In a lifetime of 70 years, and assuming a waking day of 16 hours, this amounts to about 185 billion bits of information. This number defines the limit of individual experience. Out of it must come every perception, thought, feeling, memory, or action that a person will ever have. It seems like a large number, but in actuality most people find it tragically insufficient.

(Csikszentmihalyi and Csikszentmihalyi 1988, 18)

My aim in citing these remarks is not empirical: it is not to either accept or dispute Csikszentmihalyi's figures. Instead, my aim is to highlight the ways in which a crudely economic grammar acts as a background condition for the possibility of his remarks as a whole.

Consider what defines a subject's attention for Csikszentmihalyi: a lifetime quantity of data, which is to say the data 'resources' or 'capital' the subject is capable of investing. From here, questions proliferate. For whom, for instance, could the lifetime figure of attention of '185 billion bits' really count, since no attentive subject would appear either willing or capable of quantifying the phenomenology of their attention in this way? For what type of 'quantified subject' would this putative figure 'define the limit', if not a fabricated and purely theoretical subject, in Kierkegaard's sense of the 'average man' (1978, 62) or Heidegger's sense of 'Das Man' (2005, 163–8)? And why does Csikszentmihalyi state that 'every perception, thought, feeling, memory, or action that [such] a person will ever have' must come 'out of' this quantity of 185 billion bits? If we are talking in the (vexed) terms of 'inner' and 'outer', wouldn't it make more sense to say that such items come 'into attention'? We have again reached a surfeit of rhetorical questions. Again, however, the suggestion is that these are extensions of the same grammar conditioning Csikszentmihalyi's remarks. As in the case of Le Lay, the contention is that, if these questions can be posed at all, it is because they issue from the same set of discursive conditions as Csikszentmihalyi's remarks.

Observe, further, that Csikszentmihalyi's remarks exhibit clear tendencies towards obfuscation and contradiction. This emerges most clearly in his comment that 'most people' find the putative lifetime quantity of 185 billion bits 'tragically insufficient'. This tends towards obfuscation because it is a matter of high statistical improbability that 'most people' have reflected on attention in such an artificial way, and it tends towards contradiction because it implies that, to find one's quantity of attention 'tragically insufficient', one would have to be *dead*, a state which, according to criteria employed by all current natural science, does not appear to involve the capacity for conscious attention. The point here is that Csikszentmihalyi's remarks take up an ostensibly 'everyday' grammar that frames attention in crudely economic terms, before proceeding to build elaborate and inconsistent metaphysical fictions upon it.

Consider, further, some instances of how such a grammar inflects contemporary philosophy of mind. In his *Stanford Encyclopaedia of Philosophy* article on attention, Christopher Mole writes:

Bottleneck metaphors have traditionally guided the theories that attempt to locate the cognitive resources that operate only on attended stimuli, but it has been *spotlight* metaphors that have guided the theories that attempt to say which features of a stimulus determine whether attention is being paid to that stimulus at any given moment. The central idea suggested by the spotlight metaphor is that the determinant of whether or not a stimulus is attended is that stimulus's location.

(Mole 2013, n.p.)

While reflecting on dominant metaphors that have traditionally framed philosophy of mind's theories of attention ('bottleneck' and 'spotlight'), Mole uses an even more dominant metaphor drawn from a more pervasive 'everyday' way of referring to attention: the economic metaphor that frames attention as something to be paid. In the process of being attentive to the metaphors that shape his theoretical field, then, Mole comes across as more or less oblivious to the metaphors conditioning this field on a less specialised level.

My aim in highlighting this is not to claim that Mole is being insufficiently rigorous. Unlike Crary, he is not engaged in a 'genealogical' investigation that would benefit from digging deeper into the rhetorical/grammatical background of the metaphor of attention as 'payment'. Instead, the point is that Mole's discussion is not syntactically arbitrary: while he could have referred to attention in different ways (in terms of 'being attentive', or of 'drawing' or 'giving' attention), the fact remains that he did not, and instead had recourse to the metaphor of attention as 'payment'. This, I suggest, is because although this metaphor is ultimately contingent, recourse to it is a matter of deep cultural and syntactic probability and habit.

Let me close this section by relating these reflections to Wallace's remark that '[t]oday's felt reality is overwhelmingly, circuit-blowingly huge and complex', generating a kind of 'Total Noise'. The suggestion this chapter will go on to develop is that the conditions for this perception may fundamentally have to do with an engrained tendency to frame attention in terms of the crudely economic grammar highlighted in this section. This is because framing attention as an 'asset' or as 'capital' to be invested is, contrary to the indemnity we saw Crary's genealogical account take out at the beginning of this section, not a matter of 'mere metaphor' to be alluded to. Rather, this engrained way of relating to attention has real pragmatic consequences because it carries the corollary that attention is framed as something that can become 'toxic', that can be 'exploited' or 'leveraged', and that can 'crash' and become 'bankrupt'.

Silence

The aim for this section is to consider what 'being silent' might mean today, in the midst of ostensible 'Total Noise'. Reflecting on the history of philosophy, it might be quipped that philosophers going back to Plato have often found the world too 'distracting' or 'noisy'. To torture metaphors, silence has often appeared as a kind of philosophical 'austerity measure': a way of stepping back from the world's 'idle chatter', to a metaphysical ivory tower or philosopher's armchair (Nietzsche 1998; Rorty 1991). To further explore this, consider two famously austere approaches to 'silence': from the early Wittgenstein, and Blanchot. In his 1929 'Lecture on Ethics', Wittgenstein states:

> This running against the walls of our cage is perfectly, absolutely hopeless. Ethics so far as it springs from the desire to say something about the ultimate meaning of life, the absolute good, the absolutely valuable, can be no science. What it says does not add to our knowledge in any sense.
>
> *(Wittgenstein 2014, 51)*

Although positioned at a turning point in Wittgenstein's development, these remarks are governed by the famously austere grammar underpinning the *Tractatus*, a grammar which gave rise to that text's notorious closing words: 'What we cannot speak about we must pass over in silence' (Wittgenstein 2001, 89). In both these extracts, Wittgenstein is thinking through the apparent meaninglessness of language that can be deemed 'meaningful' in any logical sense – that is, the incapacity of meaningful statements to say anything on profound issues such as the 'absolutely good' or 'absolutely valuable'. This, according to *Tractatus*' 'picture theory', is because the only truly meaningful statements are contingent ones that could be contradicted or falsified, and which therefore do not relieve the desire to say something meaningful in the sense of 'necessary' or 'profound' (89). According to the grammar orchestrating both extracts, then, the only possible recourse is silence. At most, Wittgenstein conjectures, we can hope that the absolutely good or valuable might 'show' itself, in quasi-mystical experiences that could, per definition, not be discussed in any meaningful sense (89).

Although from a different tradition, Blanchot is another philosopher who appears to indulge this austere recourse. Reflecting on Herman Melville's famous story 'Bartleby the Scrivener', he writes: '"I would prefer not to ..." the negative preference, the negation which effaces preference and which effaces itself in doing so [...]. Language silencing itself by perpetuating itself' (Blanchot 1986, 145).[3] The question arising here concerns whether the reflections of philosophers like Wittgenstein and Blanchot can emerge as 'silent' in any other sense than that of politically quietistic, elitist, or conservative. Can the limits of language be affected immanently, from within the walls of language's 'echo chamber', in such a way that we can stop perceiving silence as a philosophical 'austerity measure'?

At the risk of further torturing metaphors, perhaps the part we really need play in order to dissent from ostensible 'Total Noise' today is not that of the austere philosopher, but that of the accountant with sensitive ears; that is, someone capable of observing another, more literal, but paradoxically more forgotten sense of the term 'auditing': as *listening*. The suggestion here is that we need to develop the capacity to 'audit' ways of framing attention that, in the face of the 'Total Noise' generated by the crudely economic grammar of attention, show up as silences within this grammar. If such talk of 'auditing silences' seems too allusive, let me put it differently: what we are after is a way of recognising overlooked conditions for the possibility of the 'attention economy'.

Let me try to demonstrate what such a practice might involve. Recall Csikszentmihalyi's remark that 'we can become aware of [...] 126 bits of information in the space of one second' (1988, 18). Here, in belated response, is a speculative question: are there types of attention of which we, as conscious psychological subjects of the type quantified by Csikszentmihalyi, are unaware? Consider the following summary of a 2013 experiment to simulate the biological processing time of the human brain, by the Fujistu K supercomputer: 'It took 40 minutes with the combined muscle of 82,944 processors in K computer to [simulate] 1 second of biological brain processing time. While running, the system ate up about 1 PB of memory' (Whitham 2013, n.p.).[4] It could be objected that this summary exhibits journalistic hyperbole. This objection, however, is precisely to the point: what it draws out is the fact that this summary and Csikszentmihalyi's account exhibit isomorphisms in terms of their grammatical conditions. For example: both seek to quantify living processes (consciously directed attention in Csikszentmihalyi's case, 'biological brain processing time' in that of the summary), and both frame these in terms of more or less elaborate metaphysical fictions (a 'lifetime quantity of data' in Csikszentmihalyi's case, zoomorphisms that frame K computer in terms of 'muscle' and 'eating' in that of the summary). By virtue of these isomorphisms, both sources can, I think, be said to participate in the general grammar of the 'economy of attention', as discussed in the first section.

Despite these isomorphisms, however, the sources point towards very different conclusions on what constitutes 'attention'. Csikszentmihalyi holds that we can become aware of 126 bits of information in one second. In contrast, the summary holds that one second's worth of 'biological brain processing' requires 1 PB of computing processing power to simulate. 1 PB of processing power is 10^{15} bytes, a figure that would, assuming consistency between Csikszentmihalyi's conception of a 'bit' and that current in computer science, have to be multiplied by eight to arrive at the number of bits involved in one second's worth of biological processing time. This gives an astronomically stark difference in the orders of magnitude between the types of living process these two sources seek to quantify: 126 bits in the case of Csikszentmihalyi, and ($10^{15} \times 8$) bits in that of the summary.[5] The point about these figures, despite the huge differences between them, is that there is a case for qualifying both as attempts to quantify 'attention'. First and foremost, this is because the sources share the grammatical isomorphisms discussed above. Ontologically speaking, and more profoundly, however, it is also because the type of consciously aware attention discussed by Csikszentmihalyi must, absent a highly anachronistic Cartesian conception of mind, require 'biological brain processing' as a condition of possibility. In other words, 'biological brain processing' time must function as a necessary condition upon which attentive awareness of the type discussed by Csikszentmihalyi supervenes. From here, a case emerges for treating 'biological brain processing' time as a form of attention of which we are not consciously aware.

Suppose we call this 'unpaid attention'. By this, I mean forms of attention to which we are not 'paying attention'. This may give this concept an unfortunate appearance of paradox or wordplay. It is therefore necessary to unpack it: what I mean to highlight are necessary conditions, such as 'biological brain processing time', that must be in place in order for what we qualify as 'conscious' or 'aware' attention to supervene, but which too narrow a focus on attention as consciousness or awareness distracts us from recognising. In this sense, unpaid attention is like 'unpaid labour': it refers to conditions that contribute and work towards making the economy of attention possible, but that are exploited and not recognised as part of it by virtue of a historically engrained focus on attention as consciousness or awareness. Insofar as unpaid attention features as a necessary condition, it is inside the economy of attention; to the extent that we are distracted from recognising it, however, it appears as outside this economy, illicit.

Recognising unpaid attention in this way carries a threat and an opportunity. The threat is that it should simply show up as an untapped resource for further exploitation. In the face of an increasingly competitive contemporary economy of attention ostensibly tending towards 'Total Noise', the threat is that unpaid attention, so quantified, will merely show up as a new frontier for capturing and instrumentalising attention, framed as a 'supply' or 'resource'. The opportunity, in contrast, comes when we dissent from this grammar to read unpaid attention as a form of attention that may be irreducible to it: not as a new frontier for exploitation, but as a liminal concept that forces us to reflect on the relationship between language and economics *tout court*, and to invent and experiment with new grammars that problematise this relationship. Instead of simply making do with the terms of a crudely economic grammar that may have become too distracted, noisy, inflated, or bankrupt to make sense of the predicament of attention today, the very conceivability of something like 'unpaid attention' points towards opportunities for dissent that frame attention differently.

Consider Wallace's remark that '[f]iction's abyss is silence, *nada*' (2012, 302–3). The suggestion of this section is that silence need not be viewed as a philosophical 'austerity measure'. Rather, we can develop a dissenting practice of 'auditing silences'. This practice is not as paradoxical as it sounds, and does not amount to wilful jargon, obfuscation, or contradiction; it is not, in other words, a case of a 'mere metaphor'. Here, 'silence' refers to necessary conditions that do not register according to the frame set by a dominant and crudely economic grammar of attention that may have become too 'total' and 'noisy', yet which we can dissent from.

Philosophy as dissenting therapy

The aim for this section is to argue for a conception of philosophy as 'dissenting therapy'. By this, I mean that, before it is anything like a literary genre comparable to 'fiction' or 'nonfiction', philosophy is a critical, creative, and therapeutic practice, capable of exposing the contingency of grammars that have become ossified, toxic, or counter-productive for our forms of life. I will work through four questions: (1) Does recognising the contingency of the grammar of 'paying attention' do violence to language *per se*? (2) What is the difference between 'therapy' and 'dissenting therapy'? (3) How does 'dissenting therapy' stand in relation to the later Wittgenstein's sense of 'therapy'? (4) What alternative grammars can be used to engage a topic such as attention?

Early in *Philosophical Investigations*, Wittgenstein states that '[g]iving orders, asking questions, telling stories, having a chat, are as much a part of our natural history as walking, eating, drinking, playing' (2009, 16). Accepting Wittgenstein's contention that language can be as much a part of our natural history as 'walking, eating, drinking, playing', a question arises: is the grammar of paying attention as a much a part of our *language* as 'giving orders, asking questions, telling stories, having a chat'?

It makes manifest sense to talk about attention in economic terms today, and, as Crary highlighted (see the first section of this chapter), this way of making sense has a history.[6] Does this recognition therefore mean that I am advocating the violent 'suppression' or 'removal' of a part of the natural history of our language? Consider another famous passage from *Philosophical Investigations*: 'Think of the tools in a toolbox: there is a hammer, pliers, a saw, a screwdriver, a rule, a glue-pot, glue, nails and screws. – The functions of words are as diverse as the functions of these objects. (And in both cases there are similarities)' (Wittgenstein 2009, 9). The point I have been trying to make in this chapter is not that 'paying attention' should be violently discarded from the toolbox of language. Instead, it should be put back into the box, to be compared with the other tools. My contention, in this sense, is not that we should seek to suppress or excise the grammar of 'paying attention'. Rather, we should seek to situate and contextualise it in terms of its natural history, to see whether or not it is the best or only 'tool' for making sense of attention. Instead of perpetrating violence against the 'natural history' of language, I am advocating that we draw on this history to ameliorate distortions to our sense of the topic that may have been caused by approaching attention with one dominant tool.

Let me now turn to the second question. Commonly, but not universally, the grammar that has evolved as part of the natural history of therapeutic practices across different human cultures involves the prescription of a 'regimen'. Examples of this range from the forms of *hypomnemata* used by Stoics and Epicureans (Foucault 1988), through to contemporary courses of drugs, programmes of exercise, or diaries for recording moods in cognitive behavioural therapy (CBT). My contention here is that philosophy also involves a 'regimen', and that it is such as to qualify it as a form of potentially 'dissenting' therapy. This is because the regimen philosophy prescribes involves the critique, clarification, and creation of grammars: that is, the practice of diagnosing where faults, inconsistencies, and illusions arise by virtue of extant ways of making sense of the world, and of proposing new ways of making sense as a dissenting corrective. As Nietzsche and Deleuze have remarked, this philosophical regimen does not necessarily aim at the palliation, consolation, or normalisation of the individual (Nietzsche 2001; Deleuze 2004). On the contrary, philosophy can, by questioning extant values and ways of making sense, sweep the individual away in the morally ambiguous current of what Nietzsche called 'great health' (2001). This, I suggest, is what renders philosophy a form of potentially strong 'dissenting' therapy. To be sure, philosophy can, as per Boethius, take on the aims of consolation (2008); more fundamentally, however, its effects appear much more ambivalent.

Let me now turn to the third question, concerning how this connects to the later Wittgenstein's sense of 'therapy'. This is important because, although I have had recourse to Wittgenstein throughout this chapter, the sense of therapy discussed in this section may seem too strident in light of a more piecemeal sense of the term that his work wanted to preserve. Remark 133 of *Philosophical Investigations* states:

> We don't want to refine or complete the system of rules for the use of our words in unheard-of [*unerhörter*] ways .... The real discovery is the one that enables me to break off philosophising when I want to. – The one that gives philosophy peace, so that it is no longer tormented by questions which bring *itself* in question. – Instead, a method is now demonstrated by examples, and the series of examples can be broken off. – Problems are solved (difficulties eliminated), not a single problem. There is not a single philosophical method, though there are indeed methods, different therapies, as it were
>
> *(Wittgenstein 2009, 56–7; original emphasis)*

It is possible to read these remarks as gesturing subtly towards the beginnings of an alternative grammar for dissenting philosophical therapy. The key term in this sense is 'unheard-of', which is a translation of the German *unerhörter*. Crucially, this term also involves the sense of 'hearing'. Wittgenstein's choice of this term may seem slight, but his use of it is significant insofar as it gestures towards a switch in sensory modalities away from sight, the influence of which can noticeably be detected in the *Tractatus*' 'picture theory'. Considered in terms of hearing, Wittgenstein's injunction not to seek logical completeness becomes part of a different grammar and takes on new aspects: it can, for example, be figured as an injunction not to turn what is 'unheard' in language into 'noise'; that is, an injunction not to turn what is implicit, silent, or unspoken in language into an object of theoretical 'chatter'. Far from comprising a trivial way of restating a sense of propositions that would remain consistent across these changes, this switch is critically and conceptually revealing in that it provides a way of reshaping sense.

How, in response to the fourth question posed above, might such a grammar of 'hearing' be taken further, in ways that dissent from the crudely economic grammar discussed in the first section? Let me start with a bad pun: what consequences follow for how we relate to attention today by framing it, not as something to be 'paid', but as something to be 'played', in the sense of music?[7] Apparently slight or trivial, this shift in fact introduces a different grammar and conceptual toolbox for framing attention, and different metaphysical, epistemological, ethical, and aesthetic considerations thereby. Instead of framing attention as a resource, supply, or form of capital to be mined, exploited, or captured, it allows us to frame it as something potentially 'resonant', 'dissonant', 'tonic', 'in concert', 'harmonic', 'creative', 'processual', 'rhythmic', or 'polyrhythmic'; further, it provides an alternative standard against which to assess the successes and failures of the crudely economic model of attention. Metaphysically, the shift introduces a different set of categories, elements, and attributes. Are acts of attention better conceived on the model of 'compositions' or 'motifs'? Are acts of attention better conceived as the work of 'soloists', or 'ensembles', played in conjunction with other actors, human and nonhuman? Are musical compositions infinitely iterable, and how does this compare with acts of attention? Are musical compositions ever properly 'finished', and how does this compare with acts of attention? Why have musical vocabularies and metaphors traditionally figured in the history of metaphysics (Schopenhauer, 1969)? Accepting that musical compositions can themselves also be framed in crudely economic terms, are there aspects of these compositions that are analogous to the 'unpaid labour' of 'unpaid attention'?

Epistemologically, we introduce a new framework for justifying beliefs about attention. Are 'acts' of attention properly speaking 'acts' at all, or do they involve a passive capacity for synthesis and receptivity on the model of attending to music, in line with what Mole has called the 'cognitive unison' theory of attention (2011)?[8] How useful are the results of centuries of music theory for understanding attention? Under what conditions are we correct or incorrect to assume that playing or listening to music either aids or hinders attentiveness? What paradoxes follow from framing attention in terms of music? Is a concept such as 'cognitive dissonance' simply a figure of speech, and, if so, why did 'dissonance' suggest itself in this case as appropriate for framing the phenomenon under consideration?

Ethically and aesthetically, we introduce a new framework for considering the value of attention. What, for instance, is the role of music in generating moods and ambiences that prime us for acts of attention and concentration? What are the ethical and aesthetic dimensions of music that suggest music therapy as a candidate for treating mental illnesses, neurodevelopmental disorders, and behavioural disorders such as attention deficit and hyperactivity disorder (ADHD)? As music becomes a cheap and ubiquitous commodity in the Information Age, is this confirmation of the pervasiveness of a crudely economic grammar, or an indication of its bankruptcy, insofar as it contributes to rendering certain industries unsustainable? To what extent are music and attention to be framed in terms of part of a conception of 'everyday aesthetics' (Saito 2007)? Why does music suggest itself as a pliable vehicle for promoting crudely economic values, as in marketing and advertising?

These questions may seem too speculative. To pursue a musical metaphor, they may simply come across as 'distorting'. If so, that is fine, because the point is not to suggest the grammar of 'attention as music' as a straight-up replacement for the grammar of 'paying attention'. Instead, there are two points: to suggest this grammar as an articulate and nuanced alternative for certain circumstances; and to draw attention to the fact that it is not a distant future possibility for a highly specialised idiom yet to come. On the contrary, the grammar of attention as music is a way of framing attention that has developed, alongside that of 'paying attention', as part of what Wittgenstein called the 'natural history' of our language, in a kind of 'counterpoint' to it. In the midst of ostensible Total Noise, this alternative grammar, perhaps alongside innumerable others, is relatively silent in comparison to that of 'paying attention'. The point, however, is that auditing it (in whichever sense you please) may have strongly therapeutic consequences for making sense of the predicament of attention today, somewhere between silence and Total Noise.

Notes

1 This chapter is an attempt to develop Wittgenstein's sense of 'grammatical investigation' (2009, 47).
2 The extent to which this amounts to *ideological* complicity is beyond the scope of this chapter (see Dean 2005; Brown 2015).
3 Bartleby is the eponymous character of Melville's 1853 novella 'Bartleby, The Scrivener: A Story of Wall Street'. His dissenting phrase 'I would prefer not to' has been the focus of celebrated analyses of the intersection between politics and speech acts over the past 20 years or so (Deleuze 1998; Agamben 1999; Smith 2013; Berkman 2011).
4 The K computer is the fourth most powerful supercomputer in the world (Fujitsu 2015; Top500 2015).
5 The point here is not empirical. I am not concerned with whether these figures are correct. I am concerned with the shared grammar that recommends them as impressive or significant.
6 An important related issue that I have not explored in this chapter is the extent to which the grammar of 'paying attention' is linked to the syntax of English as the still dominant (but waning) language of the internet (See Oustinoff 2012).
7 See also Citton (2014).
8 Mole uses the metaphor of an orchestra to explain his theory of 'cognitive unison' in his *Stanford Encyclopaedia of Philosophy* article on attention (Mole 2013).

Works cited

Agamben, Giorgio. 1999. *Potentialities: Collected Essays in Philosophy*. Trans. Daniel Heller-Roazen. Stanford, CA: Stanford University Press.
Berkman, Gisèle. 2011. *L'Effet Bartleby*. Paris: Editions Hermann.
Blanchot, Maurice. 1986. *L'Ecriture du désastre*. Trans. Ann Smock. Lincoln, NE: University of Nebraska Press.
Boethius. 2008. *The Consolation of Philosophy*. Trans. H. R. James. Cambridge, MA: Harvard University Press.
Brown, Wendy. 2015. *Undoing the Demos: Neoliberalism's Stealth Revolution*. Vanderbilt: Zone Books.
Castells, Manuel. 2010. *The Rise of the Network Society, Vol. 1: Economy, Society and Culture*. Oxford: Blackwell.
Citton, Yves. 2014. *Pour une écologie de l'attention*. Paris: Editions du seuil.
Crary, Jonathan. 1990. *Techniques of the Observer: On Vision and Modernity in the Nineteenth Century*. Cambridge, MA: MIT Press.
Crary, Jonathan. 2001. *Suspensions of Perception: Attention, Perception, and Modern Culture*. Cambridge, MA: MIT Press.
Crary, Jonathan. 2014. *24/7: Late Capitalism and the Ends of Sleep*. London: Verso.
Csikszentmihalyi, Mihaly and Isabella Selega Csikszentmihalyi, eds. 1988. *Optimal Experience: Psychological Studies of Flow in Consciousness*. Cambridge: Cambridge University Press.

Dean, Jodi. 2005. 'Communicative Capitalism: Circulation and the Foreclosure of Politics', *Cultural Politics*, 1(1): 51–74.

Deleuze, Gilles. 1998. 'Bartleby; or, The Formula' in Daniel W. Smith and Michael A. Greco, eds, *Essays Critical and Clinical*. 68–90. London: Verso.

Deleuze, Gilles. 2004. *Difference and Repetition*. Trans. Paul Patton. London: Continuum.

Foucault, Michel. 1988. *Technologies of the Self*. Trans. Luther H. Martin, Huck Gutman and Patrick H. Hutton. Amherst, MA: University of Massachusetts.

Foucault, Michel. 1991. 'Nietzsche, Genealogy, History' in Paul Rabinow, ed. *The Foucault Reader*. 76–100. London: Penguin.

Fujitsu. 2015. The K Computer is Incredibly Fast. Available at: http://www.fujitsu.com/global/about/businesspolicy/tech/k/whatis/system (Accessed 21 August 2017).

Hadot, Pierre. 2001. *La Philosophie comme manière de vivre: Entretiens avec Jeannie Carlier et Arnold I. Davidson*. Paris: Editions Albin Michel.

Heidegger, Martin. 2005. *Being and Time*. Trans. John Macquarrie and Edward Robinson. Oxford: Blackwell.

Kierkegaard, Søren. 1978. *Two Ages: The Age of Revolution and the Present Age*. Trans. Howard V. Hong and Edna H. Hong. Princeton, NJ: Princeton University Press.

Le Lay, Patrick. 2004. *Le Lay: Nous vendons du temps de cerveau*. *L'Obs* 11 July. Available at: http://tempsreel.nouvelobs.com/culture/20040710.OBS2633/le-lay-nous-vendons-du-temps-de-cerveau.html (Accessed 21 August 2017).

Max, D. T. 2012. *Every Love Story Is a Ghost Story: A Life of David Foster Wallace*. London: Granta.

Mole, Christopher. 2011. *Attention Is Cognitive Unison: An Essay in Philosophical Psychology*. Oxford: Oxford University Press.

Mole, Christopher. 2013. *Attention*. Available at: http://plato.stanford.edu/entries/attention/ (Accessed 21 August 2017).

Nietzsche, Friedrich. 1998. *Beyond Good and Evil*. Trans. Marion Faber. Oxford: Oxford University Press.

Nietzsche, Friedrich. 2001. *The Gay Science*. Trans. Josefine Nauckhoff. Cambridge: Cambridge University Press.

Oustinoff, Michaël. 2012. 'English Won't Be the Internet's *Lingua Franca*' in Laurent Vannini and Hervé Le Crosnier, eds, *NET.LANG: Towards the Multilingual Cyberspace*. 55–67. Caen: C&F Editions.

Rorty, Richard. 1991. 'Wittgenstein, Heidegger and the Reification of Language' in Richard Rorty, *Essays on Heidegger and Others*. 50–65. Cambridge: Cambridge University Press.

Saito, Yuriko. 2007. *Everyday Aesthetics*. Oxford: Oxford University Press.

Schopenhauer, Arthur. 1969. *The World as Will and Representation*. Vol. 1. Trans. E. F. J. Payne. New York: Dover Books.

Smith, Dominic. 2013. 'Beyond Bartleby and Bad Faith: Thinking Critically with Deleuze and Sartre'. *Deleuze Studies* 7(1): 83–105.

Stiegler, Bernard. 2004. *Mécréance et discrédit 1. La décadence des démocraties industrielles*. Paris: Galilée.

Stiegler, Bernard, and Ars Industrialis. 2008. *Réenchanter le monde: La valeur esprit contre le populisme industriel*. Paris: Flammarion.

Top500. 2015. 'Top 500: The List'. Available at: http://www.top500.org/system/177232 (Accessed 21 August 2017).

Wallace, David Foster. 2012. 'Deciderization 2007 – A Special Report' in David Foster Wallace, *Both Flesh and Not*. 299–317. London: Penguin.

Whitham, Ryan. 2013. Simulating 1 second of human brain activity takes 82,944 processors. Available at: http://www.extremetech.com/extreme/163051-simulating-1-second-of-huma n-brain-activity-takes-82944-processors (Accessed 21 August 2017).

Wittgenstein, Ludwig. 2001. *Tractatus Logico-Philosophicus*. Trans. David F. Pears and Brian F. McGuinness. London: Routledge.

Wittgenstein, Ludwig. 2009. *Philosophical Investigations*. Trans. Gertrude E. M. Anscombe and Rush Rhees. Oxford: Wiley-Blackwell.

Wittgenstein, Ludwig. 2014. *Lecture on Ethics: Established Text of the Lecture*. Oxford: John Wiley and Sons.

4

RHETORIC OF INNOCENCE OR LITERARY DISSENT?

Franco Moretti, world-systems theory and the case of magical realism

Lorna Burns

Venturing into the 'virtually unmarked territory' shared between the disciplines of postcolonialism and world literary studies, Robert Young (2014, 213), while observing their corresponding global reach and utilisation of an expanded canon, nonetheless suggests that the two diverge around issues of politics and of dissent. World literature, for Young, evokes universal standards of aesthetic value and is defined 'as the best literature, literature of such quality and insight that it transcends its local context to establish itself as universal' (213–4), while 'postcolonial literature makes no such assertion, and indeed insofar as it involves resistance, will always in some sense be partial, locked into a particular problematic of power' (216). The postcolonial, in other words, is a literature of resistance. Aiming 'to expose and challenge imbalances of power, and the different forms of injustice that follow from such factors [...] [p]ostcolonial literature will always seek to go beyond itself to impact upon the world which it represents' (217). The notion that postcolonial literature will necessarily attempt 'to impact upon the world which it represents' is by no means an uncontested assertion as it implicitly recalls the protracted dispute within the critical wing of postcolonial studies between first-wave poststructuralists (notably Bhabha, Spivak, and Said) and the Marxist second-wave, which repudiated the former's fixation on language and discourse to the detriment of a demonstrated awareness of on-the-ground, actual, and material anticolonial struggle (cf Parry 2004). Of critical significance, I contend, is that this very division is being replicated within the contemporary field of world literary studies as the increasing visibility of structural-materialist forms of analysis are confronted with a line of enquiry that puts pressure on the relationship between world and its literary representation. As Pascale Casanova queries, '[i]s it possible to re-establish the lost bond between literature, history and the world, while still maintaining a full sense of the irreducible singularity of literary texts?' (2005, 71).

Common to materialist critiques of world literature is the assumption that their object of study is the product of the various forces that condition the literary field. Thus, for David Damrosch (2003), world literary texts must circulate beyond their culture of origin; for Casanova (2005), they are conditioned by a relatively autonomous literary field distinguished by the uneven spread of literary capital; for Rebecca Walkowitz (2015), a text will reveal its worldly status through its translatability. As Ben Etherington has remarked of this critical field, each views literature 'as a special encoder of those conditions' which structure the global literary field and, in turn, the objective of critique is to uncover 'the material base through the superstructure of literature' (2012, 539). World literature, like the postcolonial in its Marxist guise, is read as a manifestation of a more fundamental modern global capitalist and imperialist world-system. This is an approach that finds its clearest articulation to date in the recent manifesto by the Warwick Research Collective (WReC 2015), *Combined and Uneven Development: Towards a New Theory of World-Literature*, in which it is argued that the world-literary text will register the capitalist world-system. The influence of Franco Moretti, whose work will be the focus of the present chapter, can be traced in this latest development in world literary critical theory, for it is his structural premise of a world literary system that is '[o]ne, and unequal' (Moretti 2013, 46) that, alongside Casanova's contemporaneous *The World Republic of Letters*, underpins WReC's case for the literary registration of inequality. And yet, at the same time, both Casanova and Moretti continue to make the case for the specific work of language and discourse, an aesthetic sphere that cannot be reduced to its material conditions. And so the poststructuralist/Marxist debate rages on.

In this chapter I do not seek to finally resolve this debate, but rather to highlight that both tend to begin with a structural premise (language or an aesthetic sphere, for one faction; capitalism, for the other) that will explain not only the production and circulation of a text, but also the workings of plot, character, genre, and style, and, crucially, it will prefigure our interpretation of such elements. Indeed Damrosch acknowledges this much when he notes the tendency in world literature scholarship to focus on '[d]eep structures' at the expense of particularity and individual literary effects, and, as such, 'systemic approaches need to be counterbalanced with close attention to particular languages, specific texts: we need to see both the forest and the trees' (Damrosch 2003, 26). I would add, however, that the systemic approach has generated another set of conceptual problems, one that can be summarised in WReC's definition of '"world-literature" as *the literature of the world-system*' (2015, 8), 'as the literary registration of modernity under the sign of combined and even development' (17).[1] World literature and its critical analysis, by this definition, will register the signs of globalised capitalism but, crucially, WReC adds, such an endeavour 'does not (necessarily) involve criticality or dissent' (20). My counterargument to this claim is not that, by contrast, a text must (necessarily) be defined by its resistance but, rather, to suggest that just as there is no ontologically valid position to argue that a text will involve criticality or dissent (the assumption WReC resists), the reverse position is also true: there is no validity to the claim that it will not involve criticality or dissent. The question then becomes, simply, how do we read it? Do we find in the text confirmation of the all-encompassing force of global capitalism, or does it offer us the imaginative capacities to resist it and to participate in the creative positing of alternative forms of cohabitation and belonging? And, significantly, what is lost by deprioritising dissent? These questions are significant in light of the postcritical turn of scholars like Bruno Latour and Rita Felski, for whom the Marxist readings of Fredric Jameson (and by extension, I claim, the materialism of WReC) seek to uncover unconscious structures that belie a text and therefore tend to confirm the critic's predetermined expectations (Felski 2015). From this perspective, the problem with a world-systems approach to world literature is its tendency to situate a primary reality as the unconscious ground of the text: literature as epiphenomenon of the capitalist world economy. Rather than preserving the notion that it is the work of the critic to reveal the hidden structures of economy, society, or history to which the text is wholly blind, post-criticism asks us to 'place ourselves in front of the text' and reflect 'on what it unfurls, calls forth, makes possible' (Felski 2015, 12). And, of course, what it makes possible can be resistance to the hierarchies that dominate our world as much, as we shall see in the work of Moretti, as a rhetoric of innocence that anesthetises us to their acceptance.

Against the reduction of the literary text to epiphenomenon, this chapter positions itself alongside Emily Apter, who argues for a philosophising of world literature that 'work[s] against the temptation of allegories of World System or the Planet or Capital that impute subjective personalities to political entities and geographic phantasms' (2010, 184). World literature can be more than a reflection of its contemporary world contexts, and while texts need not necessarily, by definition, express 'criticality or dissent', they must always be considered as offering the potential to do so. It is a question addressed not merely to the text, but to how we read it. As Graham Harman notes, '[s]uch questions restore the proper scale of evaluation for intellectual work: demoting the pushy careerist sandbagger who remains within the bounds of the currently plausible and prudent, and promoting the gambler who uncovers new worlds' (2009, 120). This move beyond the status quo is the dissident force of critique in an era of world literature: finding in the literary text not confirmation of the structural permanence of capitalism and related forms of cultural and economic imperialism but, rather, the means to imagine a new society that functions without the opposition of self and other, oppressor and oppressed. Thus, for Harman, the effectiveness of the literary text is not simply a measure of the widest possible circulation or its literary capital: 'The books that stir us most are not those containing the fewest errors, but those that throw most light on unknown portions of the map' (120). These sentiments are at the core of this chapter's exploration of world-systems theory in the hands of Franco Moretti. His later work on world literature as a world-system, so influential on contemporary theorists such as WReC, cannot be fully appreciated apart from his earlier accounts of literature in *Signs Taken for Wonders* and in *Modern Epic*, and together they enforce an inherently conservative view of literature. In this early moment, Moretti does indeed maintain literature's affective capacity on the world that it represents: literature of the world-system, Moretti tells us, is a rhetoric of innocence, a force for ensuring our consent to the violence and inequalities that underpin the capitalist world order. This chapter will explore the ways in which Moretti sets out his case, most notably with respect to the postcolonial and world literary genre of magical realism, before finally embracing Harman's demand for a criticism that finds in the text the potential for new worlds and not simply a reflection of this one.

The rhetoric of innocence

The role of literature in producing forms of resistance and consent has long occupied Moretti's work. In the first essay of *Signs Taken for Wonders*, 'The Soul and the Harpy', literature is characterised as a branch of rhetoric both in the sense that it is political (addressed to the social) and in that that it aims to persuade, or more specifically, that it attempts 'to enlist support for a particular system of values' (Moretti 1988, 3). As rhetoric and, thus, as persuasion, literature serves to increase the transparency and, as such, the efficacy of a dominant ideology. On the level of aesthetics, literature may be innovative and creatively pose new rhetorical forms; however, 'this does not in the least "prove" [...] that "real" literature is by its nature anti-conventional' (Moretti 1988, 7). Rejecting the notion that literature is *necessarily* a source of dissent is a significant point; however, by aligning it with persuasion, Moretti is going further than like-minded critics such as WReC. In this moment he is suggesting that literature will *always* move from the pole of innovation towards that of the commonplace, and that the role of the literary critic is to trace a sociology of literary forms as they consolidate and even shape the dominant value system:

> [Rhetoric] bears witness to a society divided, in conflict. [...] Rhetorical 'daring' testifies to a will that wants to overturn the power relations of the symbolic order. 'Commonplaces' and semantic inertia, for their part, are the potential results of that daring no less than its opposite. [...] It is no longer a question, then, of contrasting rhetorical (or ideological) 'consent' with aesthetic 'dissent', but of recognizing that there are different *moments* in the development of every system of consent, and above all different *ways* of furthering it.
>
> *(Moretti 1988, 8)*

Literature, in other words, can be witness to and, indeed, instrument of the conflicts between new and old, innovative and commonplace, radical and conservative both in the aesthetic sphere, where new rhetorical forms reveal a will to challenge the accepted conventions of the 'symbolic order', and in the social sphere, where literature represents social conflicts in order to, if not resolve them, at least facilitate an acceptance of their intractability. However, in the trajectory traced in 'The Soul and the Harpy', modern literature, the literature of the capitalist world-system, is above all else a way of furthering the system of consent – literature's rhetorical function, so to speak.

Jacobean tragedy is identified by Moretti as the moment in literary history that was witness to the shift from dissent to consent, the last instance in which literature produced dissent by discrediting the concept of absolute monarchy and paving the way for the English Revolution. Tragedy, according to Moretti, 'belongs to a world that does not yet recognize the inevitability of permanent conflict between opposing and immitigable interests and values, and therefore does not feel any need to confront the problem of reconciling them' (28). The premodern world, then, is characterised by the acceptance of a hierarchical relationship of dominance and the subordination of opposed values. 'Its "tragic" quality', he writes, 'does not lie (as it would now be the case for us) in the fact that the story eventually leads to the sacrifice of one of the two values in conflict […] [but] in the fact that it has been possible to *imagine*, and put into words, an irreconcilable conflict' (28).[2] Premodern tragedy is 'an unrivalled instrument of criticism and dissent' (29) because of its capacity to imagine, at the same time, the world as it 'should be' (28) – in other words, the world in which the rightful hierarchy is secured (the resolution of the tragedy) – and (in its tragic moment) the world refigured as an irreconcilable conflict between opposed values. In other words, while the plot will always resolve itself in the triumph of one value over the other and the reconstitution of a just order, its tragic quality, as well as its capacity for criticism and dissent, stem from the possibilities of imagining a world as the perpetual conflict of irreconcilable forces. Modern literary forms, by contrast, '[see] conflict as a given fact in society' but are aligned with the aim 'of showing that mutually opposing values and interest can always reach, if not a genuine conciliation, at least some kind of coexistence and compromise' (29). It is this 'anti-tragic impulse' of modernity that lies behind, in philosophical terms, the emergence of an aesthetic sphere, which was unthinkable in a premodern society that 'did not recognize aesthetic activity as having any autonomy but believed it should always cooperate directly, immediately, in moral or cognitive purposes' (28). In aesthetic terms, premodern literature posits a direct correlation between literature and the world, between representation and reality, while modernity witnesses the advent of a relatively autonomous aesthetic sphere. In social terms, another split has been established: between a premodern world of opposed values that need no mediation or resolution because a relation of dominance will necessarily assert itself; and a modern world in which conflict tends towards some form of compromise.

This gesture towards aesthetics suggests something of the philosophical tradition that Moretti employs in his argument: both Kant's *Critique of Judgement* and Schiller's *On the Aesthetic Education of Man* are central points of reference in section four of 'The Soul and the Harpy', 'Literature, Consent'. From Kant, Moretti adopts a dualistic ontology with an aesthetic sphere distinct from that of scientific inquiry; a division between judgements of fact and value judgements; and, to turn to his wider philosophy, between phenomenon and the thing-in-itself. As Bruno Latour has argued with respect to Kant and the problem of modern thinking more broadly, post-Kantian philosophy has maintained this dualistic separation of spheres while continually searching for a means of their relation; in that sense, Hegelian dialectics is an amplified version of the Kantian separation of phenomenon and noumenon (cf Latour 1993, 56), as indeed is, as Fredric Jameson has argued, post-structuralism.[3] In one respect, this is a foreshadowing of the *a priori* assumptions noted above in relation to world-systems theory: as Jameson argues, in Kant 'the separation of the mental processes from reality encourages an explicit search for the permanent structures of the mind itself, the organizational categories and forms through which the mind is able to experience the world, or to organize meaning in what is essentially in itself meaningless' (1974, 109). The 'permanent structures' and 'organizational categories' are evident in Kantian thought, Latour claims, in a framework in which modernity is at once divided into two distinct and irreducible spheres that, at the same time, are connected. Indeed, Moretti acknowledges such when he argues that 'while capitalist society is unthinkable without the scientific and technical progress reflected in the separation of intellect and morality, it is equally unthinkable without the incessant attempt to annul that separation and remedy it, an attempt to which the extraordinary and apparently inexplicable proliferation of aesthetic activities that distinguishes capitalism bears witness' (1988, 30–1). This is remarkably similar to Latour's explanation of the efficacy of the modern world in *We Have Never Been Modern*: premodern cultures draw no distinction between reality and its representation, fact and fetish, of an aesthetic sphere apart from the social world; modernity, on the other hand, institutes these categories as separate spheres in order to distinguish themselves from premodern culture. That is what Latour refers to as the 'Great Divide' (1993, 12): the break in the flow of time that establishes one side as modern and the other as not. To expand on this point, while moderns can coexist alongside the premodern in a Blochian model of non-contemporaneity, they can do so only by inventing a paradoxical temporality in which history is conceived of as at once a rupture (a break between premodern and modern) and a teleological continuity in which the non-contemporaneous cultures of the world-system will inevitably progress towards modernity. In that sense, I suggest, the compromise that Moretti identifies as the mark of modern literature and aesthetics is problematic: by structuralising a break between premodern and modern, Moretti's theory of literature institutes a teleology by which the non-modern will necessarily progressively modernise. That said, however, modernity's separation of spheres is not dismissed by Latour in favour of a return to premodern indistinction: indeed, as Moretti argued, and Latour would agree, modernity has been remarkably successful because of its ability both to separate the scientific from the religious and the moral, and to overcome that separation. Modernity is effective because it allows both practices, but only as long as it considers them separately and as an irresolvable paradox. This is where Latour's account of post-Kantian philosophy resists Moretti's reading. Moretti can define modern literature as the reconciliation of or compromise between conflicting values (a rhetoric of innocence) only by imagining literature as a third term mediating between, but never fully reconciling, two spheres: in Kantian terms, judgement as that which connects the spheres of nature and reason. For Latour, and others before him, that misses the wider significance of Kant's philosophy and turns the philosopher that Schopenhauer and Nietzsche critiqued for too radical a separation of phenomena and the thing-in-itself into a philosopher of their relation.[4]

In order to understand Moretti's particular take on Kant, we need to return to the quotation noted above and extend it a little:

> The first function [of the aesthetic sphere] is that indicated by Kant's aesthetics: to restore the connection between the world of judgements of fact and that of judgements of value by resisting scientific 'disillusionment' and instead satisfying that deep-seated need for 'magic', which is part and parcel of the desire to see values 'rooted in facts', thus avoiding responsibility for their partiality in the secure belief that they 'stem' from the very 'reality of things'.
>
> (Moretti 1988, 33)

This is a strongly Marxist reinterpretation of Kant's philosophy. What Moretti finds in the restored connection between noumena and phenomena is not simply the intervention of aesthetics, but more specifically an idea of the commodity fetish: 'The whole mystery of commodities, all the magic and necromancy that surrounds the products of labour on the basis of commodity production' (Marx 1990, 169). It is difficult to grasp the relation that Moretti imagines between 'scientific "disillusionment"' and the 'deep-seated need for "magic"' on the one hand, and between magic and 'facts' or 'the very "reality of things"', on the other, without reflecting on the significance of Marx's term for understanding the masking of social relations between people as a relation of material things. It is the latter that connects 'magic' and the 'reality of things', even while Kant's philosophy alone leads us to consider the disjoint between an aesthetic realm of representation and that of reality. As Marx writes in *Capital*, '[t]he mysterious character of the commodity-form consists therefore simply in the fact that the commodity reflects the social characteristics of men's own labour as objective characteristics of the products of labour themselves, as the socio-natural properties of these things' (1990, 164–5), and thus 'the definite social relation between men themselves [...] assumes [...] the fantastic form of a relation between things' (165). There is, in other words, a masking or concealment at work in the commodity. When confronted with any given commodity we should, in principle, if we looked hard enough, be able to trace a whole network of actors whose labour went into its production, but the commodity itself bears virtually no trace of those relations, and its exchange-value serves to obscure them by promoting an abstract notion of universal value. What are masked are 'the social relations between the individual workers, by making those relations appear as relations between material objects' (Marx 1990, 168–9). Or, to return to Moretti, the 'magic' or fetishistic aspect of the commodity connects it to a material reality of objects rather than one of social relations. We can begin to see the deception which allows Moretti to present literature as the harpy in whose clutches the soul 'does not lower its gaze', preferring 'to delude itself about the affectionate, almost maternal nature of the creature dragging it away with her in flight' (Moretti 1988, 41). As David Harvey notes in his reading of *Capital*, Marx reveals that 'we are perpetually at risk of being ruled by fetishistic constructs that blind us to what is actually happening' (2010, 47).

It explains, too, the correlation between literature as consent proposed in 'The Soul and the Harpy', and the rhetoric of innocence, which Moretti sets out in *Modern Epic*. His contention that *lo real maravilloso* is best understood not as 'magical realism' but, rather, as 'marvellous *reality*. Not a poetics – a state of affairs' (Moretti 1996, 234) is much more than a matter of refining an awkward translation of Alejo Carpentier's original formulation. It is telling that Moretti is less concerned with the nuances of 'magic' versus 'marvellous', despite the latter signalling Carpentier's troubled association with surrealism. Rather, it is the status of the *real* that is at issue in this generic classification: not a poetics, not realism as the representation of a particular society or event, but reality. In Marxist terms, the commodity fetish (magic) is not mere illusion; it is a state of affairs, but one which masks the actual social relations that give rise to it. Its reality is one of material relations between objects and individuals rather than social relations between them. And in Moretti's case study of marvellous reality, Gabriel García Márquez's *One Hundred Years of Solitude*, what are masked are the profound inequalities produced by social relations within the capitalist world system, or, in other words, combined and uneven development. Understanding magical or marvellous reality as the literary expression of the commodity fetish helps to explain Moretti's claim that in *One Hundred Years of Solitude* 'the true magic of this novel is not magic: it is technology' (249): not flying carpets, ascending virgins, or lonely ghosts, but ice, pianolas, magnets, and the spy-glass. The novel, Moretti argues, presents magic as the products of Western modernity and thus as that which 'belongs *to the future*' (249) of those who lag behind in the temporal ordering of modernity in the periphery and semi-periphery of the world-system. The masking or duplicity of Márquez's magical reality, then, lies in its ability to confront the Western reader with the 'Weberian side of [their own] existence [...]. Nothing frightening, in the products of Western technology. They seem a game. A fantastic present sent from Europe to that faraway village: truly, a *marvellous reality*. [...] A rhetoric of innocence' (250). A fetishisation, in Marx's sense, of the commodity which disguises the real social relations between producers as a relation of benign material objects. This returns us to Moretti's Kantian claim that 'while capitalist society is unthinkable without the scientific and technical progress reflected in the separation of intellect and morality, it is equally unthinkable without the incessant attempt to annul that separation and remedy it' (1988, 30–1). Magical or marvellous reality becomes the literary expression of the attempt to 'annul that separation' of practical and pure reason, of reality and the magical, in the service of obscuring the social relations of capitalist economic production.

Read in this light, exposing the rhetoric of innocence should become the focus of world literary critique, especially if aligned with a postcolonial perspective. If Moretti's reading of *One Hundred Years of Solitude*, or more accurately, perhaps, the reception of Márquez's novel in the West, is correct, then it can be extended within the context of a contrapuntal reading that reveals the obscured social relations within the narrative as that which betrays the workings of capitalism. We can argue this point if we consider the way in which he aligns the rhetoric of innocence with imperialist expansion earlier in *Modern Epic*. It is, he argues, a function of the colonial imagination to be at once 'proud of its own world domination' and at the same time blind 'to the violence sustaining it' (Moretti 1996, 26). For example, 'Crusoe saves Friday from the cannibalism of other natives; Lord Jim protects the village of Doramin from Ali's rascally attacks; Passepartout and Phileas Fogg save Aouda from the "barbarous custom" of suttee', and of particular significance is the way in which 'all these works contemplate a marriage between the Westerner and the Native Woman: for, in marriage, conquest becomes *consent* and is thus fully legitimized' (27). Here *Modern Epic*'s rhetoric of innocence corresponds precisely with the claim of 'The Soul and the Harpy' that literature's function is to secure consent. The rhetoric of innocence is 'a strategy of denial and disavowal' (25), a displacement of the violence and exploitation that make possible capitalist modernity, and, in that sense, it is an instrument of consent: 'To make individuals feel "at ease" in the world they happen to live in, to reconcile them in a pleasant and imperceptible way to its prevailing cultural norms' (Moretti 1988, 27). This is literature's worldly effect, for Moretti. At the same time, however, this drive also creates a *narrative* of consenting subjects: in the case of the novels noted above, the marriage plot is expressly a scene of consent and thus justifies the imperialist's intervention. We can extend this motif by suggesting that imperialism creates a similar narrative through the representation not merely of expressed consent (in the case of the marriage scene), but of assumed tacit consent: as Spivak's analysis of *sati*, or in early colonial history *suttee*, revealed, '[o]ne never encounters the testimony of the women's voice consciousness', only the colonial view – 'a case of "White men saving brown women from brown men"' – or that of the traditional patriarchy – '"The women wanted to die"' (Spivak 2010, 50). Here, British and Indian perspectives both assume the women's tacit consent to a particular social order, one colonial, the other traditional. As a result, we need not rely on the presence of a legal ceremony in which consent is expressly offered. Rather, it is a function of the colonial imagination, and indeed the traditional patriarchal one, to present the reader with a cast of characters who consent, whether expressly or tacitly, to the dominant order.

Broadly, then, this maps onto Moretti's account of modern aesthetics in 'The Soul and the Harpy': premodern literature offered a genuinely tragic vision insofar as it stems from a society which accepts an organic social order (the divine right of kings, for example), but in its moment of tragedy it imagined 'an irreconcilable conflict' of two opposed values (Moretti 1988, 28). Tragedy created uncertainty, assuming the possibility that one value system could be faced with its negation and that one side would triumph over another. For this reason, it was 'an unrivalled instrument of criticism and dissent' (29). Modern aesthetics, on the other hand, is fundamentally anti-tragic since it no longer holds out the possibility that one set of values can triumph completely over another. Moretti's argument here is essentially dialectical: in the premodern era, tragedy was the dialectical negation of the dominant order and as such it resolved itself in the reassertion of one set of values conceived of as an organic (or divine) order. What distinguishes modernity, then, is a shift from Hegelian to Marxist dialectics: the modern world disregards the concept of totality (resolution and the triumph of one order over another), and dialectics proceeds by means of a constant adjustment between two opposed sides that cannot be resolved in a final synthesis.[5] The primary function of modern aesthetics, then, is to enact this unending dialectical process by which the reader is confronted with two opposed values not as the possibility of an alternative social order, but as the grounds for coexistence and compromise between the two. This in itself is a masking because, as is evident from the colonial examples above, it only *appears* as if coexistence and compromise has been achieved because of the tacit or express articulation of consent (an agreement to compromise). But when we look a little more closely at the social relations at work within a particular scene of domination, we discover the silencing or omissions enforced in order to make this possible: a rhetoric of innocence that convinces us that the subaltern cannot speak. But this leaves us with a conceptual problem: if, as Spivak implies, the work of postcolonial critique is turned towards the silences, gaps, and omissions in the historical document and in literature in order to reveal that which has been silenced or masked, then can it really do so without simply co-opting the subaltern voice into its own rhetoric of innocence? Moretti's account, while not expressly dealing with postcolonialism, would suggest that it cannot. Spivak herself was wary of intellectuals who purport to represent the dispossessed, and yet still argued that 'intellectuals must attempt to disclose and know the discourse of society's other' (1999, 249). Modernity, for Spivak, as much as it is for Moretti, is too heterogeneous a network to be reducible 'to a coherent narrative', to a single, organic or divine order of things, but as such 'persistent critique is needed' (249). Moretti, on the other hand, makes dissent and criticism a premodern activity: critique as the work of troubling and questioning the organic order, making an audience ill at ease with society. In the absence of the organic order, of an assumed totality in Hegelian terms, critique is no longer possible and the best that we can do as dissidents is to confront one system of values with another system and wish for an impossible compromise. The best approximation of critique in the moment of modernity, then, is the staging of opposed values or world-views in the hope that we can convince (or delude, Moretti might say) ourselves that a satisfactory mediation between the two can be achieved.

Magical realism and capitalist modernity

Moretti has presented us with a rather idiosyncratic reading of Kant in order to get us to this point. Broadly speaking, Kant establishes a framework for conceiving of modernity as a persistent tension between two incommensurable spheres, best formulated in his premise of the two ontological categories of noumenon and phenomenon, the inaccessible, pure thing-in-itself and the empirical world that we experience. He then introduces a third term, judgement, to connect these two aspects, and how successful that bridging has been is a matter of philosophical debate.[6] Moretti, as noted above, follows contemporary thinkers such as Latour, for whom Kant can be read as instituting a paradox in which the ontological condition of the world is one which is both split into two incommensurable categories and, at the same time, mediated by a third term – aesthetics – that connects them. If we take up Moretti's characterisation of the mediation of aesthetics between these two categories as connected to 'that deep-seated need for "magic"' (1988, 33), then we can say both that aesthetics takes on the role of the commodity fetish (as argued above) and that, as a result, it only *appears* to mediate between the two categories. Once again, this is not to say that the commodity fetish and aesthetics are merely illusions: they are the signs of a particular relation of objects, just not of their actual social relations. In other words, there is always something else going on, something other which is not visible, and as such aesthetics can only appear to mediate between a divide that it cannot actually annul. Thus, in Moretti's words, the first function of aesthetics is to satisfy 'the deep-seated need for "magic"' because we 'desire to see values "rooted in facts"', to believe 'that they "stem" from the "very reality of things"', and as such avoid confronting 'their partiality' (33). If Kant were to successfully bridge the dual categories, then everything would be at once noumenon and phenomenon, real and representation, and thus to explain one side alone would be a *partial* account. Modern thinking employs aesthetics to create consent, to reconcile us to the paradox of Kant's ontological split, by creating the appearance of coexistence and of mediation between the two spheres even while it stems from one part of reality alone, be it the reality of material relations between objects rather than social relations between individuals for Marx, or, from a Kantian perspective, the reality that we experience rather than the pure thing-in-itself. For those who read Kant's third *Critique* in a favourable light, as achieving an account of a dual ontology that is at the same time relational, the primary motivation for this manoeuvre is to show that individuals can intervene and act in the empirical world.[7] By such an account, aesthetic judgement is the primary means for achieving this since its counterpart, teleological judgement, is determined by 'preestablished [...] rules supplied by understanding or reason' (Hughes 2010, 19). Aesthetic judgement is 'the power of judgement [...] exercised in an autonomous form, detached from specific aims or objectives' (151); distinct, in other words, from judgement governed by reason (cf 23). Freed from reason or pre-established rules, aesthetic judgement, as Hughes argues, 'preserves a capacity to access aspects of the world normally lost, or at least, hidden in everyday life' (150), it opens our minds 'to the possibilities of a phenomenon without our trying to explain it' (21). Only aesthetic judgement allows us to experience the working of pure reason. This leaves us with a very different account of aesthetics than can be found in Moretti: the function of the aesthetic sphere is to provoke contemplation, which can take the form of either aesthetic or teleological judgement, or, by Hughes's reading, will proceed from a primary condition of aesthetic judgement (revealing the workings of judgement in-itself) to a secondary moment in which judgement is governed by practical reason (cf 23–25). We cannot say that in this primary moment the aesthetic sphere is intended to achieve any aim whatsoever. Moreover, freed from pre-established norms and understanding, aesthetic judgement operates for Kant, Hughes argues, through 'the transformative power of the imagination that takes up something we apprehend and finds in it much more than might initially be evident at the level of appearance' (11). Even when faced with conflict or disharmony (the Kantian sublime), 'we discover an alternative power, the capacity as rational beings to think beyond the sphere of sensible experience' (14). Hughes paints Kant as a philosopher who found in art the stimulus for mental activity and imagination freed from established norms and reason. As such, it allows us to access that which is masked by everyday life or, to return to terms used above, concealed by the 'magic' of the commodity fetish.

We might say that Moretti has offered one interpretation of Kant's notoriously difficult philosophy, and Hughes another. We might add that even Moretti felt the need to move beyond Kant and incorporate aspects of Schiller's *On the Aesthetic Education of Man* in order to show fully how aesthetics becomes an instrument of consent. However, Moretti has left us with a number of unsatisfactory propositions, in my view: a literary history that reproduces a temporal break between premodern and modern regimes; that makes modernity incapable of a critical interrogation of the existing hegemony, only able to pose alternative world-views in the hope that the compromise will settle on a better system; and that charges literature with the wholly conservative function of reconciling us to that compromise. Fundamental to his theory of literature is not only a division between premodern and modern literatures, but also a more radical separation which distinguishes art from science, magic from reality, representation from the real. As such, it reanimates anew the Kantian dualism and, as such, retains the fundamental structure that is common, as Latour and Jameson have argued, to both Marxism and poststructuralism. I maintain that the *critical* task of world literature scholarship should indeed involve the exposure of those instances where a literary text participates in a masking which obscures social relations as a relation of material objects, or which lures us into an acceptance of the exploitation and violence that maintain our way of life. However, if we align our theoretical framework with Moretti, then exposing a rhetoric of innocence is not an activity of criticality or dissent in the modern era. It is not, in Moretti's strict sense, an activity of criticality or dissent because the Kantian dualism persists: there is no dialectical resolution of the opposition of reality and its representation. As an alternative, I suggest that the dissident task of world literary scholarship can become (in Hughes's sense of Kantianism) an activity which exploits 'the transformative power of the imagination' through access to that which is hidden at 'the level of appearance' (2010, 11) but, if we are to do more than reproduce the dualism which ties both Marxism and poststructuralism to the problematic of Kant's aesthetics, then critical thinking must adjust its fundamental assumptions. Concretely, this demands a rethinking of pre-given, structured opposition and autonomous spheres as the baseline of theory, promoting instead the work of relational, constructed, and interconnected processes as they unfold in a world that too is constantly changing and irreducible to the sum of its parts or indeed their dialectical sublation. Rather than starting with philosophies which posit structural causes or totalised separate spheres of world and its representation, my approach to world literature, sketched here and developed more fully in *Postcolonialism After World Literature* (Burns 2019), draws on philosophers such as Nietzsche, Latour, Deleuze, and Rancière, whose work, while resisting totality and the predominance of dialectical thinking, especially dialectical negation, introduces an aspect of otherness into their thought, an otherness that is understood not in Kantian terms as an inaccessible realm apart, but, in the Spinozian sense, as one side of a dual reality. Moreover, each thinker uses this 'other' as the basis for theorising the emergence of newness, creativity, and dissent. While a more detailed interrogation of their philosophy exceeds the scope of this chapter, from these gestures alone I argue that we can rethink the work of literature and, indeed, literary criticism as an exercise of dissent: of recreating or exposing the production of a rhetoric of innocence, of highlighting the obscured relations at work within the text.[8] Such an act, however, should not be thought of as one strictly directed at the revelation of an unconscious 'truth' or submerged, primary reality. Rather, to repurpose Moretti, literature has the capacity to imagine an alternative society not as the dialectical negation of the present one, but as its creative refiguring: as making visible that which has been made invisible, making heard what was silenced and, as such, bringing to light the immanent possibilities of new social formations. This is the dissident function of what Deleuze and Guattari (1986) call minor literature, or Rancière (1999) dissensus, a capacity that resides in all literature as the uncovering of that which resists comprehension, which escapes us, or is in excess of everyday reality. As I shall contend in the remainder of this chapter, the postcolonial genre of magical realism, far from reproducing in literary form the processes of masking inherent in the commodity fetish and thus deceiving us with its rhetoric of innocence, constitutes an aesthetics of dissent by means of its dissensus – making visible and audible that which has been excluded by the global hegemony.

In order to understand the precise ways in which magical realism functions as a dissensus, as the refiguring of a social order that reveals silenced voices, obscured dimensions, or unperceived actions, we must first return to Moretti's discussion of the genre in *Modern Epic*. By this account, the crux of Moretti's argument rests upon *One Hundred Years of Solitude*'s critical reception in the West – it is our rhetoric of innocence – however, there is no evidence provided to support his hypothesis in that respect. Rather, he relies on close readings of the novel and through them he presents a convincing account of the plot in terms of a progression from an agrarian economy to entry into the world-system. However, in terms of the novel itself, rather than its reception, I would argue that magic does not make its presence felt primarily through the guise of technology, but rather as a dissensus. As has been noted by Shannin Schroeder, Marquez's novel as a whole can be read as an approximation of the alchemical process: it is 'the driving force' of the narrative (Schroeder 2009, 196). 'The relationship among Úrsula and José Arcadio Buendía, their family, and the town itself becomes an alchemical process – an attempt to produce "gold" [*oro*, or in the novel, Aureli*ano*] out of the marriage of Sulphur and Mercury' (207), with 'José Arcadio Buendía and Úrsula serv[ing] [...] as the sulphur and mercury, respectively', who 'set into motion the first of the six "stages" or generations of Buendías', which ends with the 'false gold' (209) that is the final Aureliano. The magical aspects of Márquez's novel circulate around Melquiades's study, home to the family's alchemical experiments. Moreover, '[a]lchemy reinforces the sense of a magically real world, stressing that what we know as science, Macondons believe to be magic, and vice versa' (197). Alchemy is, in other words, irreducible to the separate spheres of post-Enlightenment thought. Understanding alchemy as central to the novel's gesture toward 'magic' and the 'marvellous' takes us in a very particular theoretical direction, one indeed that Salman Rushdie recognised as the forbearer of postcolonial magical realism: surrealism (cf Rushdie 1992, 301–2). For the surrealists, there is a 'remarkable analogy, insofar as their goals are concerned, between the Surrealist efforts and those of the alchemists: the philosopher's stone is nothing more or less than that which was to enable man's imagination' (Breton 1972, 174). Alchemy resonated with the surrealists' interest in the unconscious and in escaping the restrictions of reason. For Pierre Mabille, whose *Mirror of the Marvellous* influenced writers of the Caribbean surrealist movement, the marvellous functioned as a pathway to unconscious, suppressed or hidden elements of reality, which, when accessed, could inspire moments of creativity and unforeseeable insight. As he writes in *Mirror of the Marvellous*,

> the marvellous is everywhere. In things it appears as soon as one succeeds in penetrating any object whatever. [...] Its form, which reveals its individual structure, is the result of transformations which have been going on since the world began. And it contains the germs of countless possibilities that will be realized in the future.
>
> *(Mabille 1998, 14)*

Corresponding to Alejo Carpentier's claim that 'everything that eludes established norms is marvellous' (1995, 101), for Mabille the marvellous is both an element in everyday reality and an otherness that lies outside of comprehension, suggested in 'the perceptible feeling [that] survives at the moment of discovery' (1998, 14), dreams (17), nature (22), and folklore as a sign of the collective unconscious (27–9). For Jung, alchemy also served as a metaphor for the functioning of the imagination, or more specifically the collective unconscious (cf Jung 1953). Together, these perspectives present alchemy as a process of creation generated by access to a not-fully-realisable but nonetheless present side of reality beyond everyday comprehension. Magical or marvellous realism when viewed from this perspective is, as Wilson Harris argued, 'an alchemical pilgrimage' (cited in Linguanti 1999, 245) – the creation of a reality that is at once, immanently, an everyday reality and an unconscious or unrepresentable otherness that can be made actual – and, as such, it allows us to think beyond a world of pre-given norms and teleological judgements.

Understanding magical or marvellous realism in such terms distances it from the rhetoric of innocence. Moretti singles out Márquez's novel for this critique: 'In Asturias and Carpentier, in Rushdie and Guimarães Rosa, magic is a thing of the past, and of the periphery. In García Márquez, however, it belongs *to the future*: to the West, to the core of the world-system' (Moretti 1996, 249). This distinction, however, relies on the temporal break between premodern and modern cultures problematised above. It is telling that Moretti cites Vargas Llosa's argument that Latin American writers 'still have great difficulty in differentiating between fiction and reality' (cited in Moretti 1996, 248): in other words, Latin American culture reveals itself as premodern insofar as it makes no distinction between fetish and fact, representation and reality, phenomenon and noumenon. Myth, the basis of the magical reality expressed in this latter version of the genre, evokes an organic and whole past to which a culture should return if it is to resist the imposition of the conflicting, imperialist culture of modernisation. Magical realism if it is modern, on the other hand, will project magic into the future as a time in which the objects of delight are fetishised commodities. However, I find it more convincing to view the magic of magical realism in terms of a dissensus or actualisation which, as such, can be aligned with the creation of dissident possibilities or alternative modes of affiliation that test the established hierarchy. Magical realism, as it is in Junot Díaz's *The Brief Wondrous Life of Oscar Wao*, as the 'zafa' – 'counterspell' (Díaz 2008, 7) – to the 'fukú' or curse of colonial history and its neo-imperialist reiteration in the present. Díaz offers a sceptical account of magical realism, to be sure: alluding to its commercialisation and acknowledging accusations of its potential exoticism.[9] Indeed, the novel offers very few moments that we could identify as magical realism (the appearance of the golden mongoose at two key events in the history of the de León family is the most obvious gesture to the genre). However, the narrative frame identifies 'this book' as the fictionalised author's 'very own counterspell' (7): as a means to resist the history of violence and oppression that is both one version of the de León family story and the curse of the New World more broadly – 'They say it came first from Africa, carried in the screams of the enslaved; that it was the death of the Tainos, uttered just as one world perished and another began' (1). The counterspell persists, in other words, despite the New World's entry into the world-system, as Moretti would see it, and moreover, it persists as the radical capacity of literature to produce dissent, to imagine the alternative forms of social organisation or accountability that are immanent within this world, not simply as its impossible transcendence.

Literature can become a conservative force that helps sustain particular relations of power. As Díaz recognised, writers and dictators can be bedfellows: 'Rushdie claims that tyrants and scribblers are natural antagonists, but I think that's too simple; it lets writers off pretty easy. Dictators, in my opinion, just know competition when they see it. Same with writers. *Like, after all, recognized like*' (Díaz 2008, 97). This reminds us of the affective force of literature, its capacity to persuade; but it is also deeply ironic. Yunior, the fictionalised persona of the writer, exerts very little authority over his novel: the stories that it contains are related to him by the individual members of the de Léon family and restricted to what they are willing or able to share – Oscar's final text, which contains 'Everything I [Oscar] think you will need' (333) to understand his life, never arrives in the mail; Belí's account of the Gangster is partial, leaving Yunior 'wait[ing] for the day the páginas en blanco finally speak' (119). Yunior himself is forced to betray aspects of his personality that he would rather conceal – 'Do you know what sign fool put up on our dorm door? *Speak, friend, and enter.* In fucking Elvish! (Please don't ask me how I knew this. Please)' (172); he has to confess the historical errors in his narrative when he is called out on them by his friends (132); he leaves the interpretation of aspects of the story wholly up to the reader – 'So which was it? you ask. An accident, a conspiracy, or a fukú? The only answer I can give you is the least satisfying: you'll have to decide yourself. What's certain is that nothing is certain' (243). Most significantly, the novel is presented as 'a *true* account of the Brief Wondrous Life of Oscar Wao' (285), and yet its veracity is tested by the improbable repetitions and coincidences (that Belí would happen to fall in love with a man so closely associated with the Trujillo family; that Oscar ends up being beaten and left for dead in a cane field in the Dominican Republic, like his mother, over the person he loves), and by the frequent allusions to fantasy and science-fiction which recur throughout. As Yunior acknowledges, his reader can either (sceptically, perhaps) accept this version of reality and keep reading, or they can reject it entirely – 'This is your chance. If blue pill, continue. If red pill, return to the Matrix' (285). This, of course, is another challenge to our perception of reality and imagination as distinct spheres: taking the red pill will signal a rejection of the version of reality offered by the novel, but it will nonetheless return us to a world of simulacra (the Matrix). The novel characterises both realities (the real account of Oscar's life and the real world of the reader) as suspect and compromised by the interruption of fantastic, improbable and magical elements. The authority of a single, coherent and realistic account of Oscar's life or the de Léon family's history is similarly compromised as a result. The 'páginas en blanco', Anna Garland Mahler has argued, often point towards suppressed histories and, as such, 'exemplif[y] the impunity that allows tyrants […] to never be held accountable for their actions' (2010, 131); 'Thus, the writer's use of ink is intended to put words of accountability on the blank pages of impunity and therefore, to put a face on the faceless. In other words, Díaz proposes writing as a means of exposing the forces of tyranny that have been hidden beneath the First World mask' (131). Or, for us, writing as the exposure of the rhetoric of innocence that says the subaltern cannot speak. For Fredric Jameson, this too is the achievement of *One Hundred Years of Solitude*. In the episode which leaves José Arcadio Segundo the only witness to the massacre of the banana company workers, the novel, Jameson argues, reveals the event to have been 'successfully, magically and yet naturally […] eradicated from the collective memory in that archetypal repression which allows all of us to survive history's immemorial nightmares, to live on happily despite "the slaughterhouse of history" (Hegel). This is the realism – yes, even the political realism – of magical realism' (Jameson 2017, 23). For Jameson, the realism of magical realism is the novel's capacity to expose the illusions that blind us to the Weberian violence that underpins our world. Márquez's text enacts the processes by which a rhetoric of innocence is created, in this case the collective amnesia of the state-sponsored massacre of Columbian workers, and as such starkly reveals the repression at work in our narrative of civilisation. Díaz's 'páginas en blanco', like Márquez's forgotten victims, confront us with a rhetoric of innocence stripped of its pretensions, but also suggest to us that an account of one side of reality alone (history rather than magic) is not enough. *The Brief Wondrous Life* presents history as a counter-narrative to the dominant, world-historical perspective of Trujillo's dictatorship, which is relegated to footnotes in the novel. Díaz's novel is quite obviously a critique of the Trujillo regime and a portrait of contemporary America that reveals its creolisation, not merely in terms of the growing constituent of peoples with non-European ancestry, but in the way in which it disrupts Standard English with the frequent intrusion of untranslated and colloquial Spanish phrases. But, recalling Spivak, it is a critique directed not simply against a single, homogeneous adversary, but one that recognises the complexity of the modern world. Resistance, in such circumstances, cannot be reduced to a matter of opposing one value system with its negation; rather, it begins with the recognition that nothing of the world is predetermined but rather constructed and partial (power and contradictions alike), and from that position the resistant world literary text creates alternative narratives of history, belonging, and living that become available to readers and critics in their ongoing renegotiation of the world. The immanent reality of both representation (or magic) and the real are necessary counterparts, not dialectically opposed spheres in this rethinking of the creative, dissident task of world literary scholarship. This capacity for dissent, I maintain, is essential if world literature and its critical analysis is to become anything more than the passive reflection of a world of global inequalities.

Acknowledgment

This chapter elaborates the section on Franco Moretti in Chapter One of *Post-colonialism After World Literature: Relation, Equality, Dissent* (London: Bloomsbury, 2019). I am grateful to Bloomsbury for permission to reproduce aspects of that work and develop them in this chapter.

Notes

1 Emphasis in the original. In all subsequent quotations, emphasis is reproduced as given in the original quote unless 'emphasis added' is noted in parenthesis.
2 For an analysis of Moretti's nuanced understanding of tragedy, see Ben Hewitt's *Byron, Shelley, and Goethe's Faust*, which addresses the Kantian basis of Moretti's argument in comparison with Lucien Goldmann's reading of Kant and as such argues for the continuing potential of tragedy to offer a source of resistance and not merely consent (cf Hewitt 2015, 25–34).
3 See Jameson's account of post-/structuralism in *The Prison-House of Language* (Jameson 1974, 108–9).

4 On this connection between Nietzsche and Schopenhauer *vis-a-vis* Kant, see John Sallis (1991, 32). The final chapter of Fiona Hughes's *Kant's Critique of Aesthetic Judgement* discusses similar responses, highlighting that for Schelling, Fichte, Hegel, and Hölderlin, Kant's philosophy was 'marred by an insuperable rift between subject and object' (2010, 154).

5 David Harvey's reading of *Capital*, for example, stresses the way in which Marx's dialectical concept of the commodity should not be read in Hegelian terms. For Marx, the commodity can be said to hold two aspects – use-value and exchange-value – in a dialectical relation; however, '[t]his is not Hegelian logic in the strict sense, because there is no final moment of synthesis, only a temporary moment of unity within which yet another contradiction – a duality – is internalized' (Harvey 2010, 26).

6 See Fiona Hughes (2010), especially the final chapter.

7 This is the aim of Fiona Hughes's *Kant's Critique of Aesthetic Judgement* (2010).

8 For a fuller account of these philosophers in relation to world literature theory, see my *Postcolonialism After World Literature* (Burns 2019).

9 'It used to be more popular in the old days, bigger, so to speak in Macondo than in McOndo' (Díaz 2008, 7). This is an allusion to Alberto Fuguet's critique of magical realism in 'I Am Not a Magical Realist': 'Unlike the ethereal world of García Márquez's imaginary Macondo, my own world is something much closer to what I call "McOndo" – a world of McDonald's, Macintoshes and condos. In a continent that was once ultra-politicized, young, apolitical writers like myself are now writing without an overt agenda, about their own experiences. Living in cities all over South America, hooked on cable TV (CNN en español), addicted to movies and connected to the Net, we are far away from the jalapeño-scented, siesta-happy atmosphere that permeates too much of the South American literary landscape' (Fuguet 1997, n.p.).

Works cited

Apter, Emily. 2010. 'Philosophizing World Literature'. *Contemporary French and Francophone Studies* 16(2): 171–186.

Breton, André. 1972. *Manifestoes of Surrealism*. Trans. Richard Seaver and Helen Lane. Ann Arbor, MI: University of Michigan Press.

Burns, Lorna. 2019. *Postcolonialism After World Literature: Relation, Equality, Dissent*. London: Bloomsbury.

Carpentier, Alejo. 1995. 'The Baroque and the Marvellous Real' in Wendy Faris and Lois Zamora, eds, *Magical Realism: Theory, History, Community*. 89–108. Durham, NC: Duke University Press.

Casanova, Pascale. 2004. *The World Republic of Letters*. Trans. Malcolm DeBevoise. Cambridge, MA: Harvard University Press.

Casanova, Pascale. 2005. 'Literature as a World'. *New Left Review* 31: 71–90.

Damrosch, David. 2003. *What is World Literature?* Princeton and Oxford: Princeton University Press.

Deleuze, Gilles and Félix Guattari. 1986. *Kafka: Toward a Minor Literature*. Trans. Dana Polan. Minneapolis and London: University of Minnesota Press.

Díaz, Junot. 2008. *The Brief Wondrous Life of Oscar Wao*. London and New York: Faber & Faber.

Etherington, Ben. 2012. 'What is Materialism's Material? Thoughts Toward (Actually Against) a Materialism for "World Literature"'. *Journal of Postcolonial Writing* 48(5): 539–551.

Felski, Rita. 2015. *The Limits of Critique*. Chicago and London: University of Chicago Press.

Fuguet, Alberto. 1997. 'I am Not a Magical Realist'. *Salon* 6 November. Available online: https://www.salon.com/1997/06/11/magicalintro/ (Accessed 25 January 2018).

Jameson, Fredric. 1974. *The Prison-House of Language: A Critical Account of Structuralism and Russian Formalism*. Princeton and London: Princeton University Press.

Jameson, Fredric. 2017. 'No Magic, No Metaphor'. *London Review of Books* 39(12): 21–32.

Jung, C. G. 1953. *Collected Works of C.G. Jung. Vol. 12. Psychology and Alchemy*. Trans. R. F. C. Hull, Ed. Herbert Read, *et al.* London: Routledge.

Harman, Graham. 2009. *Prince of Networks: Bruno Latour and Metaphysics*. Melbourne: re:press.

Harvey, David. 2010. *A Companion to Marx's Capital*. London and New York: Verso.

Hewitt, Ben. 2015. *Byron, Shelley, and Goethe's Faust: An Epic Connection*. London: Legenda.

Hughes, Fiona. 2010. *Kant's Critique of Aesthetic Judgement*. London and New York: Continuum.

Latour, Bruno. 1993. *We Have Never Been Modern*. Trans. Catherine Porter. Cambridge, MA: Harvard University Press.

Linguanti, Elsa. 1999. 'Wilson Harris: A Case Apart' in Elsa Linguanti, Francesco Casotti, and Carmen Concili, eds, *Coterminous Worlds: Magical Realism and Contemporary Post-Colonial Literatures in English*. 245–268. Amsterdam: Rodopi.

Mabille, Pierre. 1998. *Mirror of the Marvellous*. Trans. Jody Gladding. Rochester, VT: Inner Traditions.

Mahler, Anna Garland. 2010. 'The Writer as Superhero: Fighting the Colonial Curse in Junot Díaz's *The Brief Wondrous Life of Oscar Wao*'. *Journal of Latin American Cultural Studies* 16(2): 119–140.

Marx, Karl. 1990. *Capital. Vol. 1*. Trans. Ben Fowkes. London: Penguin Classics.

Moretti, Franco. 1988. *Signs Taken for Wonders: Essays in the Sociology of Literary Forms*. Trans. Susan Fischer, David Forgacs, and David Miller. London and New York: Verso.

Moretti, Franco. 1996. *Modern Epic: The World-System from Goethe to García Márquez*. London: Verso.

Moretti, Franco. 2013. *Distant Reading*. London: Verso.

Parry, Benita. 2004. *Postcolonial Studies: A Materialist Critique*. London: Routledge.

Rancière, Jacques. 1999. *Disagreement: Politics and Philosophy*. Trans. Julie Rose. Minneapolis, MN: University of Minnesota Press.

Rushdie, Salman. 1992. *Imaginary Homelands*. London: Granta Books.

Sallis, John. 1991. *Crossings: Nietzsche and the Space of Tragedy*. Chicago and London: University of Chicago Press.

Schroeder, Shannin. 2009. '"Advancing in the Opposite Direction from Reality": Magical Realism, Alchemy, and *One Hundred Years of Solitude*' in Harold Bloom, ed, *Gabriel García Márquez's One Hundred Years of Solitude*. 193–213. New York: Chelsea House.

Spivak, Gayatri. 1999. *A Critique of Postcolonial Reason: Toward a History of the Vanishing Present*. Cambridge, MA: Harvard University Press.

Spivak, Gayatri C. 2010. 'Can the Subaltern Speak?' in Rosalind C. Morris, ed, *Can the Subaltern Speak? Reflections on the History of an Idea*. 21–78. New York: Columbia University Press.

Walkowitz, Rebecca. 2015. *Born Translated: The Contemporary Novel in an Age of World Literature*. New York: Columbia University Press.

WReC. 2015. *Combined and Uneven Development: Towards a New Theory of World-Literature*. Warwick Research Collective. Liverpool, UK: Liverpool University Press.

Young, Robert. 2014. 'World Literature and Postcolonialism' in Theo D'haen, David Damrosch, Djelal Kadir, ed, *The Routledge Companion to World Literature*. 213–222. London: Routledge.

5

KHALDUNIA

The literary politics of radical Arabic humanism

Timothy Brennan

Dissent breaks from tradition by learning from it, not dispensing with it. Dissent is, to that degree, traditional. Revolutionaries are always students first – Gramsci, Marx, Ho Chi Minh, Cabral – scouring old texts for new directions, resisting the neologisms and oracular leaps of the intrepid inventors of utopia among their impatient contemporaries. An example would be Lucien Goldmann's *The Hidden God* (*Le Dieu Caché*, 1956). A Romanian student of Lukács based in France, Goldmann wrote this study – half of which is dedicated to the seventeenth-century mathematician and philosopher Blaise Pascal – in order to forge alternatives to Althusserian structuralism. He set out to show the limits of the mechanistic rationalism of Descartes, Malebranche, and Leibnitz that were, he lamented, alive and well in the vaunted dissidence of late twentieth-century France. But only 'vaunted' since that earlier scientism of the seventeenth-century rationalists had in its time, according to Goldmann, 'filled older ethical and Christian forms with an amoral and irreligious substance', and jettisoned the 'closely connected idea of the community and the universe […] replac[ing] them by the totally different concepts of the isolated individual and of infinite space' (2016, 29). Goldmann's critique was prescient, and it holds today.

This kind of rationalism was, he argued, an unequal exchange: an objectivity subjectively muscled forth, and purchased at the expense of respect for subjectivity, purging inquiry of the vagaries of human opinion under the warrant of nature. Under the unanswerable banner of the scientifically new, a prejudice against spirit could in this way pass itself off as natural law. In taking up such a strange, mediated, and at the time unfashionable project as a study of Pascal in 1960s France, Goldmann understood that every particular taste, form, and action is framed by its philosophical points of departure. It was therefore of great interest politically to revisit epistemological lineages, and to demonstrate that current debates had prior iterations. There is nothing new that is not, contextually, a rediscovery, or as Ibn Khaldūn puts it, 'the past resembles the future more than one (drop of) water another' (1967, 55). But even more, to recognise what we really believe, and what the stakes of our beliefs are, comes about only by freeing ourselves from all the tired associations that accrete around belief in the chaos and emotion of present debates. A studious distance clarifies. We learn what we think by alienating ourselves from immediate connotations and seeing them through the lens of the traditions that gave them birth. Even an incendiary term like 'communism' could no longer arrest judgment and sense – as it almost always does – if it could be seen as an event along the way of history, a latter-day manifestation of, or twist on, historical antecedents.

Ibn Khaldūn – the great fourteenth-century Maghrebian historical sociologist – is certainly one of those antecedents. If, as Erich Auerbach famously put it in his essay on *Weltliteratur* in a 1967 translation by Edward and Maire Said, 'history is the science of reality that affects us most immediately, stirs us most deeply, and compels us most forcibly to a consciousness of ourselves. It is the only science in which human beings step before us in their totality', then Ibn Khaldūn anticipated world literature very specifically.[1] He dissented from tribalism, holding out for the truth of textual evidence in the act of recording and learning from history, believing that the spirit of a people is literarily expressed and capable of later recovery. The politics of literature is not to be understood as the radical views expressed by authors, or the experiments with form that supposedly dislodge older conceptual modalities, but the role of human eloquence and articulation in the formation and sustenance of polities, as well as the textual record of the traceable patterns of the rise and decline of those polities as well as the universal striving for justice to which they testify.

According to Shafiq al Hout in *My Life in the PLO*, Eqbal Ahmad towards the end of his life returned home to Islamabad, Pakistan with the intention of founding what he called the 'Khaldunian University' (al Hout 2011, 284). He made the move in the wake of the disaster of the Oslo accords, following the symbolic gesture of his close friend Ibrahim Abu-Lughod, who had quit his job at Northwestern to return to Palestine in order to teach at Bir Zeit University for the last decade of his life. In al Hout's words, Ahmad wanted to create the university because 'he believed in the anti-imperialist role which could be played by the education sector' (284).

But why use the name 'Khaldunian'? Perhaps for the same reason that Ibn Khaldūn, the medieval Maghrebian founder of historical materialism and literary sociology, is utterly absent in today's debates on world literature. This is despite the fact of his explicit methodological statement at the beginning of the *Muqaddimah*, his masterpiece, that civilisation – which he equates with 'human social organization' – can only be studied properly if it is studied globally; that the materialist study of society is a study ultimately of *spirit* not only *matter*, that the only proper techniques of historical reconstruction are philological (in Auerbach's sense), which means – among other things – breaking down the generic boundary lines between imaginative literature and sociological or historical analysis, and giving the science of history over to a study of rhetorical figures, literary genres, and the character of language – the topics of the entire final book of the *Muqaddimah*. As Eqbal Ahmad suggests (and he is not alone), Ibn Khaldūn provided some of the clearest philosophical foundations outside of Europe for the worldliness and comparatism later found in cultural movements of anti-imperialism.

The 1200 pages of the manuscript, divided into seven books, is in every sense a work of philology in the modern, here non-technical, sense of being a science of interpretive competence based on the recovery of the historical past through texts. Do historians always get it right? Of course not, he insists. There are, he writes, questions of partisanship, prejudice, reliance on transmitters, personality criticism, unawareness of the purpose or 'why' of an event, and ignorance of how conditions shape reality. There is also a tendency for people to approach those of high rank with encomiums while ignoring virtuous people while disregarding that civilisation is not one thing, but many, and varies according to the people, the region, the culture, or historical moment. What has been lacking, he argues, is a theory of the politics of interpretation that accounts for ethnic prejudices, religious myth, obeisance to power, and historical determination – the ideas that, in ensemble, would at a later date be given the name historical materialism. It is impossible to read Ibn Khaldūn without being in awe of his improbable contemporaneity – and indeed, almost everyone who comes upon the text for the first time finds it hard to believe that they are reading a work from the fourteenth century.

The original title of the work was *Book of Lessons, Record of Beginnings and Events in the History of the Arabs and the Berbers and Their Powerful Contemporaries*. In other words, his original brief was his immediate community in relation to the world and only later, after he developed and expanded the idea, did his work morph into a proper 'universal history' – the term Ibn Khaldūn gives the work itself. In the seven volumes that make up the work, fully two of them are dedicated to the history of the Berber peoples and the nomadic Arabs of the Maghreb. The persistence with which Ibn Khaldūn throughout the *Muqaddimah* exalts the fortitude and abstinence of the Berbers, while stressing the intolerance, shortsightedness, and savagery of the Arabs, makes one suspect that he was Berber, and many have, in fact, suggested that he was. But this would be to miss the whole point of *asabiyyah* – the transcendence of blood ties.

Eqbal Ahmad was in solidarity not only with this modern voice but with the philological spirit outlined here so scientifically and completely, for he recognised its harmony with a new era of anticolonial thought and action in the twentieth-century – the very century often written off as the scene of world war, totalitarianism, and fascism. We are talking of the century often seen as the showdown between Russia and the West, between communism and democracy, which covers up what the century is much more clearly about: namely, the beginning of the ethical and rhetorical disarticulation of European and American imperial right. It is the anticolonial century. From the perspective I am outlining here, Marxism might begin to appear, along with much else, as a mode of thought and action within a broader tradition that begins in the West with Giambattista Vico, and in the Islamic West (that is, the Maghreb) with Ibn Khaldūn, whose philosophical leads guided their descendants in the key transitional period of the early twentieth century. An Arabic humanism in the postwar period – seen very visibly, for example, in the work of Sadiq Al-Azm, George Makdisi, and Edward Said – has tended to overlap with Marxism, and to draw its inspirations from it.

The symbolic attractions of Ibn Khaldūn for Arabic scholarship and activism are as unknown as they are defining. There is the case, for instance, of Mahdi Amel, a prominent philosopher, sometimes called the Arab Gramsci, a Lebanese communist who was killed in 1987 in Beirut by unknown assailants. He had moved to Algeria in 1963 in a show of anticolonial solidarity and wrote there one of his major works titled *In the Process of Ibn Khaldun's School of Thought*. Amel, one of the most outspoken critics of Said's *Orientalism* after it first appeared, was not alone. Husayn Muruwwa, an intellectual within the Lebanese Communist Party, was the editor of the newspaper *Al-Tariq* and had written a series of books that demonstrated how Arab culture was not just about religion and sentiment. It also had deep roots in science and reason. This seam of materialist culture – evident in tenth-century thinkers such as al-Farabi and Ibn Sina (Avicenna), and fourteenth-century descendants of the Golden Age of Islamist thought such as Ibn Khaldūn – had been denied by Islamist scholarship, and cancelled out with the same zeal that mainstream Western scholarship had ignored it. Muruwwa was assassinated in his hospital bed at the age of 78 for having moved scholarship of the near east in this humane and materialist direction.

World literature as such

But why does Ibn Khaldūn belong in a discussion of world literature? To begin with, drawing on Aristotle's *Nicomachean Ethics* with its turning of the question of the 'good' to practical political concerns, and representing a decisive moment in the recovery of Greek learning by Arabic scholarship (now set in the unique contexts of a cosmopolitan sympathy that the Greeks themselves never evinced), he is the first to set down the foundation of historical sociology and economics in their modern sense. At the same time, and for our purposes most interestingly, he considered the study of rhetoric, linguistics, and literature an organic part of such a study. This establishes a connection for a number of reasons, but maybe most of all because of the striking degree to which world literature over the past half-decade or so is driven by the core arguments and methods of the sociology of knowledge. It is not so much the scope of literature – national vs. world – that preoccupies its thinkers as approaches to reading and method that declare their emancipation from narrow art interpretation, poetic reverie, or the fetish of the imagination. In place of close readings of prose or poetry, these studies exhibit large institutional histories, macro-readings of book markets, computer-generated mappings of the representations of space in novels, and so on. To this degree they reflect the leads that have existed for much of the twentieth century towards the supposedly scientific methods of the social sciences.

To understand the significance of this, we have to make a distinction. In defending the essay as form, Adorno – part of whose career, remember, was spent learning the techniques of academic sociology – held out for a creative, versatile, unmanaged element in the act of critical intellectual work. He was trying to tread a delicate path between the image of the critic as an independent agent, experimenting with ideas and words, without obligation or direction, on the one hand, and, on the other, with the critic as a more trained, disciplined, knowledgeable consciousness, rigorously pursuing a method in order to arrive at perceptions that could not be dismissed as a mere personal opinion – that had about them rather the air of exactness and unanswerable authority. The ideal image Adorno projected was something like the philosopher as sociologist, the critic who is aware of the social and political consequences of their opinions and discoveries but who, for all that, does not forget the artistic dimension of what they do in the special sense of the word 'artistic' – meaning here not fictional or purely aesthetic, but retaining an element of wonder, self-interrogation, a feeling of incompleteness, an intuitive sense of the whole.

Recent examples of critical models in our circles, though – not all of them in world literature – are headed in a different direction from Adorno. They reject not only the older image of the critic as polymath, creative force, individual ethical consciousness, and so on, but also the critic as one involved in *critique* at all – as one who judges, synthesizes, assesses and evaluates as part of their essential job description. They tend rather to move the job of the critic more and more towards the social sciences and away from form in Adorno's sense, concentrating rather on macro systems: that is, the contrast is not merely between the individual and the public, but between the human and the systemic, structural, or autonomous – the *extra*-human if you will. In both cases, these two models can be seen to move in the direction of a kind of sociology very different, I will argue, from the one left us by Ibn Khaldūn, the one, I am suggesting, we should be learning from.

Because this Adornian distinction is largely unknown or misunderstood, many have rightly felt frustration with world literature of late. The neo-positivism of Franco Moretti loses touch completely with why people read at all, and treats the literary like so much coal in the furnace of contents. Based ostensibly on the Marxism of Galvano Della Volpe – which is to say a scientism in Italy proximate to that of Althusser in France – its claims on the representation of geographical space or epic in the novel, apart from being grossly inaccurate at the factual level (only one of the problems with distant reading), aspires to remove, or at least curtail, the human agent from the process of the literary. As such, Moretti's methods participate quite conventionally in the standard-issue desubjectification that has attended the anthropological anti-humanism of interwar intellectual life where Georges Bataille and Michel Leirismight be considered typical examples. The approach is not unlike the quite different, but no less misanthropic spin given to the matter in the postwar writings of structural anthropology with its macro-system of universal myth that, again, depersonalises all cultural differences (Claude Lévi-Strauss). Later, this same desubjectification acquires new life in the neo-ontologies and mathematical exuberance of a variety of theories in the humanities such as 'thing' theory, object-oriented philosophy, surface reading, and so-called 'weak thought' (Brown 2001, Bryant Harman, and Srnicek 2011, Best and Marcus 2009, Mullarkey and Smith 2012).

For her own part, Pascale Casanova (2004) posits a world republic on the thin grounds of an autonomous literary system fuelled ultimately only by taste, as though direct economic pressures, or those of cultural imperialism, were irrelevant to its course. She ignores the important regional break from that system enacted in the early twentieth century, where it would make more sense to speak of a world republic of letters that emanated from Mexico City, Calcutta, and Moscow rather than Paris, as we have seen lately from the rather unsung, but important, studies of younger scholars such as Monica Popescu, Rossen Djagalov, Marla Zubel, and Daniel Dooghan. Finally, to take a third case, the conventional Goethean motifs of David Damrosch cannot escape recycling gestures inaugurated already in 1949 by Fritz Strich, who made the same arguments within a more impactful postwar context, not to mention those of Auerbach in the 1950s and Edward and Maire Said in the 1960s, in whose wake he trails. This branch of world literature, associated with Damrosch's book *What is World Literature?* (2003), possesses no other theory of its object than that of the common sense of well-intentioned readers somehow going about their acts of reading more liberally. The new and different centres of literary production they elicit are all based on language and ethnicity rather than ideas and solidarities, and without any sustained focus on the artificial disparities of distribution and interpretation imposed by the imperial powers. And given the lineage of thought from which it is lavishly borrowing, it loses contact entirely with the Vichian and Khaldunian dimensions that motivated its predecessors.

And their most creative predecessor in this tradition, Johann Gottfried Herder, although alluded to, is discussed only glancingly, despite the fact that Herder theorised world literature before Goethe, and in much more depth (if not under that precise rubric), Goethe picking up the idea 'from the young Herder during the short period of their intense friendship in Strasbourg' (Noyes 2015). What does it matter, one might ask, whether it was Herder or Goethe who was the first in Europe to conceive the idea of world literature? Well, it matters because of the quite different, less Olympian, less vague, and profoundly more social and egalitarian direction into which Herder took the concept. Herder speaks of a 'common humanity' in a world of cultural differences, whereas Goethe, as John K. Noyes points out, was more interested in the Leibnizian interest in the manifestation of universal forces in individual human lives (Noyes 2015, 101). We are back once again, in other words, to Goldmann's critique of scientism (which so profoundly influenced Said, who leaned very heavily in his early career on Goldmann's study of Pascal).

Similarly, and once again to draw the connecting lines with which I have been working, in 1976 long before the present world literature excitements, S. S. Prawer in *Karl Marx and World Literature* had already raised up, and extensively conceptualised, the idea of world literature in its contemporary sense, speaking of war, civil institutions, and the world market, with the objective of moving literary study outside the confines of an older, Eurocentric literature, by exploring the worldliness of Marx as a reader of world literatures. And yet he, like the Russian philologist Mikhail Lifshitz who travelled the same road as early as 1933 in his study of Marx's philosophy of literature, is absent from the current discussion (Lifshitz 1973 [1938]). Vico, naturally, who anticipates the entire enterprise, is left to the footnotes of Italian specialists or students of the waning years of the Enlightenment. Ibn Khaldūn figures not at all except among certain chroniclers of historical scholarship such as Arnold Toynbee and R. G. Collingwood. He does make an entrance in the work of Said, where he plays a minor role. Indeed, the motifs in Said's work that are often taken to be Foucauldian – for example, his focus on geography and space, on institutions and instruments of governance – are as much Khaldunian according to Said himself. In his 1986 essay 'Foucault and the Imagination of Power', Said seems to say that Foucault is like Ibn Khaldūn in that he held that the historian's work 'takes place between rhetoric, on the one hand, and civil politics, on the other' (Said 2001, 240). But finally Said rejects the comparison, pointing out that Foucault's portrait of the 'unremitting and unstoppable expansion of power' sits ill with Ibn Khaldūn's innovative, and much copied, theory of the historical cycles of ascendancy and decline of states as a result of the decay of what we today would call 'hegemony' – the gradual self-satisfaction, complacency, and corruptions of empire (to borrow a phrase from Alexander Cockburn [1988]).

As early as 1976, in a roundtable with Samuel Huntington and others hosted by the American Enterprise Institute on the topic 'Can Cultures Communicate?', Said complained that 'even Arab intellectuals like Ibn Khaldoun and Averroes are widely unknown' in a West obsessed with 'the backwardness and stagnation of Islam' (Stewart *et al.* 1976). Despite being urged by his close friend, the great historian of modern Lebanon, Fawwaz Traboulsi, to take up Ibn Khaldūn and seriously incorporate his findings, Ibn Khaldūn gets only a passing reference in *Orientalism* (Said 1978, 151). And yet, in *On Late Style*, Said mentions Ibn Khaldūn in the same breath as Vico as 'the great founders of the science of history understood as "human labour"' (2008, 3).

The *literary* significance of Ibn Khaldūn arises in Said's *The World, the Text, and the Critic*, where Said observes that the celebrated 'discovery of language' in Europe by romantic philology and the rise of linguistics in the early nineteenth century was preceded by Arab intellectuals:

> Yet during the eleventh century in Andalusia there existed a remarkably sophisticated and unexpectedly prophetic school of Islamic philosophic grammarians, whose polemics anticipate twentieth-century debates between structuralists and generative grammarians, between descriptivists and behaviorists. Nor is this all. One small group of these Andalusian linguists directed its energies against tendencies amongst rival linguists to turn the question of

meaning in language into esoteric and allegorical exercises. Among the group were three linguists and theoretical grammarians, Ibn Hazm, Ibn Jinni, and Ibn Mada' al-Qurtobi, all of whom worked in Cordoba during the eleventh century, all belonging to the Zahirite school, all antagonists of the Batinist school. Batinists held that meaning in language is concealed within the words; meaning is therefore available only as the result of an inward-tending exegesis. The Zahirites – their name derives from the Arabic word for clear, apparent, and phenomenal; *Batin* connotes internal – argued that words had only a surface meaning, one that was anchored to a particular usage, circumstance, historical and religious situation.

(*Said 1983, 36*)

I will return to this preference for the 'clear and apparent' in literature later.

As Said suggests, this is – in the sense of the Goldmann example earlier – a contemporary debate recast in historical garb, not to avoid controversy by attacking opponents in a mediated way, at one step removed, but to establish the contemporary validity of the philological rediscovery of a decisive anticipation: the cycles of history playing themselves out. Partly at stake here, of course, is Said's rejection of a number of ideas that were prominent in the 1970s and 1980s – the ideas of creative interpretation, reader-response theory, the revival of Gadamerian hermeneutics with its epistemological scepticism, Althusserian symptomatic reading with its invitation to use texts as raw material so as to have them say what you need them to say, and so on. It is about Said's persistence in moving us towards the rather different idea that reading is a matter of responsibility, of discipline, in the Chomskian sense. He is here not just describing the eleventh-century Cordoban Zahirites, but allying himself with them to the extent that they, like he, were against the esotericism of words and for their social situatedness: and all this in order to arrive at (in Said's words) 'a reading system that placed the tightest possible control over the reader and his circumstances'. In short, Said – who from his co-translation and publication of Auerbach's essay on world literature is more responsible for the academic turn to world literature than any other single figure – has taken as his model the intellectual traditions that formed Ibn Khaldūn, as well as Ibn Khaldūn himself, through Vico. Because of his close resemblance to Vico, it is Ibn Khaldūn who for Said plays the largest role in establishing the Arabic and Islamic origins of humanism. The continuities and linkages are not only circumstantial or analogical. It is likely that Vico, a polymath ensconced in southern Italy and deeply schooled in Eastern Mediterranean culture, knew of his work indirectly via the excitement in Egypt, where Ibn Khaldūn's work had inspired a revival of historical scholarship in the fifteenth and sixteenth centuries; or by way of the partial translation of the Muqaddimah into Turkish in the eighteenth century. The strong parallels between Ibn Khaldūn's work and the theories of sovereignty found in Jean Bodin (1576) and Jean Chardin (1686) – both of whom Vico knew intimately – have been widely recognised by scholars from the mid-nineteenth century onwards following the first French translation of the Muqaddimah in the

1860s. Vico, however, could never have acknowledged this debt to the Muslim scholar openly given the vigour of the Inquisition in the Naples of his day.

Arabic humanism

So here is our remarkable situation: revolutionaries in Lebanon, Palestine, and Pakistan fighting in national liberation movements held up Ibn Khaldūn as an intellectual and political resource. Like the figure of Toussaint L'Ouverture in the Caribbean, he became for many a talisman, not only a historical personage. The difference, of course, is that Ibn Khaldūn was not just a dissident, but also a formidable conduit between Greek and Persian antiquity on the one hand, and European modernity on the other. Not only did he, in his very person as an Arab precursor, represent an illustrious and now forgotten past; he actually created an original theory of national liberation, cultural difference, and humanist rationalism that, under the very different conditions of mid-twentieth-century geopolitical life, expressed these revolutionaries' very goals. And, we might add, he did so while laying out a civic hermeneutics, a theory of the relationship of language to politics, which, as he expresses simply in the following terms: 'by their very nature, cooperation and social organization are made easier by proper expressions' (Ibn Khaldūn 1967, 9).

The move to reclaim Arab intellectuals of the golden age for the project of world civilisation was not limited to communists or partisans of national liberation struggles; it was part of a much larger movement whose forms we probably know best from the work of Said (although it is hardly limited to him). In the words of Kamal Abu-Deeb (who, incidentally, was the first translator of *Orientalism* into Arabic): 'the modern is not coincident with modern times, but was a subject of concern and analysis in the Arabic ninth and tenth centuries. Since Arabs recorded everything, their relationship to humanism is very easy to trace' (Abu-Deeb 1979).

George Makdisi later showed that 'classical Islam appears to have provided the model for Italian Renaissance humanism' (Makdisi 1997, 15). The *studia humanitatis* has echoes in the classical Arabic term *adab* (literally, refinement, decorum, good manners, humaneness), which was taught via 'grammar, poetry, rhetoric (as applied to letter-writing and speech-writing), history, and moral philosophy (mainly moral tracts)' (15). These, Makdisi argues, seem to have been devised first in the madrasas even if the structure of the university as such – as we know it today – is found first in medieval Europe and was not replicated elsewhere until the modern era. If humanism grew organically out of scholasticism, the latter began in the Islamic countries of the ninth century, whereas it began in Europe only in the twelfth century with Pierre Abelard. In Makdisi's account, literature holds a special place. 'Poetry', he argues, 'pervaded all intellectual products of humanism. Indeed it pervaded all of the divisions of knowledge in the classical Islamic organization of learning' (19). One might speak of 'the poetry of the intellectuals, grammarians, and so on' as well as the 'grammar, law, theology, philosophy, and so on of poetry' (19). Not all of this was good poetry, or even held to be good by contemporaries;

it was rather the form in which science, sociology, and history was expressed. But there was also poetry whose purpose was purely aesthetic, like our own sense of the word today, and this scholars gave the special name 'the poetry of poets'. Humanism was originally based, then, on the category of 'eloquence' (*bayan* – 'manifesto' or public 'declaration'), which conferred dignity on the human being (22). For this reason, eloquence is a major theme running through the *Muqaddimah*, where it is associated with a writer or speaker who is 'able to combine individual words so as to express the ideas he wants to express, and who is able to observe the form of composition that makes his speech conform to the requirements of the situation [...] conveying to the listener what he wants to convey' (Ibn Khaldūn 1967, 756). Eloquence, in this tradition, is not so much a special gift of this or that writer as it is part of the essential character of the human.

The urgency of stressing this historical fact about the Arab and Islamic contributions to humanism and rationalism is not hard to understand in a climate in which, to quote Said again, the 'backwardness and stagnation of Islam' is part of the daily news dose. It will not be lost on those who appreciate what is meant by the term 'orientalism' that this backwardness is often attributed to the Arabic language itself. Sadiq Al-Azm humorously quotes the following passage from Jonathan Raban:

> To live in Arabic is to live in a world of false turns and double meanings. No sentence means quite what it says. Every word is potentially a talisman. Conjuring the ghost of the entire family of words from which it comes. The devious complexity of Arabic grammar is legendary. It is a language perfectly constructed for saying nothing with enormous eloquence; a language of pure manners in which there are hardly any literal meanings at all and in which the symbolic gesture is everything. Arabic makes English look simple-minded, and French a mere jargon of cost accountants.
>
> *(Al-Azm 2015, 3)*

Note the conformity of Ibn Khaldūn's definition with that of the Zahirites above – 'saying what one means, clearly, and appropriately to the situation' – and note then its radical differences from Raban's charge. The latter insinuates that in Arabic's mystery and beauty, there lurks dishonesty and untrustworthiness – the very target of Ibn Khaldūn's methodological warnings against the errors of historical reporting (as Ibn Khaldūn puts it: 'the normative method for distinguishing right from wrong in historical information on the grounds of (inherent) possibility or absurdity' [1967, 38]). This aesthetic of caution against the misuse of figurative language for the purpose of concealing, or the perpetually ironic state of mind that cannot decide or choose, has profound implications for the status of literary modernism in third world literature, as I have argued elsewhere (Brennan 2014, 2017). It implies, rather, a sort of counter-modernist aesthetic of situatedness and witness that arises, after Ibn Khaldūn, in very similar terms in Vico, Hegel, and twentieth-century Marxist thinkers who form to this degree an inchoate aesthetics of the periphery based on declaration and clarity of position – on public eloquence. It might be seen here, in passing, as a riposte of sorts to the modern epic argument in Moretti, or the centre and periphery arguments of Casanova, both of which ultimately recycle the conventional tastes of literary modernism without acknowledging the vexed politics of doing so along the lines we are exploring.

For Al-Azm – in a gesture not unlike Said's implicit charges against decon-struction (which would be 'Batinist' in his terms) – goes on to make fun of Raban's critical hypocrisy. Isn't the entire critical scene of the decades we are referring to here, Al-Azm wryly asks – the ones in which Said, Ahmad, and others are making their correctives by drawing on dissident counter-traditions – all about 'the disjunction of sign, signifier, and signified, the unending shiftiness of sense, the undecidability of meaning, the paradoxes of incommensurability, William Empson's *Seven Types of Ambiguity*, the absurdities of self-reflexivity, and so on' (Al-Azm 2015, 3)? And if so, then wouldn't that make Arabic the 'ideal language for the angst-ridden *Daseins* of the postmodern condition' (3)? This kind of culture clash is very much what the *Muqaddimah* is about – a reflection on how language, in particular Arabic, is inflected by a religion founded on an inimitable text narrated by God. The (importantly spoken) language of God, on the one hand – which Ibn Khaldūn dutifully venerates, but after venerating, pushes to the margins of his inquiry – lends weight to the much vaster, and more hermeneutically interesting, language of humans, inherently capable of eloquence. Ibn Khaldūn implies that the hermeneutic elaboration and sophistication among Islamic scholars in advance of Europe derives from this fact of Arabic's special place in Islam. Its grammatical com-plexities derive from the habits and instincts of its specifically spoken form. For the Quran is a recitation, the transcription of divine speech.

The work itself

I cannot unravel the *Muqaddimah* here, given its length and complexity, but I do have time to make the following points about what makes it important to world literature.

First of all, it presents reading in the form of a legal judgment, a civic herme-neutics. *Muqaddimah*, usually translated as 'introduction', also means 'disambigua-tion' or 'adjudication'. It is a legal term, which is not surprising because of Ibn Khaldūn's training in the law. And this would seem to matter given the emphasis later in Vico, and still later in Hegel, on the civic foundations of rhetoric, and the fact that the earliest peoples in prehistory who created the first polities spoke exclusively in poetic characters.

Beginnings

Second, Ibn Khaldūn establishes both the vanity of absolute beginnings and the necessity of actively choosing a beginning, of expressing one's solidarity with a tradition. He is puzzled that others had not done what he had done before him, and so curtails his boasting. Maybe, he wonders, even his own innovations had been accomplished earlier by others. We will never know, he says, because so many discoveries have been effaced by conquerors who destroyed the historical record:

> There have been numerous sages among the nations of mankind. The knowledge that has not come down to us is larger than the knowledge that has. Where are the sciences of the Persians that 'Umar ordered wiped out at the time of the conquest! Where are the sciences of the Chaldaeans, the Syrians, and the Babylonians, and the scholarly products and results that were theirs! Where are the sciences of the Copts, their predecessors! The sciences of only one nation, the Greek, have come down to us, because they were translated through al-Ma'mun's efforts.
>
> (Ibn Khaldūn 1967, 3)

Al-Ma'mum, that is, the great intellectual patron of ninth-century Baghdad.

Group feeling (tribe vs. polity)

Third, the concept around which the entire manuscript is structured: *asabiyyah* – 'group feeling' or 'social solidarity'. Group feeling is initially based on bonds of blood and familial descent, or what we today would call tribalism: 'everybody's affection for his family and his group is more important (than anything else)' (Ibn Khaldūn 1967, 165). But here, and in many other places in the manuscript, his presentation is dialectical. For, the opening proposition on tribalism is only the start of a process unfolding in time; it is, in Hegelian terms, the false beginning to be negated in later stages of the argument. What he means to do is extend 'group feeling' to include alliances, negotiations, and like-mindedness, to turn filiation into affiliation. 'Genealogy is something that is of no use to know and that it does no harm not to know [...]. This means that when common descent is no longer clear and has become a matter of scientific knowledge, it can no longer move the imagination and is denied the affection caused by group feeling. It has become useless' (167). Ibn Khaldūn is already talking about the politics of cultural difference. Incredibly, *aasibayah* gets at something very similar to what we today call 'hegemony' in the domestic, political sense. As he puts it, 'followers share in the group feeling of their masters and take it on as if it were their own group feeling. By taking their special place within the group feeling, they participate to some extent in the (common) descent to which (that particular group feeling belongs)' (175). But then, and just as importantly, he sees it as the necessary counter-force to a people too long subject to foreign dominance. 'Group feeling produces the ability to defend oneself, to offer opposition, to protect oneself, and to press one's claims. Whoever loses (his group feeling) is too weak to do any of these things' (184).

The periphery

Ibn Khaldūn, despite the centuries separating him from us, cannot be mistaken for doing anything other than formulating a conceptual category richly developed in twentieth-century Marxism: that of the fundamental social conflict between the country and the city. He explores in great depth the mutual entanglement of the two communities – one developed, one underdeveloped – and the pros and cons of both, the slippage in both between what should be praised and what should be condemned. That is, his is not simply a conservative embrace of the noble peasant rising above the sins of Sodom and Gomorrah. 'Sedentary people have become used to laziness and ease', he writes. 'They are sunk in well-being and luxury. They have entrusted defense of their property and their lives to the governor and ruler who rules them, and to the militia which has the task of guarding them' (162). It is the Berbers and nomadic Arabs of the Maghreb, by contrast, who exhibit fortitude and self-reliance in their abstinence, which makes them less susceptible to the blandishments of ideology. In this figure of country and city, as elsewhere, he is primarily interested in questions of equality and inequality. He wants to figure out how some peoples achieve superiority over others. This question to him is crucially related to how people 'make a living', their 'gainful occupations' (1). He develops the first political economy, theorizing the first labour theory of value, but he also explains how the cultural conditions of a specific people produce specific kinds of polities, while judging the strengths on either side of the dichotomy.

The critique of home

A very crucial and unmistakable aspect of the manuscript is the deliberate, almost ostentatious anti-ethnocentrism. Ibn Khaldūn, although an Arab descended from Andalusian scholars, condemns Arabs throughout his book. In his words, they 'swarm across distant zones and achieve superiority over faraway nations' (188). They 'plunder whatever they are able to lay their hands on' (193). And further, 'the Arabs are a savage nation, fully accustomed to savagery and the things that cause it. Savagery has become their character and nature. They enjoy it, because it means freedom from authority and no subservience to leadership. Such a natural disposition is the negation and antithesis of civilization' (194). His heart is with the indigenous Berbers whom the Arabs came to dominate, for they have a strength of character that complacent city-dwellers lack.

Anticolonialism

For Ibn Khaldūn and his tradition – and this would be true of Vico later – foreign conquest is ethically odious, and leads to the wanton destruction of indigenous culture:

> The Arabs are not concerned with laws. [They are not concerned] to deter people from misdeeds or to protect some against others. They care only for

the property that they might take away from people through looting and imposts. When they have obtained that, they have no interest in anything further, such as taking care of (people), looking after their interests, or forcing them not to commit misdeeds.

(Ibn Khaldūn 1967, 194)

Politics of (world) literature in Ibn Khaldūn's 'universal history'

But finally, there is an important treatment in Ibn Khaldūn of literature itself. I have been trying to stress the unexpected and, from the Western point of view, startlingly well-developed modernity of the Islamic golden age, and particularly Ibn Khaldūn, when it comes to the early history of humanism, and the expression of that humanism by means of a literary sensibility that here, in its early form, was part of a generalist knowledge that encompassed sociology, history, and economics in a single interconnected field. How different that is from the way we approach world literature today, with all of its modernist predilections. One of the more fascinating aspects of Ibn Khaldūn's *Muqammidah* is the implicit counter-aesthetic that it suggests. Recall his earlier comments on eloquence as direct speaking, communicative action, and the precisions of the speculative mind. Creative writing is presented in the context of the book as a necessary craft. Ibn Khaldūn's long discussion of literary form, genre, and linguistics in the book follows logically from his extended analysis of economics which puts forth, as I said above, the first labour theory of value: 'The art of writing, and book production, which depends on it', he observes, 'preserve the things that are of concern to man and keep them from being forgotten. It enables the innermost thoughts of the soul to reach those who are far and absent' (508). And he continues:

> We have already mentioned in the book that the rational soul exists in man only potentially. Its transformation from potentiality into actuality is effected first by new sciences and perception derived from the *sensibilia*, and then by the later acquisition (of knowledge) through the speculative power [...]. Writing is the most useful craft because, in contrast to (the other) crafts, it deals with matters of theoretical, scientific interest. This is explained through (the circumstance) that writing involves a transition from the forms of the written letters to the verbal expressions in the imagination, and from the verbal expressions in the imagination to the concepts (underlying them), which are in the soul.
>
> *(Ibn Khaldūn 1967, 538)*

This beautifully realised defence of speculative thought, of the spirit as well as the matter that lies behind any true materialism, stakes out an attitude and direction later taken up in Hegel. It is the hostile reception of Hegel, after all – by far the most dissident intellectual source for the anticolonial liberation movements of the twentieth century (by way of Marx) and for the creation of the concept of world literature itself (by way of romance philology) – that partly explains our ignorance of Ibn Khaldūn's contribution to world literature. Our scene oscillates between the aesthetic appeals of new modernism studies, at one pole, and the macro optic of world systems, mappings, and evolutionary trees, at the other. Meanwhile Khaldunia, taken up by liberation intellectuals of the twentieth century, avoids the one-sidedness of these poles through a more sensitive, sociologically informed focus on the human being as a politically situated, speculative possibility. To go forward, we must go back in order to know what to preserve as we break the mold.

Note

1 The translation and its short introduction (Said and Said 1969) were published in 1969 but were written two years earlier. All quotations are from the short introduction, 1–2.

Works cited

Abu-Deeb, Kamal. 1979. *Al Jurjani's Theory of Poetic Imagery*. London: Aris and Phillips.

Adorno, Theodor W. 1991. 'The Essay as Form' in Theodor W. Adorno, *Notes to Literature, Vol. 1*. Trans. Shierry Weber Nicholsen. 3–23. New York: Columbia University Press.

Al-Azm, Sadiq. 2015. 'The Political Said'. Unpublished lecture, sent to the author on December 12.

Best, Stephen and Sharon Marcus. 2009. 'Surface Reading: An Introduction'. *Representations* 108(1): 1–21.

Bodin, Jean. 1576. *Les Six Livres de la République*. Paris: Jacques du Puys.

Brennan, Timothy. 2014. 'The Case Against Irony' in Ben Etherington and Jarad Zimbler eds. *The Crafts of World Literature*. Special issue of *Journal of Commonwealth Literature* 49(3): 1–16.

Brennan, Timothy. 2017. 'Against Modernism' in eds, Rashmi Varma and Sharae Deckard, *Left Turns*. London: Routledge.

Brown, Bill. 2001. 'Thing Theory'. *Critical Inquiry* 28(1): 1–22.

Bryant, Levi, Graham Harman, and Nick Srnicek, eds. 2011. *The Speculative Turn: Continental Materialism and Realism*. Melbourne: re.press.

Casanova, Pascale. 2004. *The World Republic of Letters*. Trans. M. B. DeBevoise. Cambridge, MA: Harvard University Press.

Chardin, Jean. 1686. *Journal du voyage du chevalier Chardin en Perse et aux Indes Orientales par la Mer Noire et par la Colchide. Première partie, qui contient le voyage de Paris à Ispahan*. London: Moses Pitt.

Cockburn, Alexander. 1988. *Corruptions of Empire*. New York and London: Verso.

Damrosch, David. 2003. *What is World Literature?* Princeton, NJ and Oxford: Princeton University Press.

Goldmann, Lucien. 2016. *The Hidden God: A Study of Tragic Vision in the Pensées of Pascal and the Tragedies of Racine*. Trans. Philip Tody. Foreword by Michael Löwy. London: Verso.

al Hout, Shafiq. 2011. *My Life in the PLO*. London and New York: Pluto Press.

Ibn Khaldūn, Abd al-Rahman ibn Muhammad. 1967. *Muqaddimah: An Introduction to History*. Trans. Franz Rosenthal. Princeton, NJ: Princeton University Press.

Lifshitz, Mikhail. 1973. *The Philosophy of Art of Karl Marx*. Trans. Ralph B. Winn. London and New York: Pluto Press.

Makdisi, George. 1981. *The Rise of Colleges: Institutions of Learning in Islam and the West*. Edinburgh, UK: Edinburgh University Press.

Makdisi, George. 1997. 'Inquiry into the Rise of Humanism' in Asma Afsaruddin and A. H. Mathias Zahniser, eds, *Humanism, Culture & Language in the Near East, Studies in Honor of Georg Krotkoff*. 15–26. Winona Lake, IN: Eisenbrauns.

Mullarkey, John and Anthony Paul Smith. 2012. *Laruelle and Non-Philosophy*. Edinburgh, UK: Edinburgh University Press.

Noyes, John K. 2015. 'Writing the Dialectical Structure of the Modern Subject: Goethe on World Literature and World Citizenship'. *Seminar: A Journal of Germanic Studies* 51(2): 100–114.

Prawer, S. S. 1976. *Karl Marx and World Literature*. Oxford: Clarendon Press.

Said, Edward. 1978. *Orientalism*. New York: Pantheon.

Said, Edward. 1983. *The World, The Text, and The Critic*. Cambridge, MA: Harvard University Press.

Said, Edward. 2001. *Reflections on Exile*. Cambridge, MA: Harvard University Press.

Said, Edward. 2008. *On Late Style: Music and Literature Against the Grain*. New York: Vintage.

Said, Edward and Maire Said. 1969. 'Introduction' in Erich Auerbach, *Philology and Weltliteratur*. Trans. Edward Said and Marie Said. *Centennial Review* 13: 1–2.

Stewart, Edward, Samuel P. Huntington, Laura Nader, Mustafa Safwan, and Edward Said. 1976. *Can Cultures Communicate?* An AEI Round Table held on September 23 Washington, DC: American Enterprise Institute for Public Policy Research.

Vico, Giambattista. 1968. *The New Science of Giambattista Vico*. Trans. Thomas Goddard Bergin and Max Harold Fisch. Ithaca, NY: Cornell University Press.

PART II
Dissident literatures

6

EVERYDAY DISSENT

Colonised lifeworlds in twentieth-century poetry

Nick Lawrence

The terrain of the everyday doesn't lend itself, initially, to an analysis of the possibilities of dissent, literary or otherwise. Writing in 1983 on the occasion of the centenary of Marx's death, Henri Lefebvre, who did more than anyone to theorise and promote the concept, concludes that

> the word *everyday* [*le quotiden*] designates the entry of [...] daily life into modernity: the everyday as an object of a programming [...] whose unfolding is imposed by the market, by the system of equivalences, by marketing and by advertisements. As to the concept of 'everydayness', it stresses the homogeneous, the repetitive, the fragmentary in everyday life.
>
> *(Lefebvre 1988, 87)*

Market-driven, homogeneous, repetitive, fragmentary. We are here a long way from the Lefebvre of 1945, the moment of the first volume of his career-long study of *la vie quotidienne*, with its robust defence of 'the elementary splendour of everyday life' (Lefebvre 2008a, 210) as counter to the extremes of capitalist and fascist modernization. In either case, though, 'the everyday', like the notion of 'tradition', itself must be read as an artefact of modernity − born in the split between workplace and home, public and private spheres, system and lifeworld.[1] In a 1965 encyclopaedia article, Lefebvre notes that the sectors of social life given over to the serial requirements of dailyness − commuting, working, shopping, cooking, cleaning, providing routine care and maintenance − while each distinct in their operations, share an underlying structure that unites them in their fragmentation: 'organized passivity' (Lefebvre 1987, 10). From such ground radical dissent seems unlikely to arise.

In what follows I want first to sketch a history of the passage in Lefebvre's thought between his theorisation of the everyday as a semi-autonomous realm within modernity and his growing attention to its status as occupied territory. Not because Lefebvre exists alone among thinkers who give us insights into the dissenting potential of the literary everyday – he is joined, at a minimum, by members of the Frankfurt School, ethnographers from the Mass Observation project, Edgar Morin, the pioneering feminist analyses of Simone de Beauvoir and Dorothy E. Smith, sociologists of culture such as Erving Goffman, and critics such as Roland Barthes and Raymond Williams – but because Lefebvre's focus is drawn to a particular crux in the dynamic of modernity: namely, its adherence to a logic of uneven development. In construing the everyday as a product of modernity and at the same time a 'backward', lagging, or resistant sphere within it, Lefebvre was able to grasp the constitutive unevenness of the concept at the moment when it achieves definition as a focused object of sociocultural analysis. And by adapting the analytic of uneven development to the situation of colonised lifeworlds in both metropole and periphery, he allows us to connect the experience of alienated deprivation in the colonial world with what is later experienced by those in the imperial centres of the world-system, themselves subject to unevenly imposed modernisation and accelerating commodification alike. From his supposed discovery of the concept – it occurred to him, he wrote, when his wife walked into their apartment holding a box of detergent and remarked, 'This is an excellent product'[2] – to his later elaboration of the colonial logics operative in urban planning, Lefebvre's career shows a continuing, if itself unevenly and incompletely theorised, attention to the world-systemic relations underpinning any experience of the everyday. For this reason his work constitutes a useful departure point for assessing the convergence of postwar attention to the quotidian and new forms of world-literary dissent.

Throughout his work on a critical sociology of *la vie quotidienne*, Lefebvre more than once cites Hegel's maxim, '[t]he familiar is not necessarily the known'.[3] For him – and for a generation of ethnographers, sociologists, and documentarians – the everyday initially presents itself as an undiscovered continent of the twentieth century. It is not only the realm of 'sustenance, clothing, furnishing, homes, lodging, neighborhoods, environment', but of the habitual, the recursive, the necessary but un- or under-acknowledged labour of subsistence that maintains continuity in daily life while adapting itself to changing circumstance and rationalising imperatives. It is, in another key, what a later generation of Marxist feminists will term the sphere of social reproduction, that vast sea of activity on which the narrower domain of profit production depends, but whose costs form no part of capital's accounting books.[4] As Lefebvre's encyclopaedia article is at pains to underscore, the 'generalized passivity' of this sphere

is moreover distributed unequally. It weighs more heavily on women, who are sentenced to everyday life, on the working class, on employees who are not technocrats, on youth – in short on the majority of people – yet never in the same way, at the same time, never all at once.

(*Lefebvre 1987, 10*)

Behind Marx's 'hidden abode of production' (Marx 1976 [1867], 273), an even more occulted space of ceaseless but undocumented phenomena lends its rhythms to a world against which the technologically advanced features of urban modernity stand out in sharp relief. The lines of division are gendered, racialised, and class-indexed, but also differentiated geographically according to region, above and below the level of the nation-state. Lefebvre's childhood in the shadow of the Pyrenees, together with his experience of working in the Resistance during the war, likely made him especially sensitive to the discrepancy between the modalities of urban experience and those of the rural hinterlands, the latter still formally congruent with the rhythms and processes of peasant life.[5] But it was the triangulation of these forms of experience with the dramatic introduction of an Americanised surge of consumer goods in postwar France – the really great box of laundry detergent – that catalysed his thinking about the everyday as a specifically modern, rather than residual, category.

In this light, 'the everyday' appears in Lefebvre's analyses as something like a mirage, flashing up in the moment of its alienation within a decisively different register – an afterimage, to paraphrase Walter Benjamin, of the blinding experience of the age of invasive commodification. As Kristin Ross writes in her cultural history of postwar France,

> Contrasting the French experience to the slow, steady 'rational' modernisation of American society that transpired throughout the twentieth century, Lefebvre evoked the almost cargo-cult-like, sudden descent of large appliances into war-torn French households and streets in the wake of the Marshall Plan. Before the war, it seemed, no one had a refrigerator; after the war, it seemed, everyone did.
>
> *(Ross 1996, 5)*

Alongside the accelerated modernisation of a domestic sphere now reorganised by imported commodities, the second development prompting a reconsideration of everyday life takes place overseas, in the drawn-out struggle of decolonisation. Just as the everyday is indexed to the increasing commodification of ordinary life, so for Lefebvre the postwar conclusion of formal empire predicates the rise of informal imperialism or neocolonialism, extending the logic of capital into hitherto unpenetrated territory while at the same time installing the techniques of colonial administration back in the metropole. Writing in 1961, toward the close of the second volume of his *Critique de la vie quotidienne*, Lefebvre makes emphatic his assertion that '*critique of everyday life generalizes [the] experience of the "backward" or "underdeveloped" nations and extends it to the everyday in the highly developed industrial countries*' (Lefebvre 2008b, 316, emphasis in the original). For Lefebvre, at this phase of his lifelong project, 'the everyday' arrives already riven and distorted by its constitution as the conflictual ground of forces working outside its field of vision; it is both object and subject of a process first tested and experienced in the colonies. With the example of the ongoing Algerian Revolution unavoidably in view, he writes in terms that echo Frantz Fanon:

> We know that the underdeveloped sectors do not remain quietly held back like a troop of soldiers dragging their heels far from the front line. The sectors which are destined to suffer uneven development, be it temporary or long-lasting, soon realize that they are being occupied and brutally exploited. They must regain their freedom or win it back by combat. They remain subjected.
>
> (*Lefebvre 2008b, 316*)

With its call for a 'general upheaval in the name of everyday life', Volume 2 of Lefebvre's *Critique* ends on a note quite different from its precursor volume published 14 years earlier. There, the 'critical and positive' analysis of a postwar life-world outside the sphere of systematised knowledge must lead to a 'humanism that believes in the human because it knows it' (252). At the turn of the 1960s, however, Lefebvre draws inspiration from the ferment of decolonisation to recast the theory of the everyday on a world scale, in the process forecasting with some prescience the eruption of festivalised insurrection from within the quotidian that marks the events of May 1968.

How literally are we to take the thesis of the colonised everyday? Lefebvre insists that it is no mere metaphor. His defining focus on the problem of alienation in the first volume of *Critique of Everyday Life*, augmented with intervening ethnographic work on the underdevelopment of peripheral France, alters its compass when the new realities of the postwar global order become apparent over the course of the 1950s. Far from being metaphorical, the link between colonial exploitation and 'interior colonialism' is metonymic and structural: as Ross cites a city councillor remarking during the Parisian renovation debates of the early 1960s, 'France decolonized the Third World while colonizing Paris, appointing as head of the commission charged with making decisions about the capital functionaries who had made their careers in Black Africa or in Asia' (Ross 1996, 8). If everyday life had for some time been recognised as on the receiving end of colonisation by the commodity form, grasping the context of global commodity production leads to an understanding of the processes of uneven development not only on the colonial peripheries of the world-system but in the core as well. This was certainly how Lefebvre's one-time student and collaborator Guy Debord saw it: 'Henri Lefebvre,' he wrote, 'has extended the idea of uneven development so as to characterize everyday life as a lagging sector, out of joint with the historical but not completely cut off from it. I think that one could go so far as to term this level of everyday life as a colonized sector' (Highmore 2002, 240–1).

The advantages of the optic provided by uneven development, for Lefebvre, went beyond its challenge to the complacencies of modernisation theory and related assumptions concerning *les trente glorieuses*. In its sharpened attention to the production of inequality *by means of* a subsuming homogenisation, the theory of uneven development offered ways to explore the postwar remaking of urban space; the racialised variegation of districts, zones, and regions; the transformative impact of advertising on language use in public; and the recurrence of cycles of pro-grammed abundance and planned obsolescence, among other aspects of the social geography of city and countryside alike. The contradictions, anomalies, and juxta-positions routinely thrown up by these processes at street-level could no longer be written off as accidentals on the road to progress, or signs of the 'not here/not yet' of modernity's deferred promise. This was, rather, modernity itself, an uneven combination of imposed development and lag, in line with Doreen Massey's observation: 'Much of life for many people, even in the heart of the First World, still consists of waiting in a bus shelter with your shopping for a bus that never comes' (Massey 1994, 8). Or, as Lefebvre notes, '[t]he situation of everyday life strikes us (unfortunately) as being a prime example of the law of uneven development' (Lefebvre 2008b, 316).

In parsing the implications of Lefebvre's attempt to unite his colonisation thesis with the theory of uneven development, we can note parallel contributions to an understanding of the radical implications of full commodification in postwar society. Lefebvre's productive if conflict-ridden collaboration with the younger Situationists during the late 1950s to early 1960s is well known, marking a high point in pre-1968 theorising of the irruptive possibilities of creative revolution. At the same time, the Frankfurt School's development of their critique of the wholly administered society via the mechanisms of the culture industry finds an answering chord in Lefebvre's and Debord's insistence on the takeover of everyday life by an increasingly spectaclised leisure economy. For Adorno, indeed, the distinction between the spheres of production and consumption had come under decisive pressure: time off from work, suggested the author of 'Free Time', is time structured and encased by the imperatives of the working day, not simply as necessary refuelling for the demands of wage labour, but more insidiously as a continuation of labour in other channels and by other means: 'Free time is shackled to its opposite' (1991, 162).

What Lefebvre brings to this nexus of concerns is an explicit attempt to articulate the specific parameters of postwar consumer society in dialectical relation with the moment of decolonisation (for France, a relatively brief window extending from the defeat at Dien Bien Phu in 1954 to the completion of the Algerian indepen-dence accords in 1962). In a sympathetic yet critical reading of the colonisation thesis, Stefan Kipfer and Kanishka Goonewardena note:

> With this world-wide conception of 'colonisation', Lefebvre establishes a connection between various socio-spatial 'peripheries' – underdeveloped countries, displaced peasants, slum dwellers, immigrant workers, inhabitants of suburbs, women, youth, homosexuals, drug addicts – that nourish revolt. It allows us to connect 'far' and 'near' peripheries that are subject to forms of territorial control in (ex-)colonies and metropolitan centres. It offers a way of tying geo-political aspects of imperialism and colonisation to the relations of centre and periphery within metropolitan regions themselves.
>
> *(Kipfer and Goonewardena 2013, 97)*

Kipfer and Goonewardena argue that it is only when Lefebvre moves beyond his abstract theorisation of a colonised everyday into the concrete analysis in his later work on urbanism, spatial practices, and the role of the state that the relative vagueness of his initial proposition begins to be overcome. But if we shift from matters of theory to writing practice, a different set of questions arises, having more to do with the nature of the connection that Lefebvre proposes between 'far' and 'near' in grasping the contours of the everyday, and the expressive forms – models of attention, embodied cognition, inhabitation – that might emerge in the attempt to actualise this connection in language. Can dissent be both pre- and proto-political within this frame, the frame of mundane existence?

Perhaps the most indelible example of such dissent contemporary with Lefebvre's work emerges not in France, but in the colonised Caribbean. Here is the opening of the first, less familiar version of Aimé Césaire's 'Notebook of a Return to the Native Land' published in the journal *Volontés*:

> At the end of first light burgeoning with frail coves the hungry Antilles, the Antilles pitted with smallpox, the Antilles dynamited by alcohol, stranded in the mud of this bay, in the dust of this town sinisterly stranded. At the end of first light, the extreme, deceptive desolate eschar on the wound of the waters; the martyrs who do not bear witness; the flowers of blood that fade and scatter in the empty wind like the cries of babbling parrots; an aged life mendaciously smiling, its lips opened by vacated agonies; an aged poverty rotting under the sun, silently; an aged silence bursting with tepid pustules
>
> the dreadful inanity of our raison d'être.
>
> At the end of first light [...]
>
> (Césaire 2013, 3)

We might notice in relation to Lefebvre's later concern with 'rhythmanalysis', or the cadences of everyday life, how Césaire's anaphoric iterations of the dawn of a new dead day signal not just repetition without advancement, but something closer to the nightmarish 'inanity' of colonial parrots mimicking their masters, a form of recurrence that underscores the essential struggle in the poem to break from a prevailing stasis. Where later fellow Caribbean writers will theorise an archipelagic thought whose rhythms of drift and recurrence disavow any easy assumptions of linear progress (Édouard Glissant), or argue for a region-specific 'tidealectics' rather than a dialectics (Kamau Brathwaite), Césaire's repetitions carry no redemptive charge. 'In this inert town' where Christmas is celebrated in a parodistic imitation of French custom, the colonial 'umbilical cord [is] restored to its ephemeral splendor' and the essential rhythms of island life are driven by the demands of survival, the speaker paying oblique homage to

> my mother whose legs pedal, pedal, day and night, for our tireless hunger, I am even awakened at night by these tireless legs pedaling by night and the bitter bite in the soft flesh of the night by a Singer that my mother pedals, pedals for our hunger both day and night.
>
> (Césaire 2013, 15)

It may seem perverse to cite 'Notebook', even in its original form, as exemplar of a poetry of everyday dissent. This is, after all, the paradigmatic anticolonial outcry, a work that summons not only the oppressive minutiae of contemporary Antillean existence, but also the weight of slave history, somaticising the landscape as a diseased manifestation of collective self-loathing and abandonment, giving voice to a centuries-long internalisation of colonial racism and expelling it with the force of an island volcano. Arnold and Eshleman suggest in the introduction to their translation that the first version of the poem reveals a less politicised, more spiritual preoccupation on the poet's part with the materials of his alienated homeland.[6] This may be so, but it is the powerful, sense-upending estrangement of everyday details of Caribbean life, an estrangement that is only partly accounted for by reference to Césaire's engagements with surrealism, that forms the basis of the anticolonial politics later given a more explicit edge in his postwar work, including the poetic essay-indictment *Discourse on Colonialism*. In the *Volontés* version of 'Notebook', rather than a 'purer' investigation of the poet's spiritual crisis, Césaire concentrates to a greater extent on the mundane particulars of underdeveloped colonial existence, especially as these manifest a potentially explosive arrest of colonial temporality. On these terms, the poem can be said to join in Lefebvre's call for a critique of everyday life that '*lays down the principle that the great upheaval which calls on the consciousness of those nations engaged in the drama of uneven development to emancipate themselves should reverberate through "modernity" via an upheaval of everyday life and a general upheaval in the name of everyday life, given that it is a backward sector which is exploited and oppressed by so-called "modern" society*' (Lefebvre 2008b, 316, emphasis in the original).

The historical frames for understanding this 'great upheaval' in Black francophone poetics are, notoriously, two: (1) the introduction to the second printing of 'Notebook' by surrealist *majordomo* André Breton, titled 'Un Grand Poète Noir'; and (2) Sartre's 'Orphée Noir,' the preface to Léopold Senghor's 1948 anthology of francophone Afro-diasporic poetry published first in English in the journal *Présence Africaine*. It was less Sartre's appropriation of the concept of *Négritude* than the poetry he excerpted from the anthology that drew an enthusiastic response from Frank O'Hara, the poet whose work most flamboyantly embodies the mid-century everyday in American writing. In 'Ode: Salute to the French Negro Poets', O'Hara implicitly responds to Sartre's disavowal of any connection to a white readership in the work of Césaire, Senghor, and Damas by directly addressing his fellow poets across boundaries of race, nation, and language – 'From near the sea, like Whitman my great predecessor, I call/to the spirits of other lands …' (305) – and makes explicit his solidarity with anticolonial and civil rights movements. But his series of rhetorically elevated odes are an exception to the rule of O'Hara's poetry, which otherwise tends to remain determinedly at the level of the particular and casual. To gauge the everyday as resistance in his work requires a different set of optics than those applicable to Césaire.

Unsurprisingly, everyday life in American postwar poetry often presents itself as a series of stress tests related to shopping. Randall Jarrell's aging female shopper, pausing over laundry detergent:

Moving from Cheer to Joy, from Joy to All,
I take a box
And add it to my wild rice, my Cornish game hens.
The slacked or shorted, basketed, identical
Food-gathering flocks
Are selves I overlook.

(Jarrell 1981, 279)

And Allen Ginsberg, also in the supermarket:

In my hungry fatigue, and shopping for images, I went into the neon fruit
supermarket [...]
I saw you, Walt Whitman, childless, lonely old grubber, poking among the
meats in the refrigerator and eyeing the grocery boys.

(Ginsberg 2009, 144–5)

And O'Hara, shopping for friends in midtown Manhattan:

in the GOLDEN GRIFFIN I get a little Verlaine
for Patsy with drawings by Bonnard although I do
think of Hesiod, trans. Richmond Lattimore or
Brendan Behan's new play or Le Balcon or Les Nègres
of Genet, but I don't, I stick with Verlaine
after practically going to sleep with quandariness

(O'Hara 1995, 325)

Perhaps the locus classicus of the everyday as ordinary activity, however, is
O'Hara's 1956 lunch poem 'A Step Away from Them'. The extensive commentary on the poem varies on several points, but it has reached consensus on
two: the poem is exemplary of O'Hara's 'I do this, I do that' mode of recorded
first-hand experience, taking in sights that are 'palpable, real, and closely
observed', in the words of Marjorie Perloff;[7] and its evident pleasure in these
sights is heightened or italicised by a pervasive awareness of mortality. 'It's my
lunch hour, so I go / for a walk among the hum-colored / cabs', the poem
begins, before moving on

to Times Square, where the sign
blows smoke over my head, and higher
the waterfall pours lightly. A
Negro stands in a doorway with a
toothpick, languorously agitating.

[...]

There are several Puerto
Ricans on the avenue today, which
makes it beautiful and warm.

[...]
And one has eaten and one walks,
past the magazines with nudes
and the posters for BULLFIGHT and
the Manhattan Storage Warehouse,
which they'll soon tear down.

[...]
A glass of papaya juice
and back to work. My heart is in my
pocket, it is *Poems* by Pierre Reverdy.
                    (O'Hara 1995, 257–8)

So at home in this metropolitan world does the poem appear, so insouciantly accepting of its daily variety, that any question of conflictual unevenness, not to mention colonisation, might appear literally out of place.[8] In a quest for signs of tension beneath the poem's surface, a materialist reading can all too easily be reduced to grasping at short straws: the imminent demolition of the Manhattan Storage Warehouse, signalling O'Hara's offhand revision of Baudelaire's lament over the Hausmannisation of Paris; or the apparently lazy agitation of the black man in the doorway hinting at the threshold of a new phase in the civil rights struggle (1956!); or the class markers dividing a 'lady in foxes' from half-naked construction workers, capturing the disjunction in dress codes prior to the revolution of 1960s informality in street wear; or the presence of Puerto Rican immigrants alongside Caribbean commodity-imports such as papaya juice. All the elements of US mid-century consumerist dominance, abundance shading into sheer redundancy (furs on a hot day, lightbulbs in daylight), are laid out for casual inspection. The poem blows its smoke lightly over its readers.

Rather than flip through the playbook of a hermeneutics of suspicion, then, the critic of O'Hara's work might look not for tension 'below' the surface of the poem, but instead for surface tension itself, the meniscus curve of its attention to detail and resistance to symbolic significance, embodied above all in its corner-turning line-breaks. (Hollis Frampton's 1968 film *Surface Tension*, a radically accelerated single dolly-shot tour of Manhattan from Brooklyn Bridge to Central Park, offers a resonant filmic counterpart to O'Hara's midtown peregrinations; cf. Newman 2012) Here everydayness reveals another of its aspects. For if they are scrutinised long enough, the poem's details come to seem less and less the direct transcriptions of daily witness, 'palpable, real, and closely observed', and more like a carefully assembled montage drawn from Hollywood movies: the skirt blown over the subway grate, the smartly clicking chorus girl, the loitering black man breaking into a smile, the society woman with her poodle in a taxi – these gradually acquire definition not as first-hand observations but as filmic quotations. If colonisation of the everyday is an issue in 'A Step Away from Them', it has more to do with the way experience and perception are framed according to the tropes and conventions of the culture industry than with any overt reference in the poem itself. O'Hara, as much at home with the products of Hollywood as with European art-house cinema such as Fellini's, maintained an ironic but appreciative stance on the inevitable alienations attendant on colonised experience, a structure of feeling widely analysed as camp. Yet the question of the commodity's installation at the heart of metropolitan ways of seeing here takes an additional turn, ironically reversing the mandate to see afresh so central to a modernist poetics of attention: make it new. To see instead at second-hand, through the filmic conventions of the studio system, may offer its own ambivalent Pop pleasures, but these testify to a different set of conditions for a poetry of the everyday than those faced by, for example, Reverdy. O'Hara's world is ultimately closer to what Debord will diagnose as the society of spectacle, even as memories of the poet's dead friends in its closing section preserve a counterweight to the spectacle's seductive command of attention.

The question of everyday occupation, tension, and the lyric registration of unevenness is cast in a different light in another example of the postwar quotidian, this one also titled 'A Step Away from Them':

> There's a poem called that
> by Frank O'Hara, the American,
> it begins: *It's my lunch hour so I go*
> *for a walk* …. I like the poem, sometime
> I'll write it out complete, but just for now
> I've got this OK Bazaars plastic packet
> in my left hand, and my right
> hand's in my pocket (out of sight),
> how else to walk lunch hour
> summertime Cape Town with
> one gloved hand?
>
> […] A cop van's
> at the corner. On a bench
> 3 black building workers eat
> from a can of Lucky
> Star pilchards. They're
> in various shapes & sizes. It's a fact.
> Though you'd think
> post boxes'd be all
> just one size. I'm sweating a bit
> […] but now

> I've only
> eyes for postboxes and
> my heart's in my packet: it's
> one thousand
> illegal pamphlets to be mailed.
> *(Cronin 1999, 77–8)*

This poem by South African writer and political activist Jeremy Cronin first appeared in the collection *Inside* (1983), a gathering of work written primarily while Cronin was serving a seven-year sentence for crimes against the apartheid state during the late 1970s and early 1980s. Like O'Hara's apparent distance from Césaire, the angle of vision Cronin brings to this *détournement* of O'Hara's poem appears a world away from that of its model, but what is striking is the vernacular ease with which Cronin adapts O'Hara's lightness of tone and subject matter to his mid-1970s Cape Town setting. As with the original, the South African 'A Step Away from Them' proceeds by cataloguing the sights of a city lunch hour, but like the speaker's pocketed hand kept out of sight, its secret context – the mission of distributing illegal political *communiqués* – is withheld until the final lines. En route to that reveal, the details Cronin includes continually translate between the two contexts, while pointing up shared features common to each – the presence of commercial signage, brand names for food, landmarks of the neighbourhood, bodies classified by race and nationality, above all a preoccupation with time, whose retardation signals at once the relative 'backwardness' of Cape Town in the 1970s and the slowing of perception made vivid during a moment of personal danger. If Cronin's observations, like O'Hara's, are shadowed by a looming anxiety, its source here is less the contrast between a mundane surface vitality and premature death than the overarching context of apartheid South Africa itself, which asserts itself in ways both overt (the rare 'unsegregated toilets' of the city centre) and subterranean (the speaker's obsessive focus on 'post boxes', also a term for mouths, indicates they are all one size, contravening the logic of legally mandated inequality under apartheid). Everywhere, in fact, the backlighting provided by the omnipresence of state repression and the poet's own Communist commitment contrives to pick out the significance of a string of seemingly casual details, details that together fix a moment both personal and historical; the poem documents the very activity that will lead to his imprisonment, 'inside' versus the outside of this poem's public encounters. A poem like Cronin's both indexes and embodies the connection between core and periphery underscoring even the most seemingly mundane details of everyday life – here within an unavoidably political frame.

It could be argued that Lefebvre's understanding of the colonisation of everyday life as an artefact of uneven development misses a crucial component, central to the latter's theoretical elaboration in the Marxist tradition – namely, the addition of *combination* between unlike elements within a given social conjuncture.[9] Uneven and combined: the peculiar conjunction of so-called backward (pre- or incompletely 'modern') and advanced (capitalist) social forms is what Trotsky originally drew attention to in his image of peasants 'thrown into the factory cauldron snatched directly from the plow', an instance of 'the amalgam of archaic with more contemporary forms' (1967 [1930–1932], 432). Combination in this sense heightens the objective surrealism characterising encounters between radically disparate modes of existence, including the juxtapositions of commodity proliferation and its relative absence, in a postwar world that continued to be marked by drastic asymmetries in the experience of modernity. Cronin's poem foregrounds this manifestation of the everyday surreal with reference to the specific conditions pertaining to apartheid South Africa, but its legacy extends across the map of the modernising world during the second half of the twentieth century, from the era of the Long Boom to its crisis-ridden aftermath. In each case, the linkage between combined unevenness and the advance of colonisation's logic, extending to the structures of consciousness itself, registers in poetic responses to an ongoing and seemingly inexorable process, in forms that testify at once to the particularity of individual location and a comparability of situation.

A special case among such instances of postwar unevenness concerns not the 'developing' or Third World of the world-system's capitalist periphery, but the Second World of ostensibly socialist societies during and after the Cold War. These societies come to experience the saturated spaces of advanced commodification in ways that both echo and diverge from the patterns of response associated with colonial and postcolonial areas.[10] In Cuban poet Reina María Rodríguez's 'first time', for example, a speaker again enters the testing ground of shopping, this time from the perspective of a visitor unfamiliar with the *norteamericano* culture of display:

> we went into a market – they call it a *grocery* – and you can't imagine. fruit brilliant as magazine photos. all kinds of different oranges, grapefruits, mandarins, some tiny clementines with a blue sticker – *Morocco* – they've come so far [...] i felt dizzy, the gulf between myself and this place seemed insuperable. tears welled up in my eyes, i wanted desperately to flee, to get outside so i could breathe. i wanted to explain to Phillis, the North American who had invited me, what was happening to me. i tried, but she couldn't understand: you have to have felt it yourself: the first time.
>
> *(Rodríguez 2011)*

In this testament of travel from post-revolutionary Cuba during the mid-1980s, a vision of American abundance triggers not the sexually inflected anomie of Jarrell's 'Next Day' or Ginsberg's 'Supermarket in California', but instead a specific form of vertigo, associated with the collision between two versions of the everyday. The speaker's dissent from this world, if that is what it is, expresses itself somatically and affectively, registering as a peculiar desire for escape that is at the same time bound up with the induction into a new order of knowledge. In this sense, she involuntarily undergoes something like a Global Southern version of the cognitive mapping that Fredric Jameson regarded as increasingly difficult, if not impossible, under conditions where commodity consciousness had long since become second nature.

> for the first time my mind had crossed over five hundred years of development at jet speed and arrived in the future, a cold future [...] i felt like someone from the stone age, and realized most people on the planet never know the era they're living in [...] i knew i couldn't stand this avalanche, this brilliant swarm, for long, these rows on rows of distant faces staring out at me from cardboard boxes.
>
> *(Rodríguez 2011)*

What is captured by the poem's title, then, is less an intimation of the continuity between consumer and sexual experience (a 'first time' narrative), than a kind of panic at the dissolution between these modalities – indeed, the ability to distinguish between them betrays a consciousness not (yet) fully subsumed by the logic of the commodity. This lack of subsumption, grounded in the combined unevenness of the globalised everyday, certainly speaks to Lefebvre's concern with the resistant potential of alienated awareness.[11] At the same time, the passage across 'five hundred years of development' so dizzying to the speaker compresses not simply the distance separating Cuba from the United States (the insuperable 'gulf' bridged in a state of jet-lag), but a history of colonial appropriation and market expansion – a history whose spatialised form, appearing in the guise of imported foodstuffs, Lefebvre would presumably recognise as an image of the colonised *vie quotidienne*.

For a last example of the postwar everyday, we might turn to the capital-shocked precincts of Russia in the early 2000s:

> In the Smolensky supermarket
> at the corner of the Garden Ring
> and Arbat
> among the piles
> of expensive
> luxurious
> foods
> I found a sprat paté
> for seven rubles [...]
> I took two
> figuring
> this must be a special delivery
> for neighborhood residents
> who come to the store
> every day
>
> *(Medvedev 2012, 63)*

'Incursion', by contemporary Russian poet Kirill Medvedev, details the encounter with consumerist spectacle from a different angle than in 'first time'. Here the lavish shelves of a Moscow food emporium counter the image of Soviet-era penury with such hyperbolic luxury that the speaker, self-consciously playing a variant of the socially estranged fool-naif, is moved to a curious form of pity – not for the ordinary locals unable to afford commodities like these, but for the commodities themselves ('I was very sorry / for these fish / this wine / several hundred types of wine / and all the cookies' [65]). This feeling in turn prompts critical reflection: 'I thought of the fact / that the suffocating pity I feel / for these products / is also / a form of fetishism / and also a symptom / of reification' (66). Not least of the effects of the Russian transition to plutocracy in the 1990s was the recovery, among the younger generation of dissident artists and intellectuals, of the sources of capital's critique in such thinkers as Marx, Lukács, and Lefebvre himself – this despite the institutionalised forgetting endemic under oligarchic rule.[12] For Medvedev's speaker, intentionally lost in the supermarket, an encounter with 'paté for the poor' leads to a dialectical unzipping of the perversity underwriting supermarket displays in general, in which, as he notes, 'in my confrontations / with the face / of the society of consumption / sentimentality replaces disgust' (66).

The problem with conventional lyric poetry, Medvedev has commented in an interview, is that the public/private divide on which it depends works to screen off the mundane questions of 'what you do for a living', erecting instead an architecture of personal response divorced from its material foundations. The everyday, in this scenario, becomes the site of active mystification; in its expression it is 'never able to rise to the level of saying something about society as a whole' (Medvedev 2013). Where once the terrain of dailiness offered exceptions to the rule of capitalist modernity, footholds for critique, it is now, in this reading, coterminous with it – despite the continuing and deepening unevenness of its manifestations. Colonisation of the everyday, *qua* everyday, is complete.

★

If poetic dissent in the postwar period takes a variety of forms in meeting, on the one hand, the challenge of decolonisation, and on the other, the rise of the spectacle, it has to be acknowledged that twenty-first-century writers face challenges of a different order. This is so neither because the work of decolonisation is completed, nor because the infiltration of commodity logic has slowed its pace. In a situation where the distinction between the quotidian world of consumption and the hidden abode of production has long since been effaced, verifying Adorno's prescient analysis; where 24/7 culture has restructured the politics of time through the rise of passive work, crowdsourced labour, and accelerating automation;[13] where crises of social reproduction have caught up with and outstripped the crises in capitalist growth, it is inevitable that Lefebvre's everyday no longer contains the countervailing or resistant potential that he once identified within it. The long crisis of a global regime of accumulation that now appears, in the second decade of the twenty-first century, to have reached an epochal juncture, together with a wholesale transformation of the media ecology within which writing competes to find its place, means instead that both the imperative and the scope for dissenting interventions have drastically altered. 'i just wanted to be nice, and live a normal life… but events kept forcing me to figure out ways to survive… smart enough to know whats going on, but helpless to do anything' reads the epigraph, by 'bradass87', to Anne Boyer's 2011 book *My Common Heart*, which opens with an address to 'my vital demystified art' (Boyer 2011, n.p.). If dissent is not only possible but mandatory for survival under these conditions, the question can only turn – as it has in previous moments of crisis – not to what writing, or indeed any one activity, can do in isolation from social ferment, but rather to the forms of articulation available in organisational as well as expressive terms; that is, to the coordinated activities essential to political praxis.

> […] basements
> rampant in Cincinnati occupying San Francisco of Iceland
> mostly in there's Brooklyn rioting in the basements of
> Oklahoma also in Kansas the rental houses and universities in the
> city and not the city Australia hello Texas Maine for hundreds of
> thousands or millions of dollars loans that will never be paid
> *(Boyer 2011, n.p.)*

Notes

1 Lefebvre distinguishes between everyday life [*la vie quotidienne*] and the everyday [*le quotidien*] according to the transition of the mythic register of the former into the assimilated modernity of the latter, but it can be argued that in either case 'everyday' is produced as a conceptual back-formation of self-conscious modernity (see Lefebvre 1988, 87).
2 The anecdote, from the collection of interviews in *Le Temps des Méprises*, is cited in Ross 1996, 58.
3 Its first appearance within the context of his work on the everyday is in Lefebvre 2008a, 132.
4 See the fine introduction to social reproduction theory in Battacharya 2017, 22–72.
5 Stuart Elden discusses the importance of Lefebvre's childhood and later fieldwork in the Pyrenees in Elden 2004, 127–68.
6 This interpretation is given in their 'Introduction' to Césaire 2013, xix.
7 See Perloff 1998, 107.
8 Friedlander 2000 and Lawrence 2006 offer further examinations of the complexities of race and colonialism in O'Hara's work.
9 See Davidson 2017 and WReC 2015 for discussion of the historical concept of uneven and combined development, as well as of its later applications.
10 For a consideration of the formerly communist societies of the Eastern Bloc as 'post-colonial', see Lazarus (2012).
11 Compare Jameson on the defamiliarising effect, for First World readers during the Cold War period, of speculative fiction from the Soviet orbit: '[It conveys] the radical strangeness and freshness of human existence and of its object-world in a non-commodity atmosphere, in a space from which that prodigious saturation of messages, advertisements, and packaged libidinal fantasies of all kinds, which characterizes our own daily experience, is suddenly and unexpectedly stilled. We receive this culture with all the perplexed exasperation of the city-dweller condemned to insomnia by the oppressive silence of the countryside at night' (Jameson 2005 [1982], 155).

12 For more on the intellectual context of contemporary Russian dissident movements, see
Keith Gessen's introduction to Medvedev 2012. Naomi Klein discusses the applicability
of 'disaster capitalism' to post-1991 Russia in Klein 2008, 218–262.
13 See Crary 2013.

Works cited

Adorno, Theodor. 1991. 'Free Time'. Trans. Gordon Finlayson and Nicholas Walker. In J. M.
Bernstein ed, *The Culture Industry: Selected Essays on Mass Culture*. London: Routledge.

Battacharya, Tithi. 2017. 'Introduction: Mapping Social Reproduction Theory' In Tithi
Battacharya, ed, *Social Reproduction Theory: Remapping Class, Recentering Oppression*. Foreword by Lise Vogel. London: Pluto.

Boyer, Anne. 2011. *My Common Heart*. Spooky Girlfriend Press. Available at: http://sp
ooky-girlfriend.blogspot.com (Accessed 27 July 2018).

Brathwaite, Edward Kamau. 1984. *History of the Voice: Development of Nation Language in
Anglophone Caribbean Poetry*. London: New Beacon Books.

Breton, André. 1971 [1947]. 'Un grand poète noir'. Preface to Aimé Césaire, *Cahier d'un
retour au pays natal: bilingual edition*. Trans. Émile Snyder. Paris: Présence Africaine.

Césaire, Aimé. 2013 [1939]. *The Original 1939 Notebook of a Return to the Native Land:
Bilingual Edition*. Ed. and trans. A. James Arnold and Clayton Eshleman. Wesleyan, CT:
Wesleyan University Press.

Crary, Jonathan. 2013. *24/7: Late Capitalism and the End of Sleep*. London: Verso.

Cronin, Jeremy. 1999. *Inside and Out: Poems from Inside and Even the Dead*. Cape Town:
David Philip Publishers.

Davidson, Neil. 2017. 'Uneven and Combined Development: Modernity, Modernism, Revolution'. *R21: Revolutionary Socialism in the Twenty-first Century*. Available at: https://www.
rs21test.org.uk/wp-content/uploads/2017/03/uneven-and-combined-development-moder
nity-modernism-revolution.pdf (Accessed 28 September 2018).

Elden, Stuart. 2004. *Understanding Henri Lefebvre*. London: Continuum.

Friedlander, Benjamin. 2000. 'Strange Fruit: O'Hara, Race and the Color of Time' In
Terence Diggory and Stephen Paul Miller, eds, *The Scene of My Selves: New Work on New
York School Poets*, Orono, ME: National Poetry Foundation.

Ginsberg, Allen. 2009. *Collected Poems, 1947–1997*. New York and London: Penguin Classics.

Glissant, Edouard. 1997. *Poetics of Relation*. Trans. Betsy Wing. Ann Arbor, MI: University of
Michigan Press.

Highmore, Ben, ed. 2002. *The Everyday Life Reader*. London: Routledge.

Jameson, Fredric. 1988. 'Cognitive Mapping' In Cary Nelson and Lawrence Grossberg, eds,
Marxism and the Interpretation of Culture . Urbana, IL: University of Illinois Press.

Jameson, Fredric. 2005 [1982]. 'Progress versus Utopia; Or, Can We Imagine the Future?' in
Fredric Jameson, *Archaeologies of the Future: The Desire Called Science Fiction and Other Utopias*.
London: Verso.

Jarrell, Randall. 1981. *The Complete Poems*. New York: Farrar, Straus and Giroux.

Kipfer, Stefan and Kanishka Goonewardena. 2013. 'Urban Marxism and the Post-colonial
Question: Henri Lefebvre and "Colonisation"'. *Historical Materialism* 21(2): 76–116.

Klein, Naomi. 2008. *The Shock Doctrine: The Rise of Disaster Capitalism*. New York: Henry Holt
and Company.

Lawrence, N. R. 2006. 'Frank O'Hara in New York: Race Relations, Poetic Situations,
Postcolonial Space'. *Comparative American Studies* 4(1): 85–103.

Lazarus, Neil. 2012. 'Spectres Haunting: Postcommunism and Postcolonialism'. *Journal of Postcolonial Writing* 48(2): 117–129.

Lefebvre, Henri. 1987 [1965]. 'The Everyday and Everydayness'. Trans. Christine Levich. *Yale French Studies* 73: Everyday Life, 7–11.

Lefebvre, Henri. 1988 [1983]. 'Toward a Leftist Cultural Politics: Remarks Occasioned by the Centenary of Marx's Death'. Trans. David Reifman. In Cary Nelson and Lawrence Grossberg, eds, *Marxism and the Interpretation of Culture*. 75–88. Champaign, IL: University of Illinois Press.

Lefebvre, Henri. 2008a [1947]. *Critique of Everyday Life. Vol. 1: Introduction*. Trans. John Moore. London: Verso.

Lefebvre, Henri. 2008b [1961]. *Critique of Everyday Life. Vol. 2: Foundations for a Sociology of the Everyday*. Trans. John Moore. London: Verso.

Lefebvre, Henri. 2008c [1981]. *Critique of Everyday Life. Vol. 3: From Modernity to Modernism*. Trans. John Moore. London: Verso.

Marx, Karl. 1976 [1867]. *Capital: A Critique of Political Economy. Vol. 1*. Trans. Ben Fowkes. Harmondsworth, UK: Penguin Books.

Massey, Doreen. 1994. *Space, Place, and Gender*. Minneapolis, MN: University of Minneapolis Press.

Medvedev, Kirill. 2012. *It's No Good: Poems / Essays / Actions*. Trans. Keith Gessen, with Mark Krotov, Cory Merrill, and Bela Shayevich. Brooklyn, NY: Ugly Duckling Presse.

Medvedev, Kirill and Emma Goldhammer. 2013. 'Direct Expression: An interview with the dissident Russian poet and essayist Kirill Medvedev'. *Boston Review*. Available at: http://bostonreview.net/world-poetry/direct-expression (Accessed 28 September 2018).

Newman, Andy. 2012. 'Strolling Through 1968 New York, in 160 Seconds.' *The New York Times* 8 March. Available at: https://cityroom.blogs.nytimes.com/2012/03/08/strolling-through-1968-new-york-in-160-seconds/ (Accessed 27 July 2018).

O'Hara, Frank. 1995. *The Collected Poems of Frank O'Hara*. Ed. Don Allen. Berkeley, CA: University of California Press.

Perloff, Marjorie. 1998. *Poetry On and Off the Page: Essays for Emergent Occasions*. Evanston, IL: Northwestern University Press.

Rodríguez, Reina Maria. 2011. 'first time'. Trans. Joel Brouwer and Jessica Stephenson. *Poetry*. Available at: https://www.poetryfoundation.org/poetrymagazine/poems/54757/first-time/ (Accessed 28 September 2018).

Ross, Kristin. 1996. *Fast Cars, Clean Bodies: Decolonization and the Reordering of French Culture*. Cambridge, MA: MIT Press.

Sartre, Jean-Paul. 1948. 'Orphée Noir'. *Anthologie de la nouvelle poésie nègre et malgache*. Ed. Léopold Senghor. Paris: Presses Universitaires de France.

Trotsky, Leon. 1967 [1930–1932]. *History of the Russian Revolution. Vol. 1*. Trans. Max Eastman. London: Sphere Books.

WReC. 2015. *Combined and Uneven Development: Towards a New Theory of World-Literature*. Warwick Research Collective. Liverpool: Liverpool University Press.

7

FACEBOOK POET

Poetic dissent and social media in contemporary India

Anindya Raychaudhuri

On 19 March 2017, the most populous state of India, Uttar Pradesh, saw the inauguration and swearing-in of its thirty-second and latest Chief Minister, Yogi Adityanath, in a ceremony that *The Times of India* described as being 'graced by a plethora of BJP luminaries, including Prime Minister Narendra Modi, senior opposition politicians, and a raft of *sadhus, sanyasis* and *sanyasinis*' (Times of India 2017). The swearing-in ceremony was an example of the highest levels of leadership of the Hindu Right showing off after a truly historic victory. It had been preceded by many months of campaigning and a phased two-month-long election period, during which more than 86 million people had cast their votes. The Bharatiya Janata Party (BJP) emerged from these elections with a landslide victory, winning 312 of 403 seats, an increase of 265 since the elections five years previously. The BJP had gone through the entire elections without naming a chief ministerial candidate, and, at least in mainstream media, the perception had been that the elections were a referendum on the performance of the Prime Minister Narendra Modi and his central national government in New Delhi.

Even for a party with the Hindu nationalist credentials of the BJP, the elevation of Adityanath to the post of Chief Minister came as a shock. *The Guardian* was representative of most national and international media when it described him as a 'firebrand Hindu priest' who 'has regularly stirred controversy – and significant personal popularity among rightwing Hindus – with incendiary rhetoric about Indian minorities, particularly Muslims' (Safi 2017). Adityanath is on record recommending that Hindu men seduce Muslim women and persuade them to convert – a reversal of what the Hindu Right sees as the Muslim conspiracy of Love Jihad.[1] At a rally in the town of Gorakhpur in 2007, Adityanath had said: 'If one Hindu girl marries a Muslim man, then we will take 100 Muslim girls in return […]. If they [Muslims] kill one Hindu man, then we will kill 100 Muslim men' (quoted in Gupta and Gowen 2017). An undated but widely circulated video shows Adityanath on stage at a campaign rally, while one of his supporters calls on Hindus to rape dead Muslim women (Anand 2015).

On the same day that Adityanath was being sworn in as the Chief Minister of the most populated state of the largest democracy in the world, Bengali poet Srijato Bandopadhyay posted a poem on his own Facebook profile. Called 'Curse', this poem was an explicit attack on what Dibyesh Anand has identified as the porno-nationalist nature (Anand 2008) of Adityanath and the Hindu Right's Islamophobia:

> Where patriarchy and sainthood merge into one
> And I, as a woman, am hunted beyond death
> For as long as you rape my body out of the grave,
> Your devout trident will always stand condom-ed.[2]
> *(Bandopadhyay 2017)*

Very soon after publication on Facebook, the poem achieved notoriety – attracting both praise and condemnation. Two days after publication, a student-member of the fringe Hindu Right group Hindu Samhati in the northern Bengali town of Siliguri filed a police complaint (known as a First Incident Report) against the poet accusing him of 'deliberate or malicious acts intended to outrage religious feelings of any class by insulting its religion or religious beliefs'. According to at least one contemporaneous media report, an anonymous police official responded to the complaint by saying: 'As soon as we get confirmation of the hardware and authenticity of the account from which the poem was uploaded, the writer will be arrested' (quoted in Chanda 2017).

The police's efforts in attempting to victimise and silence Srijato was not the only example of censorship, however. Along with the nation-state, other forms of censorship were also visible. In a timely reminder that social media is not a space that is beyond normative control, Facebook itself removed his original post, accusing it of having contravened Facebook's Community Standards (Hindustan Times 2017). By 26 September, however, Facebook restored the post with an apology – blaming a 'member of our team [who had] accidentally removed' it (quoted in Dasgupta 2017). Whether or not the furore caused by the police complaint had an effect on Facebook's decision to restore the post is of course impossible to say, but in either case it reinforces the contested nature of Facebook and the obvious truth that, even on Facebook, not all things are equally speakable.

Meanwhile, in Kolkata, Srijato himself filed a formal complaint about death threats that he had received on Facebook and over the phone. In response, the police in Kolkata provided extra security for the poet and his wife, amid continuing formal and informal, named and anonymous complaints and threats of violence (Indian Express 2017). Srijato's case got caught up in local parliamentary politics, as the incumbent Chief Minister of West Bengal, Mamata Banerjee, anxious to buttress her at-times questionable anti-BJP credentials, spoke out in his support.[3]

Other poets also rallied round in support, including Mandakranta Sen, whose own poetic response was also published on her Facebook page, leading to explicit and specific threats of gang-rape. Mandakranta's poem was published on 27 March 2017, and was clearly a response to the wider and increased attack by religious fundamentalists on intellectuals and poets:

> RSS on one side, Jamaat and HuJI on the other,
> From whom from whom from whom can I get freedom?
> Diabolic dark times, humanity is under attack
> [...]
> What is this theatre of cruelty?
>
> *(quoted in Ali 2017)*

While the screenshot of this poetic response to Srijato has been captured in several journalistic accounts, the original post seems to either have been deleted or had its settings changed to 'Private'. Poems published on Facebook might at times be able to evade the economic strictures of traditional literary publishing, but they do often pay for this evasion through increased precarity. Elsewhere on WhatsApp and on various Facebook groups, other poetic responses by Mandakranta Sen to Srijato's situation have also circulated:

> Write, poet, write more. Give us more such weapons
> [...]
> The mob is suing, jail for you without bail
> But how? Am I not here, my shoulder to yours?
> No, no – not me, but us. Let's see what they can do
> They might be able to threaten and curse, we write poetry.
>
> *(quoted in Biswas 2017)*

As of the time of writing, Srijato's poem 'Curse' has been reacted to more than 20,000 times, commented on by 7,000 people, and shared more than 5,000 times – though the actual numbers are in fact much higher, as many more people have posted screenshots of the original post rather than using Facebook's 'share' function. These poems and many others of a similar nature have been shared widely on WhatsApp as well, in numerous private conversations which are impossible to track or quantify.[4]

Fast forward ten months. In January 2018, Asifa Bano, an eight-year-old girl from the Bakarwal community – a nomadic mostly Muslim tribe in Kashmir, was abducted, drugged, raped, and then murdered in Kathua – specifically inside the local village temple, allegedly under the instigation of the temple's custodian, Sanjhi Ram. According to the official charge sheet, the gang of men who raped and murdered Asifa were trying to drive out the Muslim tribespeople from the local area. When the official charges were filed in April, the story achieved national prominence, inspiring protests all over India and beyond, and further calls for strengthening India's penal code when it comes to rape and other sexual offences (see, for example, Eltagouri 2018).

In the past few weeks since the Kathua rape case, the two poets I have already mentioned and many others have continued to write protest poems on Facebook, which have then been circulated widely. As an example, we can look at this poem, written by poet Mandakranta Sen. Published on her Facebook profile on 22 April 2018, she responds to Asifa's rape, and to the increasing use of rape as a weapon by the Hindu Right:

> Will I get used to rape one day?
> For as long as I survive, not being raped,
> Will I wonder if that will be my fate?
> [...]
> Words will drink our blood, wipe their mouth
> And lie down in the dictionary.
> My screams will drown out
> All staged speeches songs poems.
>
> *(Sen 2018)*

Another similar poetic response is this poem called 'Kathua', written by an amateur poet under the pseudonym Aarjyatirtha. It is not easy to pinpoint where the poem was first published. The poet does have a Facebook account, but his posts are set to private. On 13 April 2018, Aarjyatirtha posted it on the Facebook account of a couple of literary groups, and since then it has been shared multiple times on Facebook and WhatsApp:

> Whether she was murdered or died in the end
> Only the stone idol knows
> Big-shot lawyers snort in anger
> The guilty have the insurance of faith.
> The cows in the field chew on grass and think
> These are the people who think us holy
> Everything could have gone so wrong, if only
> A capricious God had made us woman.
>
> *(Aarjyatirtha 2018)*

While Hindutva as a potent political force has made its presence felt for many decades now, the election of Adityanath and the rape and murder of Asifa Bano took place in the context of both a quantitative increase in its power and a qualitative change in how this power is manifested across large sections of the country. Since 2014, and Narendra Modi's elevation to the Prime Ministership of India, there has been a marked rise in violent attacks on Muslims and other minorities, and on dissenting intellectuals and their freedom of speech. In September 2015, Mohammed Akhlaq of Dadri, Uttar Pradesh was lynched by a Hindu mob because he was suspected of stealing and slaughtering a neighbour's calf. As part of the official investigation into Akhlaq's death, the authorities considered it appropriate to analyse the meat found in his house and in a garbage dump nearby to determine if it was indeed beef. A month after Akhlaq's murder, the progressive intellectual and academic M. M. Kalburgi was assassinated in his own home in Dharwad, in the southern Indian state of Karnataka. Kalburgi's assassination was in fact the second example in con-temporary Indian history of a progressive intellectual being murdered for their beliefs. Almost exactly two years previously, a medical doctor who had campaigned against superstition and religious fundamentalism, Narendra Dabholkar, was assassinated in Pune, Maharashtra. In February 2015, left-wing politician and author Govind Pansare was shot in identical fashion in Mumbai, while in September 2017, journalist and activist Gauri Lankesh was shot outside her home in Bangalore. As of writing, these murders remain unsolved.

Writing in 2011, Dibyesh Anand provides a cogent definition of the Hindutva project, which is the intellectual and political movement against which these writers are dissenting:

> Hindutva ('Hindu-ness,' shorthand for Hindu national-ism) in India is a chau-vinist and majoritarian nationalism that conjures up the image of a peaceful Hindu Self vis-à-vis the threatening minority Other. Hindu nationalism nor-malizes a politics of fear and hatred by representing it as a defensive reaction to the threats supposedly posed by Muslims to the security of the individual Hindus as well as of the Hindu collective. Hindutva is porno-nationalism in its obsessive preoccupation with the predatory sexuality of the putative Muslim figure and the dangers to the integrity of the Hindu bodies. The proponents of Hindutva mobilize and generate negative stereotypes of Islam and Muslims to legitimize violence against actual Muslims living in India.
>
> *(Anand 2011, 1)*

One can see this ideology in action in Adityanath's rhetoric, in the rape and murder of Asifa Bano, in the cycle of assassination of dissenting voices, and in the terrifying increase in both organised and random violence against Muslims and other minorities. As early as 1993, Partha Chatterjee was warning against the majoritarian and totalitarian tendencies of the Hindu Right, arguing that '[t]he idea of the singularity of national history has inevitably led to a single source of Indian tradition, namely ancient Hindu civilisation' (Chatterjee 1993, 115). In the words of journalist and commentator Subhash Gatade, 'any impartial, objective student of Indian society and state would agree that the idea of Hindutva and its paraphernalia of numerous organisations posit the biggest threat to the cause of justice and peace in the Indian subcontinent' (Gatade 2011, 31). In the years since Chatterjee, Anand, and Gatade were writing, the Hindu Nationalist movement has grown much stronger, and has solidified its connection to the nation-state to a much greater extent. Cyclical waves of anti-Muslim violence – Ayodhya in 1992, Gujarat in 2002, and Muzaffarnagar in 2013, to name but a few – have made the position of Indian Muslims even more precarious and have strengthened the hold of the Hindu Right over the machinery of the Indian nation-state.

In this context, between September 2015 and February 2017, at least 39 authors from across India returned their Sahitya Akademi awards, one of the most prominent prizes awarded by India's National Academy of Letters. As one of the people who returned her award, Nayantara Sahgal, put it: 'In memory of the Indians who have been murdered, in support of all Indians who uphold the right to dissent, and of all dissenters who now live in fear and uncertainty, I am returning my Sahitya Akademi Award' (quoted in Indian Cultural Forum 2015). During the same period, a further 24 figures form the world of cinema returned their national awards. This included filmmakers, cinematographers, and writers. This symbolic gesture was, in the words of one of the open letters addressed to the Prime Minister and the President, a demand that they 'pay attention to our fears, that the warp and weft of our robust democracy might be coming apart in the current atmosphere' (Financial Express 2015). The dissent, then, is specifically against the dictatorial tendencies of Hindu nationalism, and the twinning of statist and religious intolerance that represents. Given the statist nature of the Hindu Right in contemporary India, dissent against Hindutva necessarily involves dissent against the State, and the various statements released by the dissenting poets, writers, and intellectuals demonstrate this awareness of the mutually reinforcing relationship Hindutva and the nation-state have been enjoying for the past few years.

It is thus not surprising that countering the hegemony of religion features prominently as a theme in the kind of dissenting poems that are being shared across social media as well. These are written by established and unknown poets alike, shared with or without attribution. Although renowned Bengali poet and novelist Sunil Ganguly died in 2012, in the context of the upsurge in religious fundamentalism in the past two years, his poem 'Proletarian Unbelievers' has been shared across Facebook and WhatsApp multiple times:

One shouldn't offend the faith of others
One shouldn't offend the faith of others
So much faith, everywhere,

Ever-deepening, every day

Faiths of so many hues
The saffronite who has decided

That the heathen child's blood should flow down the streets,

Licked by dogs
That too is his deep faith
[…]
All of them are the believers united
All believers, believers, believers
Sometimes I feel like raising

My own fragile voice
Wake up unbelievers
Proletarian Unbelievers of the world unite.

(quoted in Abedin 2018)

In the same manner as these poems by established poets, the following anonymous lines have been widely circulated on WhatsApp as well:

Hunger has no religion, the stomach knows
[...]
Who killed later, who killed first
Two religions united only in smears of blood

Smart phone in hand, but primitive in heart
The country drowns in the sickness of hate.

Another poet, Tapabrata Bhaduri, shared multiple poems on his own profile, such as 'God' published on 29 March 2018, and clearly in reference to Asifa's murder:

Have any of you seen God?
If you have,

Then ask Him from me –
Why so much murder in His name?
Tell him from me,
I am scared of Him, I hate Him,
I do not want to see His face

(Bhaduri 2018)

Rather than uploading the poem as a text on his Facebook status, as most of the other poets I am looking at have done, Bhaduri uploads the poems as images, which can make tracking the extent to which they have been shared even more difficult.

All of these poems, and many more besides, constitute this form of poetic dissent on Facebook and WhatsApp, shuttling back and forth in multiple online conversations, becoming extraneously attached to images and videos, featuring in multiple different conversations in multiple ways, and cumulatively forming a notable and novel form of literary activism that deserves further examination.

While it is clear that these two forms of dissent – the online version of poetry-as-memes and the offline version of returning awards bestowed by the nation-state – are connected, it is my contention that they are operating in very different ways. The returning of awards is an act that implies authorial privilege and leaves little space for readerly interaction, while the transformation of poetry into memes begins to undercut authorial privilege, blurs the lines between author and reader, and in the process creates a precarious but potentially radical poetic community of dissent. The process of transformation of poetry into a meme represents a challenge to definitions of poet, poem, and reader, which in turn transforms the ways in which this poetic relationship can produce dissent. The former can be seen to reinforce what Michel Foucault called 'author function', while the latter, albeit in at times a limited fashion, challenges and undermines it. The community of readers on Facebook and WhatsApp can receive the dissent in diametrically opposite ways – disagreeing with the poet, often sending them abusive messages and threats of violence, filing official police complaints, and, of course, thus reinforcing the message of dissent even further; or agreeing with the poet and their statement about the hegemonic Hindu nationalism in contemporary India, and then strengthening and multiplying this act of dissent by sharing it within and across their networks.

Shared and re-shared again and again, these poems assume the status of memes. Sometimes they are shared with the poet's name, at other times the phrase 'As received' or 'Collected' stands in for an authorial attribution. Often, and again like memes, one encounters the poem multiple times in multiple different contexts – as numerous Facebook friends post it as their status, or as WhatsApp contacts share it in several groups. I often encounter these poems across many of my own net-works – friends, family, professional colleagues, and political comrades, many of whom might not know each other, but all of whom have been interpellated into this poetic community of dissent through the act of reading and sharing these poems. Unmoored from the authority of the poet, these poems assume afterlives that are beyond the control of the poet, as readers introduce the poems into dif-ferent Facebook or WhatsApp conversational contexts, which therefore change the ways in which the poems might or might not be received. Readers sometimes use Facebook's 'Share' function, which allows us to track the ways in which the poem has been used. At other times, readers will copy and paste, provide their own ad-hoc translation, share a screenshot on Facebook, or copy and paste it in WhatsApp. Trying to follow the various ways in which this poem has been shared on Face-book is like trying to trace the original of a simulacrum. The poem becomes a meme, a copy-without-an-original. Indeed, often one simply must assume at face value the 'truth' of the authorial attribution, as there is little or no corroborating evidence to firmly establish the provenance of any individual poem. There are so many fora in which these poems can be shared – Facebook, WhatsApp, YouTube, blogging sites; and so many ways in which the poem can be shared – as text, image, video, audio, that it is impossible to say with any certainty where and how it first entered the online world, let alone when and where it was first written.

In the remainder of this chapter I am going to use a number of contemporary Bengali poems by both established and amateur poets, which have made an appearance on Facebook and WhatsApp, to think about how the use of poetry in social media helps change the production and consumption of literature, and how this transformation in turn encourages us to rethink the relationship between lit-erature and dissent. I argue that Facebook and WhatsApp can be seen to represent a kind of remediation – not just of the poem as an object, but also a transformation of both poet and reader. In the process, the use of social media to transmit poetry helps construct a distinctive poetic community. The poem becomes a property of this community, which potentially helps to erase or at least challenge the authority of the poet. Works of an award-winning, established poet and an amateur or even anonymous poet can be shared on an equal footing, validated not by the economics of literary publishing but by the recognition of a temporary and precarious community of readers. This community of literary producers and consumers represents the potentiality of dissent. This potentiality may be never actualised, but in its very nascence it still encourages us to rethink the relationship between writers and readers, and how the relationship between the two can be mediated and remediated in diverse and productive ways.

Writing in 1999, Jay David Bolter and Richard Grusin defined remediation as 'the formal logic by which new media refashion the prior media forms' (273).[5] Writing the year after, Bolter goes on to argue that remediation could be thought of as 'a more complex kind of borrowing in which one medium is itself incorporated or represented in another medium' (Bolter 2000, 65). In other words, 'the very act of remediation, however, ensures that the older medium cannot be entirely effaced; the new medium remains dependent upon the older one in acknowledged or unacknowledged ways' (67). As early as 2000, Bolter was able to claim that though remediation 'might seem at first to be an esoteric practice, [it] is so widespread that we can identify a spectrum of different ways in which digital media remediate their predecessors, a spectrum depending upon the degree of perceived competition or rivalry between the new media and the old' (65). What interests me for the moment is how remediation reveals the economically and technologically contingent nature of authorship, readership, and therefore the possibilities of literary dissent. In *Grundrisse*, Karl Marx famously asked if the *Iliad* was possible in the world of the printing press. Marx's point, of course, is that 'Greek art and epic poetry are bound up with certain forms of social development' (1975–2004, 28:47). In other words, the evolution of art is intrinsically bound up with, and affected by, the economic and technological development of society as a whole:

> It is even acknowledged that certain forms of art, e.g. epos, can no longer be produced in their epoch-making, classic form after artistic production as such has begun; in other words that certain important creations within the compass of art are only possible at an early stage of its development. If this is the case with regard to the different arts within the sphere of art itself, it is not so remarkable that this should also be the case with regard to the entire sphere of art in its relation to the general development of society.
>
> *(Marx 1975–2004, 28:46–7)*

As Hadjiafxendi and Mackay have written in explaining Marx's argument: 'Marx's theory of the disappearance of the epic poet (as a performer) and his public (as spectators) exemplifies the role that changes in the material conditions of production play in the evolution of literary genres (for example, epic poetry) and their reception (from viewing to reading)' (2007, 2). Economics and technology affect the kind of art that may be produced, and societal conceptions of the identities of the producers and consumers of said art. Just over 100 years later, Michel Foucault made a similar argument in his lecture 'What is an Author?':

> a sociohistorical analysis of the author as an individual [...] [would reveal] how the author was individualized in a culture such as ours; the status we have given the author, for instance, when we began our research into authenticity and attribution; the systems of valorization in which he was included; or the moment when the stories of heroes gave way to an author's biography; the conditions that fostered the formulation of the fundamental critical category of 'the man and his work'.
>
> *(Foucault 1977, 115)*

Following Marx and Foucault, it is my contention that the advent of the dissenting Facebook poet in the context of the rise of Hindu nationalism in contemporary India represents a challenge to the concept of authorship. It seems to me that the act of sharing on Facebook or WhatsApp has the potential to recalibrate the relationship between author and reader in a way that, while not unproblematic, nevertheless carries with it the potential to construct a precarious but dissenting poetic community. To give a concrete example, I have witnessed numerous exchanges on WhatsApp that have taken the following form: Person A shares a poem, sometimes with an attribution, sometimes without. Person B reads the poem, assumes it is written by Person A, and praises them for writing it. By the time Person A has responded to disclaim credit, it has been shared on as a poem written by Person A. Every time a poem is shared and reshared, the distance between it and the authorial source grows larger and larger, and the dividing line between poet and reader is further and further blurred. While the sharing of creative work without attribution has many problems, of which copyright infringement is only one example, it does also have this perhaps unintended benefit – the line between reader and poet often becomes blurred. Under such conditions, the poem shared on Facebook or WhatsApp, the poem-as-meme, becomes the 'anonymous poster attached to a wall' postulated by Foucault, which 'may have a writer, but he cannot be an author' (1977, 124). If Foucault is correct when he argues that 'the function of an author is to characterize the existence, circulation, and operation of certain discourses within a society' (124), then the discourse of the returning of literary awards is characterised by this 'author-function', while the discourse of the poetry-as-meme carries within it the potential to transform an authoritative author into a mere writer.

In other words, what the poem-as-meme can be seen to challenge is what Walter Benjamin famously described as the aura of art. In 'The Work of Art in the Age of Mechanical Reproduction', Benjamin describes aura 'as the unique phenomenon of distance, however close it may be' (2007, 222). Or in the words of Bolter, MacIntyre, Gandy, and Schweitzer: 'Aura is the sense of the "here and now" that each work possesses because of its history of production and transmission.

This uniqueness lends to each painting or sculpture a special quality, which can in turn evoke an attitude of reverence on the part of the viewer' (Bolter *et al.* 2006, 24). Famously, in a move that reminds me of Marx's argument about the impossibility of epic poetry in the age of printing, Benjamin argues:

> that which withers in the age of mechanical reproduction is the aura of the world of art [...]. One might generalize by saying: the technique of reproduction detaches the reproduced object from the domain of tradition. By making many reproductions it substitutes a plurality of copies for a unique existence. And in permitting the reproduction to meet the beholder or listener in his own particular situation, it reactivates the object reproduced.
>
> *(Benjamin 2007, 221)*

Marx and Benjamin both recognise the economic and technological contingency of the figure of the author and the power that he or she wields. Marx and Benjamin both further recognise the role that technology (whether it is the printing press or the camera) might play in rendering this figure ontologically unstable. The role that the printing press might have played for Homer, or the role that Benjamin affords the camera, is the role that I am suggesting Facebook and WhatsApp might play in challenging the reifying discourse of the cult of the author and the literary establishment that is underpinned by it.

This is not to say that literature on social media will necessarily present such a challenge. Rupi Kaur's transition from Tumblr through Instagram to global publishing phenomenon demonstrates the fact that it is perfectly possible to replicate the cult of the author in the remediated world of social media (see, for example, Kruger 2017). Even among the poets I am looking at, Srijato Bandopadhyay's recent book *Srijato's Facebook* (2018b) demonstrates the fact that social media is not immune to the cult of the poet, but rather can easily become just another avenue for the poet to re-establish their identity and therefore their authority.

After the notoriety that Srijato gained in September 2017, he launched a new collection of assorted writings that had started life as status updates on his Facebook profile. Called *Srijato's Facebook*, this book was launched at that most iconic of events in the Bengali literary establishment calendar, the Kolkata Book Fair, in February 2018. On the one hand, this publication clearly reinforces Srijato as a Facebook poet, and to that extent, it reinforces the auratic cult of the poet and his authority. On the other hand, Srijato and his publishers are clearly and deliberately using Facebook to create a poetic community that includes poet and reader in something approaching a non-hierarchical relationship. On 22 January 2018, Srijato announced the launch of *Srijato's Facebook* on his own Facebook profile:

> I can never agree with those who think that Facebook is not to be trusted. While I have had to go through some turmoil because I write on Facebook, it has also allowed me to get to know so many people, gradually they have taken on the mantle of friends. Well-wishers have pointed out mistakes in my

writing, so many others have expressed their satisfaction and support. I don't have the arrogance to dismiss all of this just because it takes place on social media. I have no such desire. Only the desire to preserve this ever-growing family. To cling onto them … No matter how little importance I might place on my writing, I have always felt Facebook to be all-powerful as a medium to help my writing reach people, and I still do. For me there is no such special separate thing as a 'Facebook poem' or a 'Facebook author'. Poetry is poetry, the writer is a writer. Whether they write on the streets or in the King's court. Similarly, it would be laughably condescending to relegate those who give me their opinion having read my writing on Facebook, to the category of 'virtual reader'. Readers are readers. I remember how many events I have reacted to on Facebook … for three, three and a half years, I have prattled on here, on my wall…

(Bandopadhyay 2018a)

There is a lot to unpack here, and some of it is clearly contradictory. Srijato is at once idealising Facebook as a medium, while at the same time insisting that it does not represent any real difference in the act of writing, or in the relations between writer and reader. He is self-deprecating about the value he places on his own writing, but lauds Facebook because it allows him to deliver this same writing to his readers. He is aware of the reception of this writing, however, and clearly values it enough to, as he puts it, 'give it the honour of placing it between covers'. For all of his idealising Facebook, then, there is also an implicit acknowledgment of the hierarchy between online and traditional publishing.

I think a way to conceptualise, if not to resolve, the contradictions of Srijato's claims is to view them in terms of the crisis of aura that remediation involves. When a poem is published using the full weight of authority that traditional publishing and the label of an officially-recognised poet carries, it emanates the Benjaminian distancing aura − ownership of the poem within the covers of a book might reduce the physical distance between reader and poet, but the aura of the published poem reinforces and therefore increases this distance. When the same poem is published on Facebook, when it is shared across Facebook and WhatsApp, it helps to increase the distance between poem and poet. The poetic authority is rendered unstable, the poem is brought much closer to the reader, who can now do more than just read the poem. In sharing it, the reader is able to, if only fleetingly, assume something akin to the role of the poet. In the process, the aura of the object that is the poem is rendered unstable. This instability is not, however (and *contra* Benjamin), final. Through official social recognition such as the 'Facebook Poet', not to mention through official censorship, the poet's aura and therefore the aura of his or her poetry, both online and offline, can be re-affirmed. In the words of Bolter *et al.*, remediation of poetry on social media creates 'an ongoing crisis, in which the experience of aura is alternately called into question and reaffirmed' (2006, 22).

Rather than aura withering away, it ends up in a permanent crisis of desacralisation, as Bolter *et al.* have argued in their different context of Virtual Reality: 'the permanent crisis of aura that began in the age of mechanical reproduction and continues with digital technology has had the effect of desacralizing aura' (36). As poems become separated from the persona and control of the poet, as they are shared and re-shared across Facebook and WhatsApp, in the process helping to create a Facebook readership as well as a Facebook poet, this remediation suggests an uneasy and unstable relationship between the virtual and the real. Tom Boellstorff, among others, has pointed out that the 'division between virtual and actual is unsustainable because so much of what takes place in virtual worlds draws from the actual worlds' (2008, 27). Ilana Gershon agrees, reminding us that 'the virtual and the real are socially constructed divisions' and that 'studying media ideologies also means studying the remediation at the heart of people's media ideologies' (2008, 13).

Returning to Srijato's evocation of his virtual readership, then, it is interesting how he uses particular spatial language – Facebook helps him 'reach' his reader, he is like an author 'on the streets', his readers have joined him in an 'ever-growing family', even his use of the Bengali '*dewal*', literally a wall, to refer to his Facebook profile, or what is now called time-line – suggests that, at least in this particular case, the remediation between the real and the virtual is not just a matter of social contingency, but also a matter of space and scale. With the creation of a Facebook readership and a Facebook poet, Benjamin's auratic quality of distance-no-matter-how-near is being replaced with an equal but opposite nearness-no-matter-how-far.

Conceptualising this auratic crisis as one of space and scale allows us to intervene in one of the most pressing questions of world literature – that of scale. The object of poem-as-meme allows us to think through a possible answer to Robert Dixon's question:

> What *is* the appropriate scale for the study of literature? This is another way of asking, where is literature best *located*? Is it desirable or even possible to study a text or the phenomenon of literature in general on a world scale? [...] [W]hat are the consequences for the degree of resolution or accuracy that we might achieve from such a perspective?
>
> (Dixon 2015, 1)

Similarly, Nirvana Tanoukhi has pointed out that 'distance has long been a thorny issue of comparative literature' precisely because of the 'very fact of incommen-surability' (2008: 599). Tanoukhi's identification of the problem of scale in world literature rests on the apparent assumption that 'for [comparative] crossings to be attempted, each book, each author, each device – each canon, nation, or inter-pretive community – would assume its rightful place' (599). Both Dixon and Tanoukhi are quite right in their diagnosis of the problem, and in their use of human geographers like Neil Smith and Derek Gregory to remind literary scholars that 'events and processes [do not] take place "*in* space" but rather that space and spaces are produced as an expression of these social and natural processes' (Smith 2004, 196).

Rethinking the remediation process that produces the poem-as-meme as helping to bring about an auratic crisis that can be conceptualised in spatial terms can, I think, help us to situate literature, and literary dissent in particular, as part of the social processes that help to construct space, and therefore think of scale as specifically contingent on a precarious dissenting literary community. The community of readers may be far apart, but they have been brought together through Facebook, through the ways in which Facebook has helped Srijato's poem to reach his readers – nearness-no-matter-how-far. These readers might then send the poems on to others, creating a further chain of nearness over which Srijato himself would have little or no control. The reversal of the Benjaminian formula of distance serves to remind us of the contingency of space and scale – the notion that these are human, political terms and therefore when we use them to locate literature in space, we are always already making political decisions.

At every point in this chain of nearness, each individual encounter with each poem happens in the immediate space of each reader, but it is an immediacy that can connect one sharer to another. This immediacy is at once deeply private and intensely public; it is at once specifically localised and can transcend whole time zones. One finger presses a button and shares a poem in Kolkata or New Delhi, and at the same time (somehow in the same space) another finger in Edinburgh scrolls down a screen, reads the poem, and then shares it around again, perhaps to be read by someone else in Kolkata and New Delhi. Whether these fingers belong to the reader or the poet becomes immaterial for this literary connection to exist. In a sense, this is reminiscent of Djelal Kadir's argument for the immediacy of literature:

> literature is in your present (that is why we are taught to always refer to narrative events in the present tense); the world is in your time (etymologically, 'world' means 'man in time'); and theory is invariably localized and situated wherever you happen to be (since its origins in Greek antiquity, *theoría* means to witness for oneself and for one's city-state the rituals of others). I deliberately situate these claims in your chronotopic immediacy, in your predicament.
>
> *(Kadir 2016, 72–3)*

Through the interactivity of sharing, copying and pasting, liking, and commenting, through the ways in which this sharing helps to create a dissenting community of chronotopic immediacy across time and space, these readers represent the kind of literary resistance that Stephen Slemon was evoking when he asked:

> Is literary resistance something that simply issues forth, through narrative, against a clearly definable set of power relations? Is it something actually *there* in the text, or is it produced and reproduced in and through communities of readers and through the mediating structures of their own culturally specific histories?
>
> *(Slemon 1990, 31, emphasis in original)*

Following Slemon, we could say that literary dissent is mediated through the spe-
cificities of the communities of readers, remediated through the technology that
allows these readers to engage with and intervene in the literary acts of dissent, and
through the ambiguity of space that alternately distances them and brings them
closer together. This form of literary dissent can also be seen in American poet
Brian Kim Stefans' anti-Iraq War initiative *Circulars*, which, in his words, was intended to 'critique and/or augment some conventional modes of expressing political
views [...] by creat[ing] a dynamic, persuasive idiom that can work in a public
sphere, mingling elements of rhetoric and stylistics associated with the aforemen-
tioned modes— analytical, ironic, or humanistic' (Stefans 2006, 66). While the work
collected in *Circulars* is different from the poems I am examining, in that the former
were conceived as part of a coherent project rather than having emerged as a loose,
uncollected, and uncurated conglomeration of poems by multiple different poets,
they do share something important as well. They both help to create a similarly
precarious dissenting community:

> Email stories and jokes, not to mention political cartoons based on 'remixes' of
> found material, were being zinged around daily on the Internet at that time. I
> thought: with the mere pressing of the 'send' button to one's entire address
> book, one of these poems would be picked up by one of the many visitors to
> the site and turned into an anthem of dissent for millions—a lofty dream, of
> course, but nonetheless the guiding principle behind the name of the site.
>
> *(Stefans 2006, 72)*

These objects that are 'being zinged around daily on the Internet' are what Darren
Wershler has described as findables: 'the kind of amusing crap that surfaces in our
inboxes all the time – altered and unaltered images, funny infographics, viral videos,
even spam – in terms of the conditions of its circulability, iterability and form'
(Wershler 2012, n.p.). Like the objects zinging around the Internet, these findables
depend on iterability for their very existence. They become something recognised,
something we might today describe as a meme, through this process of iteration. This
necessity of repetition for any 'amusing crap' to become a meme has been noted by
scholars of new media. Patrick Davison has defined the meme as 'a piece of culture,
typically a joke, which gains influence through online transmission' (2012, 122), while
Daniel Dennett argued that memes 'replicate at rates that make even fruit flies and
yeast cells look glacial in comparison' (1993, 205). Knobel and Lankshear have
defined memes as 'contagious patterns of "cultural information" that get passed from
mind to mind and directly generate and shape the mindsets and significant forms of
behaviour and actions of a social group' (2007, 199). These definitions of the meme
help me to concretise the rather loose poetry-as-meme narrative that I have been
constructing so far. Because if the meme depends on iteration, on the fact of its circulation around the internet, then one could argue that this is something it shares
with poetry. As Homi Bhabha has written about the repeated use of W. H. Auden's
'September 1, 1939' in the context of post 9/11 New York:

Poetry does not rest in the realm of the 'idea' or 'emotion'; it survives through recitation, by being passed from mouth to mouth, in an embodied circulation. The *utterance of meaning* is the psychic and affective *happening* of the poem; and the 'emotional tone' sets the note for this mnemonic iterability of meanings-in-performance. The *imminence* of poetry, the renewal and surprise that emerges in every recitation – makes something remarkable *happen*: It keeps redrawing the contingent boundary between what we represent as 'public' and what we designate as 'private'.

(*Bhabha 2016, 64, emphasis in original*)

If sharing can be seen as a similar act of embodied circulation, if the smiling, or crying, pressing of a button, or scrolling down a screen can be seen as a similar act of recitation, then perhaps Bhabha's analysis might help us to redraw another contingent boundary – the boundary between offline poetry and online poetry. N. Katherine Hayles has argued that through remediation in the digital world, the poem can be 'eventilized', or 'made more an event and less a discrete, self-contained object with clear boundaries in space and time' (2006, 182), but perhaps Bhabha helps reveal the potential for such a transformation that was there in the pre-digital poetry all along.

The poem exists in my immediacy as a reader because the poem has always been an event for me, an event that takes place in multiple immediacies of multiple readers, creating a poetic community that, in the case of poetic responses to Hindu nationalism, is physically scattered in space, but brought together through similar acts of literary dissent. Dissent here helps to create what Mark Surman and Darren Wershler-Henry have described as commonspace:

The Internet isn't even about technology. It's about us. The *collective* us. The real power of the Internet lies in *the collective* – the vital, thrilling interconnection of people and ideas that happen online. The juice that makes the Internet hum is the direct result of people talking, sharing, collaborating, aggregating, and playing [...] It's the sparks that fly when a million great ideas collide in one place. People. Connected. *Commonspace*.

(*Surman and Wershler-Henry 2001, 2, emphasis in original*)

Similarly, writing in the context of black women's use of hair blogs, Latoya Lee has borrowed from bell hooks to coin the phrase 'virtual homeplace':

Virtual homeplace is a (real or imagined) place that offers comfort and nurture, where one can seek safe harbour against the racial and sexual oppression they may face on a daily basis [...] a site of affirmation, a space to discuss issues of concern, provide support, elevate spirits and also resist hatred; a site of networking, a space providing economic independency (and dependency); and as a site of recovery, a space of healing.

(*Lee 2015, 93, emphasis in original*)

At this point, it could be fairly argued that I am painting an impossibly Utopian vision of social media. After all, at the time of writing in 2018, Facebook's reputation has never been so low. As the precise fallout of the Cambridge Analytica scandal is still uncertain, and as even leading figures of virtual reality and computer philosophy such as Jaron Lanier are calling their readers to be pioneers by deleting their Facebook accounts and 'beating the addiction, making a political statement and redefining social life' (Lanier 2018), my attempt to explore the dissenting potential Facebook may provide seems quixotic at best, naïve at worst. But what seems to me to be missing from much of the discourse about Facebook and its use of personal data is the possibility of agency on the part of its users. Even those who are dismissive of the #deleteFacebook movement often base their suspicion on Facebook's apparent omnipotence: 'Facebook feels too big to leave […]. In effect, Facebook is a monopoly' (Statt 2018). The central question that this analysis leaves unanswered is this: does Facebook get to have complete say over what Facebook is for? If the answer is to be in the negative, then maybe we can begin to open up the possibility of dissent and resistance that may lie within even the most highly-regulated and coercive forms of communication.

To phrase it another way: if Surman and Wershler-Henry's, and Lee's, accounts of the online world sound impossibly Utopian, it is only because we mistakenly take the commonspace or the virtual homeplace as inevitable. Instead, we could highlight the discursive nature of these communities, following Jacques Rancière's lead, and think of them as literary communities:

> The creation of such communities is made by words. In that sense, the notion of 'literary community' goes far beyond the production of an art named 'literature'. A literary community exists whenever human beings are gathered by the power of certain words. A religious community (structured by obedience to the Word of God) or a political community (shaped by the power of words such as liberty or equality) are literary communities in that sense.
>
> (Rancière 2016, 93–4)

The emphasis then is on precarity and contingency. Shaped around the immediacy of language-as-event, this community is always loose and limited, impossible to quantify or know, but nevertheless real, both online and offline. This literary community is Srijato's family of readers. What Srijato, Mandakranta, Tapabrata, and the many other anonymous poets are able to do, what writers and sharers are able to do with poems by Sunil Ganguly years after his death, what the connective technology of Facebook and WhatsApp allows us all to do, is to conceptualise and therefore perhaps help create a new and novel literary community of dissent.

Marx said that the 'social revolution of the nineteenth century cannot take its poetry from the past but only from the future' (Marx 1975–2004, 11:106), that the content needed to go beyond the phrase. In the twenty-first century, the content can go beyond the phrase in ways that Marx could never have imagined. In the twenty-first century, Facebook and WhatsApp allow not just for a new kind of poetry about the future, but also for the possibility of a new kind of dissenting poetic community. Using the poem-as-meme, we are able to construct a community of dissent, linked in time and space, connected through the shared, optimistic insistence on the power of language to challenge hegemony, the shared belief that the sharing of a poem can challenge the nation-state, can reverse the tide of oppressive religious fundamentalism, of majoritarian dictatorship. We are connected through this shared belief in ourselves as Facebook readers and poets, and the potential we believe we have as a collective to change the course of history and redefine how one might use Facebook and WhatsApp and, perhaps, what it might mean to be Indian in the twenty-first century.

Notes

1 See, for example, Gupta (2009).
2 All translations are my own.
3 Mamata Banerjee's governing Trinamool Congress Party has entered into alliance with the BJP numerous times over the past few years, including serving in the National Government as part of the BJP-led National Democratic Alliance for a number of years.
4 This clearly causes difficulties for academic discourse as well. Many of the poems I am using here are impossible to cite, let alone to attribute to any original, authoritative source. The difficulty of having to bend the referencing system to allow for academic discussion of such poems speaks to the challenge that this form of poetry represents.
5 I am grateful to Chris Jones for pointing me towards this concept, and for allowing me to see an unpublished version of his chapter where he borrows from and adapts this term (Jones 2017, 173).

Works cited

Aarjyatirtha. 2018. 'Kathua', 13 April. Available at: https://www.facebook.com/groups/237253063438912/permalink/369839076846976/ (Accessed 21 May 2018).
Abedin, Anal. 2018. '"Proletarian Unbelievers" by Sunil Ganguly', 13 April. Available at: https://www.facebook.com/anal.abedin/posts/2003518799897884 (Accessed 21 May 2018).
Ali, Arshad. 2017. 'Poem against Adityanath: Poet Mandakranta Sen Receives Rape Threats for Supporting Srijato Bandopadhyay', *DNA India* 29 March. Available at: http://www.dnaindia.com/india/report-poem-against-adityanath-poet-mandakranta-sen-receives-rape-threats-for-supporting-srijato-bandopadhyay-2374242 (Accessed 10 May 2018).
Anand, Dibyesh. 2008. 'Porno-Nationalism and the Male Subject: An Ethnography of Hindu Nationalist Imagination in India' in Jane Parpart and Marysia Zalewski, eds. *Rethinking the 'Man' Question in International Politics*. 163–180. London: Zed Books.
Anand, Dibyesh. 2011. *Hindu Nationalism in India and the Politics of Fear*. Basingstoke, UK: Palgrave Macmillan.
Anand, Kunal. 2015 'Yogi Adityanath's Men Telling Hindus To Rape Dead Muslim Women Is Beyond Shocking', *India Times* 3 March. Available at: https://www.indiatimes.com/news/india/yogi-adityanaths-men-telling-hindus-to-rape-dead-muslim-women-is-beyond-shocking-230679.html (Accessed 10 May 2018).
Bandopadhyay, Srijato. 2017. 'Curse', 19 March. Available at: https://www.facebook.com/srijato.speaks.3/posts/1912563035681688 (Accessed 10 May 2018).

Bandopadhyay, Srijato. 2018a. 'I can never agree with those who think that Facebook is not to be trusted', 22 January. Available at: https://www.facebook.com/srijato.speaks.3/posts/2085808471690476 (Accessed 21 May 2018).

Bandopadhyay, Srijato. 2018b. *Srijator Facebook* [*Srijato's Facebook*]. Kolkata: Patra Bharati.

Benjamin, Walter. 2007. *Illuminations*. Trans. Harry Zohn. Edited by Hannah Arendt. New York: Schocken Books.

Bhabha, Homi K. 2016. 'Poetics of Anxiety and Security: The Problem of Speech and Action in Our Time' in Thomas Claviez, ed, *The Common Growl: Toward a Poetics of Precarious Community*. 57–71. New York: Fordham University Press.

Bhaduri, Tapabrata. 2018. 'God', 29 March. Available at: https://www.facebook.com/tapabrata.bhaduri.3/posts/1261094970689923:0 (Accessed 13 November 2018).

Biswas, Rasmita. 2017. 'Mandakranta Sen', 23 March. Available at: https://www.facebook.com/groups/282377818859735/permalink/282390742191776/ (Accessed 10 May 2018).

Boellstorff, Tom. 2008. *Coming of Age in Second Life: An Anthropologist Explores the Virtually Human*. Princeton, NJ: Princeton University Press.

Bolter, Jay David. 2000. 'Remediation and the Desire for Immediacy'. *Convergence: The International Journal of Research into New Media Technologies* 6(1): 62–71.

Bolter, Jay David, and Richard Grusin. 1999. *Remediation: Understanding New Media*. Cambridge, MA and London: MIT Press.

Bolter, Jay David, Blair MacIntyre, Maribeth Gandy, and Petra Schweitzer. 2006. 'New Media and the Permanent Crisis of Aura'. *Convergence: The International Journal of Research into New Media Technologies* 12(1): 21–39.

Chanda, Aishik. 2017. 'Controversial Bengali Poet Srijato May Face 3-years Jail'. *The New Indian Express* 22 March. Available at: http://www.newindianexpress.com/nation/2017/mar/22/controversial-bengali-poet-srijato-may-face-3-years-jail-1584529.html (Accessed 10 May 2018).

Chatterjee, Partha. 1993. *The Nation and its Fragments: Colonial and Postcolonial Histories*. Princeton, NJ: Princeton University Press.

Dasgupta, Priyanka. 2017. 'Facebook Apologizes to Srijato for Deleting Poem', *The Times of India* 27 March. Available at: https://timesofindia.indiatimes.com/city/kolkata/fb-apologizes-to-srijato-for-deleting-poem/articleshow/57845800.cms (Accessed 10 May 2018).

Davison, Patrick. 2012. 'The Language of Internet Memes' in Michael Mandiberg, ed, *The Social Media Reader*. 120–134. New York: New York University Press.

Dennett, Daniel. 1993. *Consciousness Explained*. London: Penguin.

Dixon, Robert. 2015. 'National Literatures, Scale and the Problem of the World'. *Journal of the Association for the Study of Australian Literature* 15(3): 1–10.

Eltagouri, Marwa. 2018. 'An 8-year-old's Rape and Murder Inflames Tensions between Hindus and Muslims in India'. *The Washington Post* 11 April.

Financial Express. 2015. '"Intolerance" Controversy: Arundhati Roy, Kundan Shah, Saeed Mirza, Others Return National Awards', *Financial Express* 6 November. Available at https://www.financialexpress.com/india-news/intolerance-controversy-arundhati-roy-24-kundan-shah-saeed-mirza-national-awards/162127/ (Accessed 21 May 2018).

Foucault, Michel. 1977. *Language, Counter-memory, Practice: Selected Essays and Interviews*. Trans. Donald F. Bouchard and Sherry Simon. Edited by Donald F. Bouchard. Ithaca, NY: Cornell University Press.

Gatade, Subhash. 2011. *The Saffron Condition: Politics of Repression of Exclusion in Neoliberal India*. Gurgaon, India: Three Essays Collective.

Gershon, Ilana. 2008. 'Email My Heart: Remediation and Romantic Break-Ups'. *Anthropology Today* 24(6): 13–15.

Gupta, Charu. 2009. 'Hindu Women, Muslim Men: Love Jihad and Conversions'. *Economic and Political Weekly* 44(51): 13–15.

Gupta, Swati and Annie Gowen. 2017. 'Modi's Party Picks Yogi Adityanath, Strident Hindu Nationalist Priest, as Leader of India's Biggest State', *The Washington Post* 19 March.

Hadjiafxendi, Kyriaki and Polina Mackay, eds. 2007. *Authorship in Context: From the Theoretical to the Material*. Basingstoke, UK: Palgrave Macmillan.

Hayles, N. Katherine. 2006. 'The Time of Digital Poetry: From Object to Event' in Adalaide Morris and Thomas Swiss, eds, *New Media Poetics: Contexts, Technotexts, and Theories*. 181–209. Cambridge, MA and London: MIT Press.

Hindustan Times. 2017. 'Facebook Removed the Controversial Poem from my Wall: Srijato Bandopadhyay', *Hindustan Times* 26 March 2017. Available at: https://www.hindustantimes.com/kolkata/facebook-removed-the-controversial-poem-from-my-wall-srijato-bandyopadhyay/story-hsmw9Af9oWnQy2QHKfK5rI.html (Accessed 10 May 2018).

Indian Cultural Forum. 2015. 'Nayantara Sahgal Returns Her Sahitya Akademi Award', 6 October. Available at: http://indianculturalforum.in/2015/10/06/nayantara-sahgal-returns-her-sahitya-akademi-award/ (Accessed 21 May 2018).

Indian Express. 2017. 'Police Security to Poet Srijato Bandopadhyay after He Alleges Threat to Life', *Indian Express* 24 March 2017. Available at: http://indianexpress.com/article/cities/kolkata/kolkata-police-security-to-poet-srijato-bandopadhyay-after-he-alleges-threat-to-life-4583033/ (Accessed 10 May 2018).

Jones, Chris. 2017. 'Digital Mouvance: Once and Future Medieval Poetry Remediated in the Modern World' in Bettina Bildhauer and Chris Jones, eds, *The Middle Ages in the Modern World: Twenty-First Century Perspectives*. 168–185. London: Oxford University Press/British Academy.

Kadir, Djelal. 2016. 'Literature, the World, and You' in Thomas Claviez, ed, *The Common Growl: Toward a Poetics of Precarious Community*. 72–89. New York: Fordham University Press.

Knobel, Michele and Colin Lankshear. 2007. 'Online Memes, Affinities and Cultural Production' in Colin Lankshear and Michele Knobel, eds, *A New Literacies Sampler*. 199–228. New York: Peter Lang.

Kruger, Sasha. 2017. 'The Technopo(e)litics of Rupi Kaur: (de)Colonial Aesthetics and Spatial Narrations in the DigiFemme Age'. *Ada: A Journal of Gender, New Media and Technology* 11. Available at: https://adanewmedia.org/2017/05/issue11-kruger/ (Accessed 21 May 2018).

Lanier, Jaron. 2018. 'Be a Pioneer – Delete Facebook'. *The Guardian* 27 March. Available at: https://www.theguardian.com/commentisfree/2018/mar/27/pioneer-delete-facebook-addiction-social-life (Accessed 21 May 2018).

Lee, Latoya. 2015. 'Virtual Homeplace: (Re)Constructing the Body through Social Media' in Keisha Edwards Tassie and Sonja M. Brown Givens, eds, *Women of Colour and Social Media Multitasking: Blogs, Timelines, Feeds and Community*. 91–112. Lanham, MD: Lexington Books.

Marx, Karl. 1975–2004. 'Economic Manuscripts of 1857–1858' in Karl Marx and Frederick Engels, *The Collected Works of Karl Marx and Frederick Engels*. 50 vols. Trans. Ernst Wangermann, *et al.* London: Lawrence and Wishart.

Rancière, Jacques. 2016. 'Literary Communities' in Thomas Claviez, ed, *The Common Growl: Toward a Poetics of Precarious Community*. 93–110. New York: Fordham University Press.

Safi, Michael. 2017. 'Controversial Hindu Priest Chosen as Uttar Pradesh Chief Minister'. *The Guardian* 19 March. Available at: https://www.theguardian.com/world/2017/mar/19/uttar-pradesh-yogi-adityanath-hindu-priest-chief-minister (Accessed 10 May 2018).

Sen, Mandakranta. 2018. 'Examination', 22 April 2018. Available at: https://www.facebook.com/mandakranta.sen/posts/1704377406304446 (Accessed 21 May 2018).

Slemon, Stephen. 1990. 'Unsettling the Empire: Resistance Theory for the Second World'. *Journal of Postcolonial Writing* 30(2): 30–41.

Smith, Neil. 2004. 'Scale Bending and the Fate of the National' in Eric Sheppard and Robert B. McMaster, eds, *Scale and Geographic Inquiry: Nature, Society and Method*. 192–213. Malden, MA: Blackwell.

Statt, Nick. 2018. 'Boycotting digital monopolies like Facebook is harder than it seems'. *The Verge* 22 March 2018. Available at: https://www.theverge.com/2018/3/22/17152922/delete-facebook-boycott-cambridge-analytica-tech-monopoly-data-privacy (Accessed on 21 May 2018).

Stefans, Brian Kim. 2006. 'Toward a Poetics for Circulars' in Adalaide Morris and Thomas Swiss, eds, *New Media Poetics: Contexts, Technotexts, and Theories*. 65–72. Cambridge, MA and London: MIT Press.

Surman, Mark. and Darren Wershler-Henry. 2001. *Commonspace: Beyond Virtual Community* London: Financial Times Management.

Tanoukhi, Nirvana. 2008. 'The Scale of World Literature'. *New Literary History* 39(3): 599–617.

Times of India. 2017. 'BJP's Adityanath Sworn in as UP Chief Minister with 2 Deputies', *The Times of India* 19 March. Available at: https://timesofindia.indiatimes.com/elections/assembly-elections/uttar-pradesh/news/bjps-adityanath-sworn-in-as-uttar-pradesh-chief-minister/articleshow/57716008.cms (Accessed 10 May 2018).

Wershler, Darren. 2012. 'Best Before Date', 4 April. Available at: http://www.alienated.net/poetics/best-before-date/ (Accessed 21 May 2018).

8

WRITING THE NECROPOLITICAL

Notes around the idea of Mexican anti-world literature

Ignacio M. Sánchez Prado

In the two decades or so between the revival of the idea of world literature and its current state, somewhere between conceptual euphoria and institutional stasis, the world to which the category refers remains a site of contention and an open signifier. The world is the site of world literature's utopian promise. It brings up the ideas of a democratic spatial imagination and an experiential cosmopolitanism that have been at the core of comparatism, at least since the postcolonial turn challenged the self-evidence of cultural Eurocentrism. As Edward W. Said put it in a foundational essay, the world is that which opposes cultural imaginations irradiating from hierarchical cultural systems: 'criticism is worldly and in the world so long as it opposes mono-centrism, a concept I understand as working in conjunction with ethnocentrism, which licenses a culture to cloak itself in the particular authority of certain values over others' (Said 1983, 53). And yet, even if this declaration of principle was aimed at the foundation of what Said called 'secular criticism', its spirit remains untenable, ungraspable. Said was aiming at the development of a transcendental signifier – worldliness – that meant to capture, in its untranslatability, two ideas of the world in constant tension with each other. The first one related to extension, the sense of a planetary culture that was rendered visible in the epistemic decentring brought about by the coincidence of Third-World decolonisation and post-structuralist decon-struction. The second one had to do with the everyday experience of the human, with the mundane sense of the common materiality of life. Said theorised this ideal, however, during a moment in which the theoretical revolutions that made his the-orisation possible – postcolonialism, poststructuralism – were beginning to show their limits, and in the early days of a neoliberal world that would subsume the post-colonial into the economic order of globalisation and territorialise significant parts of the poststructural revolution into the realm of semiocapitalism.

Said, like much of the debate on world literature, missed the point of yet another untranslatable, a romance-language distinction illegible in English, between globe and world, between *globalización* and *mundialización*. Reflecting on the French version of this difference, Jean-Luc Nancy established a distinction between *globalization* as 'the idea of an integrated totality' in contrast to *mondialisation* understood as a '*process* throughout the expanse of the world of *human* beings, cultures and nations' (2007, 28, emphasis in the original). The residual persistence of this distinction, of the undecidability of the world as a totality or as a process, is a matter of major debate in world-literature theory. Of course, all worlds are always-already historical, rooted in their present and in their genealogies. The compact world of globalisation and neo-liberalism is a stage in the totalisation of multinational capitalism. As David Harvey suggests, it contains in itself a 'utopian design' (2005, 19), a design contradictory with the ideas hegemonic within the literary humanities. In contrast, the romance-language untranslatable holds firmly the notion of another utopia that may be thinkable (depending on the perspective that one sustains) either as autonomous from, or as irrevocably intertwined with, the logic of capital. Personally, I think that the notion of world literature is most productive when one does not resolve this tension, but rather thinks through, and against, the blind spots and indeterminations that reside in the space between both ideals.

My aim in this chapter is not to linger on this question, much less resolve it, but rather to traverse the idea of what I call here an 'anti-world literature', a set of formal and ideological stances against the axioms and ideologies of world literature theories and practices. My frame of reference is contemporary Mexican literature, which will function throughout this chapter as a referent to reflect upon the theoretical gaps and aporias in recent theorisations of world literature. In citing Mexico as a reference point, I do not seek to enact a recovery of the national or the local. And I certainly do not intend this to be yet another exploration of semiperipheral literature as the resisting kernel against modernism or capital, as it is often portrayed in world-literary studies of all kinds. Rather, I contend that specific interventions within contemporary Mexican literature render visible a significant problem in the double utopia of the world in world literature, creating forms of writing that engage the world without any kind of utopian promise. It is remarkable that Mexican literature is trending in this direction, particularly in the moment in which a translation boom is bringing significant amounts of Mexican literature into the neoliberal exchange of literary commodities. Mexico's necropolitical neoliberalism opens a space to think – and to formalise – writing practices against the grain of both globalisation and *mundialización*. Yet, before getting to key Mexican texts, the first pages of this chapter must engage with a Heideggerian trend of rendering the world in world literature from the idea of 'world-making', an updating of the Saidian notion of worldliness as experience, even if it is not always recognised as such. To understand anti-world literature, it is necessary to disclose the politics and aesthetics informing the project of world literature in the current junctures. I contend, as a matter of conceptual framework, that a necropolitical site like Mexico opens the space for anti-world writing, understanding 'anti-world' as a political and aesthetic engagement against the self-evidence of the world's purported utopian promise in any of its guises. In these terms, the first part of the chapter rehearses a critical reading of the idea of the world in world litera-ture as posited by recent theorists like Eric Hayot, Pheng Cheah and Debjani Ganguly, who put forward versions of a concept of 'world-making' to challenge the spatial core of institutionalist world-literature theories.

The second part of the chapter brings to the table Sayak Valencia's idea of 'gore capitalism' and Cristina Rivera Garza's theories of 'necrowriting' and 'disappropria-tion'. I will engage the literary implications of necropolitics, both as lived reality and conceptual framework in the writing of Mexican literature through a set of inter-ventions. I will thusly discuss the theorisation of the ideas of 'necrowriting' and 'disappropriation' in the work of Cristina Rivera Garza as alternative forms of engagement with canonicity, which I will further illustrate through the work of Sara Uribe. The chapter will conclude by bringing to the fore the reimagining of Mex-ico's historical engagement with various formations of the world through the work of Julián Herbert. The Mexican literature I consider here, implicitly in the first half of the chapter and openly in the second half, exists in different spaces of the Mexican literary field, although the different works are connected by an oppositional aim against the 'world' as embodied in the two utopian projects described above.

This chapter follows work I have previously done on the concept of world lit-erature, first by editing the earliest compilation that sought a collective response to the Moretti–Casanova paradigm from Latin American Studies (Sánchez Prado 2006), and much more recently by studying 'Mexican world literature' as a device to understand the intersection between cosmopolitanism and the neoliberalisation of the book market between the 1960s and the 2000s (Sánchez Prado 2018a). Because of this preceding work, and work by other Latin Americanists (Siskind 2014; Hoyos 2015; Gras and Müller 2015; Müller, Locane, and Loy 2018, to mention the most notable), I will not address here the question of world literature 'from Latin America' nor articulate a Latin American or Mexican perspective on world literature. Rather, I will depart from a contention set forward by Nancy, which will, as I hope to show, give sense to the cultural production – the creation of meaning in Nancy's own terms – that is rendered possible when one takes the parallactic step of moving outside the hegemonic spaces of formulation of world literature – namely Anglophone academic debates and related Francophone interventions – into the practice of a literary writing against the world itself: 'To create the world means: immediately, without delay, reopening each possible struggle for a world that is, for what must form the contrary of a global injustice against the background of general equivalence' (Nancy 2007, 54). Mexico's anti-world literature, as presented here, is a politics of writing that recognises, with Nancy, that 'this world is coming out of nothing, that there is nothing before it and that it is without models, without principle and without given end, and that it is precisely *what* forms the justice and the meaning of a world' (55). The writers I discuss here take this contention a step further: in anti-world literature, this world, which Nancy poses as potentiality and utopia, is in fact an impossibility, an unreachable horizon against which the writer in the necropolitical present must position her struggle.

The persistent question of the world in world literature has essentially divided the theoretical field in roughly three camps. First, and perhaps more straightforwardly, it is defined as a 'mode of circulation and reading' to which literary works enter insofar as two conditions apply: 'being read *as* literature' and 'by circulating into a broader world beyond its linguistic and cultural point of origin' (Damrosch 2003, 5–6, emphasis in the original); or as a relatively autonomous 'World Republic of Letters' in which the mode of circulation described by Damrosch is layered by the recognition of inequality within languages (Casanova 2004). Secondly, various theorists go beyond the idea of a mode of reading and of relative cultural autonomy by openly or implicitly identifying the 'world' in world literature with the world in world-systems theory or with global capital. This notion of the world poses it as a space that is 'one and unequal' (Moretti 2013, 46), or as a system superstructural to the dynamics of 'combined and uneven development' (WReC 2015). I will not rehash here a full critique of these approaches, but in my previous work I have argued that the conception of world literature as one, embedded in all of these approaches, is apt to describe what I call 'hegemonic world literature', that which indeed circulates in the neoliberal book markets and the circuits of agents, fairs, and translations. Contrariwise, it fares poorly when departing the book-market centre and moving into different linguistic ecosystems (like the Spanish language) and national literary fields (like Mexico) where world literature in particular, and the world in general, are conceived and represented in ways that depart from the deterministic and one-directional accounts favoured by many Anglophone and Francophone theoretical interventions.

A third camp, more to the point of my aims here, is represented by theorists who, like Nancy, have followed the Heideggerian idea of a world as inhabited site, which thinks it, in Debjani Ganguly's formulation, '*as related to but not synonymous with its material and chronotopical coordinates*' (2016, 21, emphasis in the original). This is a way of saying that the world in world literature can be something other than the 'one and unequal' system of capitalist modernity and globalisation, or even its close relative, the world of geopolitics and global war. In this realm, one can recall Eric Hayot's idea of the 'aesthetic world' as 'the *diegetic totality* constituted by the sum of all aspects of a single work or work-part constellated into a structure or system that amounts to a whole', but that nonetheless is 'among other things a relation to and theory of the lived world whether as a largely preconscious normative construct, a rearticulation, or even an active refusal of the world-norms of their age' (2012, 44–5, emphasis in the original). In this formulation, Hayot does not so much engage the romance-language tension of globalisation and *mondialisation* when he borrows from Nancy, but rather sidesteps the untranslatable altogether by locating worldliness in the realm of aesthetics and form. Ganguly, in turn, expands upon Hayot to pose that 'the actual world is but one of the conditions of possibility of the fictional world' and notes that even Moretti and Casanova's approaches describe 'not the actual world of material and territorial expansion but a world constituting system of literary production' (2016, 22). I do not dismiss at all this notion of the autonomy of a world-constituting literary system that operates in its own dynamic relative to the actual world – a canonical idea posed by Pierre Bourdieu (1996) and revisited here through a Heideggerian lens. Ganguly's tensioning between the world as a space defined by 'global violence' and the novel as a world-form defined by 'its long thinking of the human' (2016, 36–7) is relevant, as we will see below, to the study of the necropolitical setting of Mexican anti-world literature. In a similar vein, Pheng Cheah (2016) takes a Heideggerian–Marxist stance to develop a temporal theory of world literature centre in the idea of 'world-making' and the possibility of imagining and enacting social change, which, in his view, is a critique of the cultural violence of the capital world-system and a fundamental mode of thinking postcolonial literatures.

Read from the stance of Mexican literature of the twenty-first century, particularly the anti-world literature that is my focus here, the wilfully humanistic and utopian bent of Heideggerian world literature theory is significantly flawed. It replicates the idea, present in the work of neo-Heideggerian critics of neoliberalism like Byung-Chul Han (2017a, 2017b), that the dynamics of capital can be countered either by an idea of beauty (or literary form in the case of criticism) as truth; or by an argument for a *vita contemplativa* in which the careful attention to the human is a counter to the demands of late capitalism. In literary criticism, this approach has fostered the notion that utopian world literature – or at least literary world-making – resides in the autonomy of literary form, which in turns holds an epistemological privilege for the rendering of a notion of the human against the grain of capitalist globalisation and geopolitical war. In Cheah's formulation, this is attributed concretely to 'postcolonial world literature', understood as a 'continuing pertinence, not only as an expression of humanity's ideals or suffering, but as an active force for the emergence of new subjects in the world' (2016, 330), while Ganguly reads her corpus from the contention that 'the contemporary world novel is not a literary simulacrum of our current geopolitical world order' but rather 'contains many worlds that travel, haunt, layer and disrupt other worlds even as it is informed in our present time by technologies that amplify our sense of the interconnections among these myriad possible worlds' (2016, 84–5). I am fairly sceptical that the identity-centred novels favoured by Cheah, which fall squarely into what Graham Huggan (2006) calls 'the postcolonial exotic', or that writers as territorialised into the global literary market as Rushdie or Ondaatje, analysed by Ganguly, operate that kind of against-the-grain literary world-making, but that is a discussion that exceeds my purposes. Rather, what I seek to question here, informed by the work of Mexican writers confronted with this very question, is whether the novel-form remains a site to perform this kind of utopian work – even live up to what David Palumbo-Liu (2012), in a different conceptual constellation, describes as the ethics of the 'deliverance of others' in global-age literature.

The experience of Mexican literature in the twenty-first century indicates otherwise. Back in the 1990s, the Mexican literary field very much sustained a similar view. Just to mention a notable stance, the Crack literary group, which included writers of great international renown like Jorge Volpi and Ignacio Padilla, released a manifesto in 1996 that defended the universal and human values of the novel against its territorialisation into global corporate markets and advocated cosmopolitanism as an antidote to the commoditisation of magical realism (Chávez Castañeda *et al.* 2016). In 2018, this idealism seems to have disappeared, and some of the most significant literary writing today, including the one that I will discuss briefly, has moved to post-fictional and non-fictional modes of writing due to a sense, I think, of either the exhaustion or the insufficiency of the novel-form to deal with the intensities of Mexico's necropolitical present. Just to provide a very simple example, Jorge Volpi's claim to fame stemmed from his defence of the cosmopolitan novel from Latin America, and his most famous work, *En busca de Klingsor* (*In Search of Klingsor* 1999; Volpi 2002), was an exploration of the nature of humanity and evil against the backdrop of the relationships between Nazism and science. Even if he did not circulate as widely in English, Volpi was in fact the first Mexican writer to successfully enter world-literary markets in years (Carlos Fuentes and Octavio Paz did so decades before), and his work, translated into various languages and subject to bidding wars at the Frankfurt book fair, became the signal of a new Latin American novel that was finally overcoming magical realism, and that would become even bigger when Roberto Bolaño came onto the global stage. Two decades later, in 2018, Volpi won the Alfaguara literary award, one of the most visible and money-endowed prizes in the Spanish language, with *Una novela criminal* (*A Criminal Novel*; Volpi 2018), a thoroughly nonfictional work based in an extensive documentary investigation of the controversial case of a French woman, Florence Cassez, who was accused of kidnapping in Mexico, to later become an icon of the country's manufacturing of legal cases and mismanagement of the justice system, and the centre of a major diplomatic conflict between Mexico and France. Volpi's career followed a significant trajectory during the first 18 years of the twenty-first century. From the universalist fiction of *Klingsor* and other sprawling books reflecting on the global experience of the twentieth century, *El jardín devastado* (*The Devastated Garden*; Volpi 2008), a short novella first released in a blog and later in book form, was a departure, one which very much fits within Palumbo-Liu's (2012) ethics of the 'deliverance of others' by connecting a Mexican and an Iraqi woman during the second Iraq war. A decade later, Volpi shifts in the opposite direction, writing a long novel that moves away from the devices of fiction and imagination, and from the novel's ability to deliver others, into the realm of a documentary work where the novel-form is a secondary device mostly aimed at filling narrative gaps in his references. Volpi's latest work, bearing the marks of a writer who represented in many debates the exceptionality and power of the novel-form, points to the acceptance that the concrete reality of Mexico, or even its horizon of world-making, is perhaps unthinkable from the epistemological perspective of fiction. When Volpi departs the realm of global otherness and returns to the materiality of the nation, the novel-form no longer enjoys any kind of proper epistemological privilege.

For all the copious discussions in two decades of academic vogue, it is clear that the world in world literature is ultimately a horizon of utopian will, a shared Idea or potentiality that materialises with different politics, but with a similar aim in form. The utopian will manifests itself in the faith that world literature will allow literary writing to overcome the constrictions of the national, or that there are forms of writing from semiperipheral or dominated areas that can break out of the inherently unequal structure of modernity, or that literary form is a technology that remains firmly grounded in its exceptional capacity for accounting for the human as such. The common thread is that the most valued cultural form of capitalist modernity – one that has been thought from Lukács (1971) onwards as the genre that narrates the gap between subject and totality – has an epistemological strength and an insight on the human that remains strong through the different modes of capitalist modernity. In various sites of Mexico and Latin America (and I would suspect elsewhere too, but I do not have a corpus to affirm it), the rise of forms highly sceptical of literature's purported cultural autonomy and epistemological exceptionalism signals the possible decline of the novel as privileged aesthetic form for the representation of the human as such. Thusly, the literary writer's task becomes an engagement with contemporaneity through the full embrace of the terms and consequences of this realisation. There is no room here for a full description of the reasons why Latin America at large is a site where this has taken place in recent years. One can list the work of the polarising Roberto Bolaño and his pushing the very idea of literary modernity and its forms to crisis – something discussed by Oswaldo Zavala (2015) in intelligent terms, although I do not share his enthusiasm for the Chilean writer. The exhaustion of testimonial literary genres and magical-realist modes of literature as cultural tools for political engagement is also relevant, as it points to the growing scepticism regarding the correlation between history, memory, and human rights as a master narrative of the relationship between literature and civil society (a mode discussed in depth by Rosenberg 2016).

The Mexican case presents particularities because the country's relationship to the world-system and to globalisation has been defined in what theorists in Mexico and elsewhere identify with neoliberalism and the idea of necropolitics. Achille Mbembe's (2013) foundational essay on the matter has encountered significant reception, even if the three major sites of his analysis – late colonialism, the Iraq War, Palestine – are not fully analogous to Mexico's situation. Theorist Sayak Valencia openly engages with Mbembe's concept, and notes the need for an expansion of the idea of necropolitics and necropower (Valencia 2018, 211–12). A fully-fledged discussion of Valencia's work is beyond the scope of my analysis. Yet her theorisation leads, in one of its central lines of organisation, to the articulation of cultural dynamics underlying what I call anti-world literature. In her characterisation of necropower as dystopian, and thus inherently opposed to the two utopias in the world of world literature described above, Valencia notes that a cultural dynamic of gore capitalism, which she identifies particularly with Hollywood cinema, resides in the technologies of 'spectralization' and 'derealization'. Of particular interest is Valencia's description of derealisation and the idea of the 'Third World':

derealization attacks the concept of the Third World itself, designating it as politically incorrect and arguing that the term has no place in contemporary discourse because it is not applicable to current conditions [...]. In this way, it also thwarts any possibility of articulating a discourse that might lead to agency and empowerment for subjects whose daily lives take place in Third World territories. This denial of discourse and agency has a derealizing effect on these subjects, depicting them as silent, articulate and ineffectual.

(Valencia, 2018, 249)

What Valencia calls the 'Third World' is a political cartography of space which in world-literary imaginaries has been captured by more contemporary categories, such as the Global South or the postcolonial. Valencia suggests here that global modes of cultural representation, intertwined in the spectacularised violence of gore capitalism, exercise symbolic violence on the very ability of world-making from below, from the peripheries. Translated to my discussion here, this means not only that the world in world literature is always-already enunciated from concrete positions in the cartography of the global, but also that the very utopian or dystopian character of world-literary writing very much depends on whether utopianism is thinkable from any given site. Furthermore, one can claim that, much like Valencia's version of Hollywood cinema, hegemonic modes of world literature, enunciated from the global corporate publishing apparatus and sustained by academic and critical structures in the Western academy, oftentimes exercise spectralisation and derealisation of the modes of writing from the Third World, the Global South, the postcolonial, the periphery, or however one chooses to name less-than-hegemonic sites of literary enunciation.

While foundational interventions in world literature like the ones articulated by Damrosch, Moretti, and Casanova generally admit the inequality of the system or the distortions in intercultural translation as a mere fact to be accounted for, the Heideggerian approaches hold a more proactive view of the agency of less-than-hegemonic world literature in imagining alternative world-making. Cheah, for instance, notes in a Hegelian key that literary works from the postcolonial peripheries 'confront the irreducible reality of violence in the world-system and they express the belief that literary forms are part of the world's objective structure' (2016, 56). This is later elaborated in a Heideggerian key that recognises that '[w]orldliness is the constitutive ontological structure of our existence' but that normative forms of world literature based on extension rather than world-making align with a 'de-worlding' or 'unworlding' that the worldliness of postcolonial literature challenges (2016, 98–9). This approach, like Ganguly's 'human', imagines world literature as an alternative technology of world-making because the concept of the possible is either related to the ontological possibilities of world-making (Cheah) or to geopolitical modes of warfare (Ganguly). Valencia's notion of gore capitalism – and Mexico's theoretical engagement with the concept of necropolitics in general – discloses the possibility that the postcolonial and the peripheral in itself are not always-already sites of the production of alternative world-making, but rather sites for the imagining of the impossibilities and aporias of that world-making.

The analysis of gore capitalism in the context of world literature theory points towards the need to direct our critical and theoretical eyes to dystopian forms of cultural enunciation in sites peripheralised by hegemonic understandings of world literature, and to acknowledge that the territorialisation of non-hegemonic literatures into world literature theories sometimes requires the erasure of the socio-political conditions and materialities embedded in literary writing. In her suggestive study of Orhan Pamuk's relationship to world-literature systems and criticism, Gloria Fisk notes that the distance between the reading of a writer in her local context and her appropriation to world-literary circles in English translations renders visible paradoxes such as the existence of 'literary critics who write with a broad consensus against neoliberalism and global capitalism in research that secures their employment in cultural and educational institutions that operate by precisely that logic' (2018, 7). Obviously, the point here is not to silence criticism (even if Fisk and I are also workers in neoliberal educational institutions), but rather to challenge the self-evidence of the anti-neoliberal politics derived from the reading of postcolonial and world-literary texts. Fisk's answer is to study the arrival of Pamuk to the English-dominated structures of world literature and academic criticism, thus highlighting the very tension between the intellectual labour of the writer in a fraught national context like Turkey, and the concurrent intellectual labour that said writer performs when addressing Western audiences and literary fields. In my case, the question is rather to think how literary writing in necropolitical contexts like contemporary Mexico enacts more than the forms of resistant world-making that Western critique assigns to peripheral countries in world-literature's international division of existential labour. The untroubled association of peripheral cultural labour with resistance is an ostensible problem in models that flatten the tensional relationship between the literary sphere and the sociopolitical realities of (semi)peripheral countries in the name of reading a differential politics of literature *vis-á-vis* dominant Western models. One example is the flat rendering of Latin America's tension between realism and vanguardism in the Warwick Research Collective's model, which recognises the global commodification of magical realism, but still sees in the regional version the promise of literary forms 'capable of capturing more adequately the experience and temper of social life' and to express 'the scepticism of intellectuals towards their distorted state formations' (WReC 2015, 80).

The idea of anti-world literature derives from the recognition that regions like Latin America and countries like Mexico produce literary texts that engage with the question of the world in forms and practices not reducible to either the geo-spatial idea of the world as a circulation of cultural capital and commodities, or the Heideggerian notion of world-making and its implications of the human, authenticity, and other reifications of the purported epistemological privilege of the Other. Many important theories of Latin American literature today are attempts to cope with this situation, as is the case of Argentine Damián Tabarovsky's (2004) *Literatura de izquierda*, a manifesto against the imperatives of literature's intellectual labour in the region, and against the forms of writing inherited from the cultural politics of the twentieth century. In Mexico, one of the most important theorisations is that of Cristina Rivera Garza (2013), which directly engages the aesthetic and political consequences of necropolitics for literary writing. Rivera Garza's reflections emerge from the confluence of two phenomena: the increasing horror of violence and necropolitics in contemporary Mexico, and the emergence of the digital as a paradigmatic change in literary writing. Rivera Garza argues that the Adornian idea of literature as a way to articulate language against mercantilisation, and its corollaries in practices such as 'indirect denunciation, the rejection of the transparency of language or of the idea of this as a mere vehicle for meaning, a certain distorted syntax, the constant critique to referentiality, the undermining of the position of the lyrical self, the continuous defeat of the reader's expectations' have been rendered obsolete and even become integrated into necropolitical power strategies (2013, 21, my translation). One can take Rivera Garza's point even further and note that the territorialising machine of neoliberalism has severely undermined the utopian projects of language that underlie world literature theories, both in the guise of global translation and circulation, and in the world-making idea of Heideggerian perspectives. To face this, Rivera Garza proposes two modes of writing. The first one, necrowriting (*necroescritura*), speaks to the dissolution of the subjective privilege of the author and favours collective modes of writing, while the second one, disappropriation (*desapropiación*), refers to the idea of writing beyond the idea of property (2013, 22). In Rivera Garza's rendering, these modes of writing imagine the possibility not so much of the positive world-making of experience, but rather of the dissolution and delay of the territorialising practices of writing – from the subjectivity of the author to the marketability of the work – that have been fully folded into the realm of capital, even when they may seem to be critical of it.

Rivera Garza coincides in this with other forms of Latin American critical theory that challenge the neoliberal ideological mechanism of common sense, which, as Irmgard Emmelhainz (2016) notes, has become a tyranny of a politics of knowledge tied to the cultural turn of late capitalism. It is of course well known by now that the strongest critics of the idea of world literature usually underscore issues such as untranslatability (Apter 2013), its intertwining with market dynamics (Brouillette 2016), or its continuation of Orientalist politics (Mufti 2016), generally signalling either the subsumption of the literary to late capitalist dynamics such as the 'creative economy' (Brouillette 2014), or even the simple notion that literature is more complex than its world literary version. Rivera Garza's challenge widens the discussion, as it points to the necropoliticisation of everyday life, on the one hand, and the radical material transformations of the platforms that support literary writing, on the other. Read against world literature debates, Rivera Garza's perspective suggests that the utopian projects embedded in any notion of literature construed as critical of neoliberal capitalism must be thoroughly tested to see if the critical act actually identifies an alternative or resistance, or if theories and criticism are simply built around the symbolic restoration of forms of writing that remain active, but are either no longer contemporary or whose contemporaneity no longer carries any kind of resistant kernel. Rivera Garza, who is clear to assert that 'necrowritings' is a plural noun, pushes us to the idea that the world in world literature cannot be thinkable as a contemporary entity if one continues to assert that a literary world can be more than, or autonomous from, the socioeconomic world of capital, as Hayot and Cheah affirm. Rivera Garza derives from a large number of sources whose common thread is the idea that the digital changes the concept of writing in itself: these include Antoine Volodine's notion of exoticism (2015), Tabarovsky's 'literatura de izquierda' (2004), or Vanessa Place and Robert Fitterman's work on conceptualism (2009), which she translated into Spanish. She cross-lists these theoretical efforts with Mbembe's theorisation of necropolitics (2013) and Adriana Cavarero's work on horrorism (2011). In this juncture, Rivera Garza shows how literary narratives that historically have been thought to create counter-narratives to capitalist culture, like the much beloved and much maligned idea of 'national allegory' (Jameson 1986), may in fact refer to forms of culture that are thoroughly incorporated to neoliberalism (one can indeed find national allegories all over the commercial literary circuit). More importantly, though, the validation of these forms of literary politics, which are deeply embedded in world literature theory of all stripes, misread the possible political and resistant labour that literature may perform, or, even if one resists the notion that this labour is even possible any more, fail to recognise the possibilities for literature to reflect upon the limits of representation as politics. I would venture further, as my examples below will illustrate, that part of the reason why this happens is because the novel genre, which as a material practice is tightly bound to the gradual incorporation of cultural commerce to the logic of capital, remains the central point of reference for most world literature theories.

It is at this point in the argument where Mexican anti-world literature, as a set of projects that directly or indirectly engage with the challenges described by Rivera Garza, or that criticise Rivera Garza's account in endeavours to further radicalise the idea of literature, can be introduced. The world in Mexican anti-world literature is a horizon of impossibility, defined by the unnameable violence of history – both national and global – and by the recognition of the epistemological limitations of the literary in world-making. This not to say that anti-world literature denies the possibility of the commons or the political. Quite the contrary, the commons are an element that may be embedded in the act of writing itself, as Rivera Garza posits by adopting the idea of *tequio* or the collective work one gives back to the community, as discussed by Mixe theorist Floriberto Díaz (Rivera Garza 2013, 278–9; Díaz 2007, 58–60). The labour of literature is, in this rendering, the constitution of ephemeral communities of writing that, in lieu of reifying literature as a machine for world-making, displace and reorganise the literary as such in a time when literature's potential for resistance may already be fully subsumed into the logic of capital (or at least when such full subsumption has become thoroughly thinkable), and when the predominance of necropolitical horror has rendered obsolete the politics of aesthetic world-making. From this perspective, one could perhaps assert that the Heideggerian wager in world literature theory names the reluctance to think the challenges that late neoliberal contemporaneity brings into literary writing, by embedding the ability of disclosing Being or the world into literary forms that are exhausted or superseded at the very moment of their enunciation.

The 'anti' in anti-world literature thus brings into the fore two negative moves. It posits a negative in the idea of the realm of world-making, which Jean-Luc Nancy, in his work about community, characterises as interruption: 'Literature interrupts itself: this is, essentially, what makes it literature (writing) and not myth' (1991, 72). Rivera Garza brings Nancy's notion of literature, which, in her rendering, is notable for its notion of communication as a bringing-together and not as an intersubjective exchange, along with Díaz's notion of communal labour or *tequio* to characterise the horizon of literary writing in these terms (Rivera Garza 2013, 275). In other words, in the negativity of a world that can never be made by literary writing, it is the act of writing, the in-common of what Nancy calls the 'inoperative community', where another function of the literary may emerge. Yet the anti- is also the inscription of a negative against the grain of the double utopia of frictionless neoliberal capitalism and the imagined alternative worlds to counter it. It is the possibility that either dystopia or the void left by the impossibility of utopia are the ways in which the world can be engaged in anti-world literature. In Rivera Garza this is achieved by arguing that the ethical and critical relation to literature in a necropolitical time can only be so when a communal practice is thought *vis-á-vis* the material condition of writing. As Brian Whitener notes, Rivera Garza goes even further than other Latin American attempts – like the *cartonera* publishers of the early 2000s – to ask crucial question regarding infrastructure and literature: 'What are the specific material means that writing can use to confront terminal crisis and state violence? What are our options in terms of platforms and means of production?' (2018, 272). In this rendering, if the politics of world literature is to grant the literary the epistemological privilege of alternative world-making, anti-world literature assumes the literary as an unprivileged and communal labour whose material infrastructure has the duty to confront the full consequences of the necropolitical present.

To move towards the conclusion of this chapter, I will discuss some key works of contemporary Mexican anti-world literature in order to show the material stakes of literary writing in necropolitical neoliberalism. It is important to note that Mexican anti-world literature no longer operates under the critical primacy of the novel, and even authors who have written major novels (like Rivera Garza) have gradually moved to writing in ways that challenge the idea of genre itself. One such work is *Antígona González*, in which Sara Uribe (2016) openly follows Rivera Garza's reflections on disappropriation and necrowriting to engage in the literary representation of the dead. The book is formally a poetry collection, although its origins are in a communal act of writing. Its original publication in Mexico in 2012 was the result of theatre director Sandra Muñoz's invitation to Uribe to write a play on Antigone dealing with the rising violence in their state of Tamaulipas and with reference to a famous kidnapping case (Villeda 2017). The project came into fruition after the gruesome discovery of the bodies of 72 Central American migrants in San Fernando, a case that obtained unusual visibility among the brutality of killing in Mexico. I will not speak of the content of the book and the political work it performs in mourning the victims and in thinking through its poetic form, as Tamara Williams (2017) has written an exceptional study on this matter. For my purposes, *Antígona González* is notable because it shows the intersection between the anti-world literary labour I have laid out so far and various issues related to world-literature theory. The undecidability of the text in terms of genre is telling. *Antígona González* is a poetry book that is also a gathering of disappropriated voices and a text that is meant to be performed. Thus, it inscribes in itself various forms of the communal. The book's 'I' is not authorial. In some cases, it is the director of the play: 'I am Sandra Muñoz. I live in Tampico, Tamaulipas and I want to know where the missing bodies are. For all those lost to appear' (Uribe 2016, 9). In other cases, it is the character Antígona González seeking the body of her brother Tadeo. And, in other instances, it is an unfolding of Sara Uribe, who is one with other voices in the communal concern for the work of justice: 'I am Sandra Muñoz, but I am also Sara Uribe and we want to name the voices behind the stories that take place here' (2016, 167). The general structure of *Antígona González* is that of a literary un-work, a textual site with many subjects and none, and with a slippery, always deferred, formal structure.

Roberto Cruz Arzabal reads *Antígona González* by connecting the work to its particular place of enacting mourning, focusing on what he calls the 'interface' of the book: 'we can think *Antígona González*'s grieving poetics as a deferral between writing and materiality; its production conditions as the mediation of a specter that is none other than the violence triggered by the necropolicies that support the reproduction of capitalism' (2018, 248–9). This, Cruz Arzabal asserts, makes the book's 'engagement with grief focused more on memory than on ghosts; what persists isn't what occupies space, but rather the attempt to reconstruct it' (2018, 249). The central issue is that *Antígona González* never seeks to be an alternative as such or to tell any kind of redemptive story. Rather, as Cruz Arzabal explains, the disappeared 'acquire a floating form between the book's materiality (the act of reading, the performance) and its deferral. Only this way can the grieving and the missing become part of a new community, the community of grief – which only exists as an event in order to disappear once again' (2018, 249–50). In these terms, it is possible to claim that *Antígona González* resists the kind of labour that world literature theorists of different stripes assign to the literary work of the periphery: it does not perform allegory, national or otherwise, nor does it deploy a tensional realism connected to the politics of the nation-state. It is precisely in what Cruz Arzabal calls the 'deferral', or what we can call with Nancy the 'interruption' of the work itself, that the politics of the work are rendered visible. *Antígona González* does not engage in world-making, but rather takes over the rubbles and ruins of a community subject to violence – in the form of texts of others, of different voices, of the different cadavers that the many Antigones of contemporary Mexico reclaim – to reflect in its performance the impossibility of a world, the community of the world-less (victims and mourners) for whom utopian restitution or any horizon of justice is always-already impossible.

A reader could be tempted to locate in the book's disappropriation of the Antigone character a world-literary device that connects the violence of contemporary Mexico into the networks of what Wai Chee Dimock (2009) calls 'deep time', a set of relations across temporal moments that break the borders of the nation-state. Yet, this reading would miss the point of Uribe's invocation. Uribe cites Rómulo Pianacci's encyclopedic *Antígona: Una tragedia latinoamericana*, which recounts the extensive appearance of the Greek tragic character in the theatre of most Latin American countries (Uribe 2016, 177–81; Pianacci 2015). Uribe's disappropriation of Antigone traverses both the Latin American cultural history that has invoked her to engage the memories of the disappeared in dictatorships and other events, and the theoretical interventions of figures such as Judith Butler, Giorgio Agamben, and Joan Copjec around the Antigone myth. In these terms, *Antígona González* is not a relation of Mexico to the Western canon as such, but rather to a political history of writing on Antigone that exceeds the time and space of the nation-state, aligning itself with an anti-worldly tradition: the reflection of the justice that never was, the restitution that never happened, the never-told stories that are buried alongside the bodies of the victims. This is the sense of Uribe's necrowriting. Rivera Garza cites Uribe as part of a canon that asks questions about the ethics and possibilities of memory and mourning (2013, 121–2). More importantly the reflection is part of what Rivera Garza calls 'documentary fiction' in contradiction to 'historical fiction'. Documentary fiction understands the limits of the archive, in Rivera Garza's telling, and it

> does not rescue voices but unveils (and produces by unveiling) authors. Better said, authorships. That is perhaps the reason why documentary fiction is incapable to confirm our present. In a tight relationship with both the form and the content of the document, making the document and its context the very source of the questioning that produces them in the present, documentary fiction disrupts.
>
> *(Rivera Garza 2013, 114–15)*

Facing the (in)existence of other stories, the impossibility of reading the archive against the grain, as there is not even an archive sometimes, writings like *Antígona González* exist in the impossibility of world-making.

One of the fundamental senses in which the unthinkability of utopia permeates Mexican anti-world literature is in the way in which some works begin to grapple with the gaps and voids connected both to the country's relationship to the world as global, and to the writer's relationship to the world as *mundo*. A prime example of this is the recent work of Julián Herbert, whose work in poetry and narrative challenges the possibility of deploying the archive for the purposes of world-making. The first instance of this work is the poetry collection *Álbum iscariote*

(Herbert 2013). Each of the core sections of the book is a reflection on the impossibility of creating meaning from materials borrowed from the present and past. Some of these materials are Mexican and include covertly-taken photos of a decaying cultural centre intervened by ironic captions (to enact the collapse of state-centred culture in Mexico [Herbert 2013, 33–51]), and fragments of the Boturini Codex, a Pre-Columbian text that only remains in fragments, and that Herbert interprets by writing free associations to the text's images (79–150). Herbert's poetic devices do not cite Rivera Garza's conceptual work, but, as some critics have noted (particularly Íñiguez Rodríguez 2017), the book's work with the idea of death, the disappropriation of texts, and the creation of communal readings is fully readable as a form of necrowriting. It is also very conscious in its visibilisation of the materiality and the insufficiency of writing, using devices like crossing-outs and obliterations that refuse to hide in correction the insecurities of the text (Ballester and Higashi 2017). Herbert's work in this regard questions the ability to create discursive and literary continuities between past and present, the possibility of deploying archives to allegorise the Mexican imagined community.

Herbert's work goes into world-cultural archives too, and in these cases we can see him disputing the procedures of cosmopolitanism and world literature. In the poem regarding the Boturini Codex, a piece of Nahua graphic writing from the sixteenth century, Herbert writes an intermission ('*intermedio*' in the sense used in old cinema screenings) where he replaces the images of the Codex with a series of anonymous photos he purchased in a flea market in Berlin's Mauerpark. This unexpected venture into a worldly context in the middle of an engagement with a foundational national text is sparked, in the poem, by the poetic voice's sudden awareness of the necropolitical: 'I suddenly lost my inspiration / The problem is that The Here is very quickly exhausted / the *Here they kill people*' (Herbert 2013, 130, my translation). The idea that he is writing from a site (from a 'here') where a murder takes place links him, almost like a Proustian flashback, to Nazi Germany: 'For example: / in the Flohmarkt of Mauerpark they killed people / (I want to think they did so with the clean shot of a rifle)' (130, my translation). Yet, the archive that is presented to us is not a direct archive of the German murders, but rather random images from old photographs purchased at the site of killing. We see, for instance, two verses reflecting on the idea of history ('History always happens many times. / First, as chaos' [132, my translation]) followed an undated photo of a military garrison that may or may not be from the 1940s. Another verse/caption follows: 'The following ones, as karaoke' (133, my translation). In the following two pages, we are confronted with an album of four photographs showing Germans, likely in the immediate postwar era although no date is provided, living their everyday life: children building a sand castle, a group of young women in what appears to be dance classes, a group of young girls at a picnic in a park or forest, and an older woman standing in a field next to a fence. The only text in the two pages reads: 'Human fragments almost always smile out of focus' (135, my translation). The poem immediately connects back to Mexico: 'Especially if you call them by their name: / "Today they dropped / 49 corpses / in Cadereyta

Jiménez, / Nuevo León'" (136, my translation). After reflecting further on human fragments and photographs, the poem concludes: 'In the Flohmarkt of Mauerpark / I bought two cheap trinkets: / a shirt and a jacket from the German Army / The uniform of a sniper' (137, my translation).

Herbert's poem is a manifestation of anti-world literature at one of its moments of highest radicality. It constructs a chain of trauma and cultural texts by enacting in every single step the impossibility of using stories for any kind of redemptive purposes, and the inability of performing literary world-making with the precarious materials at hand. It is a set of interruptions, in the sense discussed above, that chain of moments of unworlding: the impossibility of connecting the past with the present that informs Herbert's work with the Boturini Codex is interrupted by the consciousness of necropolitical killing, which is in turn once again interrupted by another archive (the flea market photos) that are nothing but human fragments, until another killing (the 49 corpses in Cadereyta) interrupts the narrative. History does not have the unifying dialectical sense that Marx invests in his famous sentence 'first as tragedy, then as farce'. Herbert remixes this common expression to indicate that meaning was never there to begin with (first as chaos) and that any attempt at revisiting the history does not deliver the comedic reinterpretation of farce, but rather just karaoke, a vapid, extrapolated, ephemeral performance. Like Sara Uribe, Herbert deploys a consciousness of the materiality of his sources, but fully reflects on their pure ephemerality. The people who appear in the 'intermission' are merely fragments, documental remnants of lives that are no longer tellable and that the literary voice does not seek to tell, signalling the futility of imagination as world-making. It is the same procedure as the one used by Guatemalan writer Rodrigo Rey Rosa in his novel *El material humano* (Rey Rosa 2009), where the lives indexed in the cards of the National Police Archives have fragments of their actions and signs of their identity but no underlying story. Herbert's human fragments, like Rey Rosa's human archives, can only be materialised in necrowriting because there is no possible writing about them. The persistence of the past is something that exists solely in ruins, in fragments, and in objects like the German army jacket that reminds us of the violent persistence of the past and the necropolitical nature of the present, but which do not, cannot, constitute a literary world.

As poetry, *Álbum Iscariote* is an exploration of the linguistic and material connotations of necropolitics and provides a good theoretical approximation to the workings of anti-world literature. Yet, the full power of Herbert's aesthetics vis-á-vis the question of the world is deployed in his nonfictional work *La casa del dolor ajeno* (*The House of Someone Else's Pain*, Herbert 2015). The book is a hybrid essay-memoir-narrative in which Herbert explores a silenced event in Mexican history: the massacre of around 300 Chinese people in the city of Torreón, half of the Cantonese colony at the time, from 13 to 15 May 1911. The killing was done by the Maderista revolutionary troops (although many locals attribute it in their memory to the Villistas). Herbert's exploration brings to the fore a series of reflections on Mexican modernity: the project of turning Torreón at the time into a vanguard industrial city (which is the reason why Chinese migrants and capital were present), the role of Sinophobia in the formation of Mexico's nationalist ideas of race and *mestizaje*, and the open and consistent acts of erasure of this past (for instance, the house of Walter Lim, one of the most prominent members of the Chinese community and a victim of the massacre, is now the local Museum of the Mexican Revolution). The formal innovation of the book has been discussed in different terms. In a study I wrote on the book, I argued that one could read its use of potential history, memory, and form in relation to the consciousness of failed modernity in Mexico (Sánchez Prado 2017). From a different perspective, Nieves Marín Cobos (2017) argues that Herbert displaces the idea of writing a 'historical novel' through devices of autofiction, hybridity, and metafiction, thus refusing to establish a historical truth. Although Marín Cobos and I differ on the technicalities of Herbert's work with form, the core idea of breaking with historicist accounts of the Revolution and the ethics of thinking through ways of engaging the past beyond neoliberal historicity are shared. It is relevant here that, just as *Antígona González*'s writing was triggered by the finding of the 72 corpses in San Fernando, Herbert attributes the final impulse of the book to the forced disappearance of 43 students in Ayotzinapa, Guerrero in 2014, another case that galvanised attention to Mexican necropolitical logics. Rather than telling the story of the Chinese victims or creating a restitutive literary world, Herbert works here with processes of interruption similar to the ones present in *Álbum Iscariote*, including moving back and forth between the memory of the 303 Chinese victims and the 43 Ayotzinapa students, the mnemonic performance of the spaces where violence takes place, the open engagement with an archive of fragments (which in this case includes significant academic historical work on the Chinese experience in Mexico), and even some *Gonzo* interludes in taxi cabs during his research. By making visible the historical trauma of present and past that informs the writing, the materiality of the research down to the transportation from one place to the next and the uncertainties and gaps in his information, Herbert does not write an alternative story or a literary world that fills the historical void with allegorical meaning, but rather brings to the necropolitical present the spectre of another necropolitical modernisation, in the cusp between the Porfirian and the Revolutionary eras.

In the context of the present argument, there is an additional point to be considered in *La casa del dolor ajeno*. In her brilliant reading of the work, Laura Torres-Rodríguez (2018) notes that the Chinese theme is related to significant structures of Mexican capitalism. Torres-Rodríguez argues that 'Orientalism is a liberal phenomenology' and, as such, what Herbert enacts is the way in which Orientalism can be countered through the study of 'the history of migration and the experience of different diasporic groups in the Americas; the conceptualisation of war; and the construction of external and internal borders' (2018, 23). Indeed, Torres-Rodríguez continues, the book takes our understanding of Orientalism beyond Said's work, which generally has significant blind spots in reading East Asian diasporas in the Americas, to render visible 'its connection to forms of accumulation and the organisation of labor in nonimperial contexts' (23). The fact that Herbert is building a history of the necropolitics of capitalism in relation to unthinkable stories from the Pacific migration circuit confronts a concrete form of contemporary neoliberal world-making developing at the same time as the Trans-Pacific Partnership. Following Torres-Rodríguez's insights, one can see that *La casa del dolor ajeno* openly refuses to present an alternative utopian history of the Chinese community in Mexico, or to imagine a literary world in which the richness of individual lives of the victims allows us to think history otherwise. Rather, the book tells us a story that is always-already necropolitical and from which there is no alternative. Necrowriting, in this case, is a device through which the stories of those killed, and the literary platforms that bring them into the present, seek to undermine the politics and epistemics of the idea of the world as such.

Works cited

Apter, Emily. 2013. *Against World Literature: On the Politics of Untranslatability*. London: Verso.

Ballester, Ignacio, and Alejandro Higashi. 2017. 'Tachaduras y borraduras en la poesía mexicana contemporánea (Albarrán, Herbert, Alcantar)'. *Signos Literarios* 25: 8–43.

Bourdieu, Pierre. 1996. *The Rules of Art: Genesis and Structure of the Literary Field*. Trans. Susan Emanuel. Stanford, CT: Stanford University Press.

Brouillette, Sarah. 2014. *Literature and the Creative Economy*. Stanford, CT: Stanford University Press.

Brouillette, Sarah. 2016. 'World Literature and Market Dynamics' in S. Helgesson and P. Vermeulen, eds, *Institutions of World Literature. Writing, Translation, Markets*. 93–106. London: Routledge.

Casanova, Pascale. 2004. *The World Republic of Letters*. Trans. Malcolm DeBevoise. Cambridge: Harvard University Press.

Cavarero, Adriana. 2011. *Horrorism: Naming Contemporary Violence*. New York: Columbia University Press.

Chávez Castañeda, Ricardo, *et al.* 2016. *Manifiesto del Crack (1996). Postmanifiesto del Crack (1996–2006)*. Miami, FL: La Pereza.

Cheah, Pheng. 2016. *What is World? On Postcolonial Literature as World Literature*. Durham, NC: Duke University Press.

Cruz Arzabal, Roberto. 2018. 'Writing and the Body: Interfaces of Violence in Neoliberal Mexico' in Ignacio M. Sánchez Prado, ed. *Mexican Literature in Theory*. 243–259. London: Bloomsbury.

Damrosch, David. 2003. *What is World Literature?* Princeton, NJ: Princeton University Press.

Díaz, Floriberto. 2007. *Escrito. Comunalidad, energía viva del pensamiento mixe. Ayuujktsënää'yën – ayuujkwënmää'ny – ayuujk mëk'äjtën*. Comps. Sofia Robles Hernández and Rafael Cardoso Jiménez. Mexico City: Universidad Nacional Autónoma de México.

Dimock, Wai Chee. 2009. *Through Other Continents: American Literature Across Deep Time*. Princeton, NJ: Princeton University Press.

Emmelhainz, Irmgard. 2016. *La tiranía del sentido común. La reconversion neoliberal de México*. Mexico City: Paradiso Editores.

Fisk, Gloria. 2018. *Orhan Pamuk and the Good of World Literature*. New York: Columbia University Press.

Ganguly, Debjani. 2016. *This Thing Called the World: The Contemporary Novel as Global Form*. Durham, NC: Duke University Press.

Gras, Dunia, and Gesine Müller. 2015. *América Latina y la literatura mundial: Mercado editorial, redes globales y la invención de un continente*. Madrid: Iberoamericana Vervuert.

Han, Byung-Chul. 2017a. *Saving Beauty*. Trans. Daniel Steuer. Medford, MA: Polity.

Han, Byung-Chul. 2017b. *The Scent of Time: A Philosophical Essay on the Art of Lingering*. Trans. Daniel Steuer. Medford, MA: Polity.

Harvey, David. 2005. *A Brief History of Neoliberalism*. Oxford, UK: Oxford University Press.

Hayot, Eric. 2012. *On Literary Worlds*. Oxford, UK: Oxford University Press.

Herbert, Julián. 2013. *Álbum Iscariote*. Mexico City: Ediciones Era.

Herbert, Julián. 2015. *La casa del dolor ajeno*. Mexico: Literatura Random House.

Hoyos, Héctor. 2015. *Beyond Bolaño: The Global Latin American Novel*. New York: Columbia University Press.

Huggan, Graham. 2006. *The Postcolonial Exotic. Marketing the Margins*. London: Routledge.

Íñiguez Rodríguez, Edgardo. 2017. 'Poesía, muerte y tejido social: Necroescrituras en *Álbum Iscariote* de Julián Herbert'. *Mitologías hoy* 15: 21–34.

Jameson, Fredric. 1986. 'Third-World Literature in the Era of Multinational Capitalism'. *Social Text* 15: 65–88.

Lukács, György. 1971. *Theory of the Novel*. Trans. Anna Bostock. Cambridge, MA: MIT Press.

Marín Cobos, Nieves. 2017. 'La autoficción como contrapunto a la "novela histórica" de los vencedores. Hibridismo y metaficción en *La casa del dolor ajeno* (2015) de Julián Herbert'. *Impossibilia* 14: 74–92.

Mbembe, Achille. (2013) 'Necropolitics' in Timothy Campbell and Adam Sitze, eds, *Biopolitics. A Reader*. 161–192. Durhamm NC: Duke University Press.

Moretti, Franco. 2013. *Distant Reading*. London: Verso.

Mufti, Aamir. 2016. *Forget English! Orientalisms and World Literatures*. Cambridge, MA: Harvard University Press.

Müller, Gesine, Jorge J. Locane and Benjamin Loy. 2018. *Re-Mapping World Literature: Writing, Book Markets and Epistemologies between Latin America and the Global South*. Berlin: De Gruyter.

Nancy, Jean-Luc. 1991. *The Inoperative Community*. Ed. Peter Connor. Minneapolis, MN: University of Minnesota Press.

Nancy, Jean-Luc. 2007. *The Creation of the World or Globalization*. Trans. Francois Raffoul and David Pettigrew. Albany, NY: State University of New York Press.

Palumbo-Liu, David. 2012. *The Deliverance of Others. Reading Literature in a Global Age*. Durham, NC: Duke University Press.

Pianacci, Rómulo E. 2015. *Antígona. Una tragedia latinoamericana*. Buenos Aires: Losada.

Place, Vanessa, and Robert Fitterman. 2009. *Notes on Conceptualisms*. New York: Ugly Duckling Presse.

Rey Rosa, Rodrigo. 2009. *El material humano*. Barcelona, Spain: Anagrama.

Rivera Garza, Cristina. 2013. *Los muertos indóciles. Necroescrituras y desapropiación*. Mexico City: Tusquets Editores.

Rosenberg, Fernando. 2016. *After Human Rights: Literature, Visual Arts, and Film in Latin America, 1990–2010*. Pittsburgh, PA: University of Pittsburgh Press.

Said, Edward W. 1983. *The World, the Text and the Critic*. Cambridge, MA: Harvard University Press.

Sánchez Prado, Ignacio M., ed. 2006. *América Latina en la 'literatura mundial'*. Pittsburgh, PA: Instituto Internacional de Literatura Iberoamericana.

Sánchez Prado, Ignacio M. 2017. '*La casa del dolor ajeno* de Julián Herbert. No-ficción, memoria e historicidad en el México contemporáneo'. *MLN* 132(2): 426–440.

Sánchez Prado, Ignacio M. 2018a. *Strategic Occidentalism: On Mexican Fiction, the Neoliberal Book Market and the Question of World Literature*. Evanston, IL: Northwestern University Press.

Sánchez Prado, Ignacio M., ed. 2018b. *Mexican Literature in Theory*. London: Bloomsbury.

Siskind, Mariano. 2014. *Cosmopolitan Desires: Global Modernity and World Literature in Latin America*. Evanston, IL: Northwestern University Press.

Tabarovsky, Damián. 2004. *Literatura de izquierda*. Rosario, Argentina: Beatriz Viterbo Editora.

Torres-Rodríguez, Laura. 2018. 'Into the "Oriental" Zone: Edward Said and Mexican Literature' in Ignacio M. Sánchez Prado, ed, *Mexican Literature in Theory*. 11–31. London: Bloomsbury.

Uribe, Sara. 2016. *Antígona González*. Trans. John Pluecker. Los Angeles, CA: Les Figues.

Valencia, Sayak. 2018. *Gore Capitalism*. Trans. John Pluecker. Los Angeles, CA: Semiotext(e).

Villeda, Karen. 2017. '¿Me ayudas a levantar el cadáver? Diálogo con Sara Uribe'. *Nexos en Línea*, February 16. Available at: https://cultura.nexos.com.mx/?p=12147. (Accessed 15 April 2018).

Volodine, Antoine. 2015. *Post-Exoticism in Ten Lessons: Lesson Eleven*. Trans. J. T. Mahany. Rochester, NY: Open Letter.

Volpi, Jorge. 2002. *In Search of Klingsor*. Trans. Kristina Cordero. New York: Scribner.

Volpi, Jorge. 2008. *El jardín devastado*. Mexico: Alfaguara.

Volpi, Jorge. 2018. *Una novela criminal*. Mexico: Alfaguara.

Whitener, Brian. 2018. 'The Politics of Infrastructure in Contemporary Mexican Writing' in Ignacio M. Sánchez Prado, ed, *Mexican Literature in Theory*. 261–278. London: Bloomsbury.

Williams, Tamara. 2017. 'Wounded Nation, Voided State: Sara Uribe's Antígona González'. *Romance Notes* 57(1): 3–14.

WReC. 2015. *Combined and Uneven Development: Towards a New Theory of World-Literature*. Warwick Research Collective. Liverpool, UK: Liverpool University Press.

Zavala, Oswaldo. 2015. *La modernidad insufrible: Roberto Bolaño en los límites de la literatura latinoamericana contemporánea*. Chapel Hill, NC: North Carolina Studies in the Romance Languages and Literatures.

9

'DREAMS OF REVOLT', THE 'REVOLT OF NATURE'

World literature and the ecology of revolution

Sharae Deckard

In an article provocatively entitled 'Why Postcolonialism Hates Revolutions', Tabish Khair once criticised the poststructuralist strand of postcolonial studies' disavowal of 'all claims of universality', warning that such an emphasis 'makes impossible [...] the possibility of change in any revolutionary (and, hence, democratically collective) sense' (Khair 1999, 7). This chapter comes from two motivations: firstly, to investigate the capacity of contemporary world literature to represent revolution, both historical and imagined, as explicit subject and content; and secondly, to explore the ecology of revolution. I begin by imagining a world-literary criticism that seeks to take account of the revolutionary political potential of literature to challenge our global present. My critical framework combines world-systems and world-ecology approaches to world literature as the literature of the capitalist world-system, while drawing on the Warwick Research Collective's conceptualisation of this world-literature as mediating and figuring combined and uneven development (WReC 2015). However, world-systems approaches can tend towards a critique of domination that emphasises the top-down effects of inter-state competition, and thus it is urgent that world-literary critics read not only for critique of the totality of capitalism, but also the ways in which texts imagine and represent the making-of-history-from-below.

What is the capacity of world literature not only to mediate world-systemic asymmetries and register dissent towards capitalism – but also to literally represent revolution and imagine future insurgent possibilities? How can the periodic recurrence of certain cultural forms, genres, or aesthetics at different points in the systemic cycles of capitalist accumulation be read not only in relation to the cyclical *crises* of capitalism, but in relation to the world-culture of 'world-revolutions', defined by world-systems theorist Christopher Chase-Dunn as those 'clusters of social movements and rebellions that break out in different regions of the system during the same time periods' (Chase-Dunn 2017, 738). These questions redirect focus both to the anticolonial liberation struggles that have been central to the materialist strand of postcolonial studies – and which might risk being obscured in the 'world-literary turn' – and to the ongoing attempts of critically-conscious world literatures to represent class struggle and anti-capitalist resistance in the postcolonial era. Asking questions like these also helps us to see how literary aesthetics and form might themselves invoke periodic clusters of resistance, imagining revolution in terms not of exceptional rupture but of continuity and return across transhistorical contexts.

In Michael Löwy's classic book *The Politics of Combined and Uneven Development*, he emphasises the significance of the theory of uneven and combined development as inextricable from Leon Trotsky's idea of 'permanent revolution', arguing that the social ruptures that result when advanced and archaic elements collide or fuse create new political possibilities for the oppressed to change the world, particularly in those semi-peripheral situations where sociocultural innovation plays a significant role in both representing and constituting new forms of political, anti-capitalist consciousness (Löwy 1981). The significance of the semi-periphery, therefore, is not only as a zone of hierarchal subordination and exploitation where value is extracted and transmitted to the core, but also in terms of its dialectical potential to function counter-hegemonically as an incubator of political resistance, a space from which new forms of solidarity and international consciousness can be transmitted and circulated across semi-peripheral situations. World-literary criticism, if it takes the capitalist world-system as the political horizon of world-culture, must also seek to discover how world-literature imagines new forms of internationalist consciousness or post-capitalist futurity, and whether new imaginaries tend to arise with particular salience in semi-peripheral and postcolonial situations.

As an example of this critical praxis, this chapter will compare four texts by Amitav Ghosh, Lindsey Collen, and Merle Collins that employ symbolic imaginaries of the typhoon, the cyclone, and the hurricane to represent moments of collective transformation and revolution. These contemporary texts wrestle with the problem of historicity in a neoliberal present seemingly emptied of political alternatives to late capitalism, in which the representation and imagination of revolution carries a peculiar urgency. Written in the late twentieth and early twenty-first centuries, in a period when literature with explicit political intent has become unfashionable, often dismissed as didactic and less aesthetically accomplished, they are unabashed in their commitment to both the recuperation of past legacies of liberation movements and the attempt to imagine future contexts of insurgency. In all four, storm events function as both plot and metaphor, mediating and emplotting revolution on the level of form and content.

Figuring revolution

Storms appear as a plot device throughout Amitav Ghosh's fiction. At the climax of *The Hungry Tide*, a cyclone batters the Sundarbans, resulting in the epiphanic transformation of the social conscience of its bourgeois protagonist Piya (whose preservation from the storm is problematically attained through the literal sacrifice of a lower-caste character, Fokir). At the same time, the cyclone serves to materialise the incremental violence of climate change and the intensified exposure of precarious human and non-human inhabitants of the Asian mega-delta to the perils of uneven disasters. At the conclusion of *Sea of Poppies*, the first historical novel in Ghosh's Ibis trilogy of the Opium wars, a typhoon in the Indian Ocean enables the success of a shipboard mutiny of indentured Indian labourers – 'coolies' from the province of Bihar who once worked on the opium plantations and are now bound for the sugar plantations of Mauritius. *River of Smoke*, the second novel in the trilogy, returns to the typhoon in its opening, describing the storm as a pivotal moment that transforms the agency of all involved in it, focalising its narration this time through the perspective of Deeti, the wife of one of the mutineers, later to become a runaway. Deeti mythologises the typhoon, creating a story which she narrates aloud to her descendants and enshrines in her 'Memory-Temple', high in the Mauritian hills:

> It was as if the tufaan had chosen her to be its confidant, freezing the passage of time, and lending her the vision of its own eye; for the duration of that moment, she had been able to see everything that fell within that whirling circle of wind. [...] [I]n the same way that a parent leads a child's gaze towards something of interest, the storm had tipped back her chin to show her a craft that was trapped within its windy skirts [...]. In the brief interval before the passing of the storm's eye and the return of the winds, it was as if another tempest had seized hold of the Ibis, with dozens of feet pounding across the deck, running agram-bagram, this way and that.
>
> *(Ghosh 2011, 16)*

For Deeti, the eye of the typhoon seems to provide not only the external conditions for the escape of the mutineers but a prophetic vision that later becomes the symbolic basis of her family's multi-generational resistance to the sugar plantation.

In Lindsey Collen's *There is a Tide* (1990), the cyclone functions as a literal event that impacts the entirety of the social stratum in Mauritius, a plot element that enables the novel to construct a unified view of the social totality. It is perceived differently according to the different socio-economic conditions of those it impacts, whether the caneworkers who are drowned in the storm after they set fire to a local sugar plantation in protest against the lack of secure employment or fair wages and flee out to sea in their pirogue, or the woman who gives birth during the cyclone even as her shanty is blown down around her. But the cyclone also serves as a symbolic motif for the novel's insurrectionary history of anti-capitalist resistance, which moves from the anticolonial movements of the independence struggle, through the industrial actions and general strikes of 1937, 1943, 1971, 1975, and 1979, while at the same time envisaging other kinds of dissent: the arson of the caneworkers against the neocolonial plantation, the slow work tactics and mass fainting of women workers in sweatshop clothing factories, to the hunger strike of an adolescent girl who refuses food in protest against patriarchal gender norms, to the dancing of a mother in protest against police brutality as she shouts 'Revolution!'. These varied forms of dissent, both collective and individualised, intertwine concrete historical contexts of institutionalised left organisation, with more personalised, spontaneous acts of resistance, thus collating a genealogy of the 'deep anger of generations ... interspersed with moments of open, proud rebellion' (Collen 1990: 190).

This punctuated history of clusters of periodic revolt is conjoined with the imagination of a post-capitalist future ushered in by a world-revolution, after an international socialist revolution, called CREATE, in the year 2031. In a trick of temporal *legerdemain*, the text's science-fictional frame narrative, set in 2050, presents the novel as a ready-made, found object constituted from three testimonial narratives from twentieth-century Mauritians assembled into one text by the fictional editor Koko Bi Panchoo, and assigned on school curriculum in the post-CREATE society because of 'its image of a cyclone', of a capitalist society 'trapped in mindlessness':

> People at the time thought that all the effects of cyclone were more or less inevitable. Some thought it the work of the hand of a bad-tempered god. Others thought it the work of an indifferent nature. It didn't strike anyone that people's reality defines the effects of a cyclone. But Koko Bi Panchoo's characters, however, questioned the cyclone and its meaning. Right in the middle of the cyclone, the author on one single occasion expresses his opinion. He helps us to understand the particular blindness, immorality and callousness of the Second Dark Ages, and to remind us that we, too, could revert to barbarism if we are not careful. There, as it were, but for the grace of CREATE and IKLI, go I.
>
> *(Collen 1990, 10–11)*

The novel's mixing of genres is an experiment in the invention of what Fredric Jameson calls 'totalizing retrospect' (2013, 311): the attempt to invent a science-fictional far future that will make history of the bad present, casting it as the 'Second Dark Age' and thus revitalising the capacity of the reader, even in the face of multiple defeats of moments of class and gender insurgency in the neoliberal present of the novel's composition, to imagine a post-capitalist, post-patriarchal future after world-revolution finally transforms the capitalist world-system. At the same time, the novel rejects both determinist and fatalistic views of nature – the 'inevitable' effects of the cyclone, the work of a 'bad-tempered god' – in favour of an experiential understanding of environmental history, in which the socio-ecological conditions shaping the 'people's reality' define both the cyclone's material effects and its symbolic meaning.

In *Mutiny* (2001), Collen again uses a cyclone as plot device, which coincides with an island-wide general strike and facilitates a mutiny of women prisoners forced to engage in unpaid labour in prison sweatshops assembling electronic components for American transnational corporations, after an electricity blackout enables them to break open their doors. The megacyclone's name emphasises the degree to which it combines destructive power with a prophetic temporality that disrupts the seemingly unmoveable real: 'The two cyclones have united into a single megacyclone. [...] They name it *Doorgandra*. The giver and taker, Doorgawatee, has united with the teller of the future, Cassandra' (Collen 2001, 326). Juna, one of the leaders of the mutiny, imagines the storm as providing a material basis for the very capacity to imagine revolt, as she describes the wardens' fear in the face of the cyclone:

> It's not the *storm* of the cyclone that makes them lose confidence, like the storm makes officers in charge of a cargo of slaves fear the elements as a leveller [...] It's the storm that has got *into us* today, galley slaves all. It's the fear of mutiny. [...] What if we break our chains and shout.
>
> *(Collen 2001, 325)*

At the novel's conclusion, when the prisoners break free to dance in the streets, Collen returns to the image of the spinning cyclone in conjunction with a planetary consciousness of the Earth:

> What is the point of a mutiny in *just this one neck of the woods, Jay?* In our prison, our country, our region? Would they not snuff us out like a candle? In the wind?
>
> A small island, our earth is. So green and blue and turquoise you could cry. I've seen it through the eyes of a satellite so often.
>
> Could it be everywhere? Our mutiny, Jay?
>
> Round and round? Could we call it a revolution then? Turning around?
>
> *(Collen 2001, 275).*

Unlike in her earlier novel, where the 'useless' gyres of the cyclone signalled the paralysis of thwarted social transformation, here it puns on the literal meaning of revolution, as a turning around of seemingly intransigent conditions, and a circling out from the localised instant moment of spontaneous mutiny to global consciousness of the necessity for world-revolution.

My final example, Merle Collins's '*Tout Moun ka Pléwé* (Everybody Bawling)' (2007), a poetic essay which she calls 'a true piece of fiction', narrates a popular history of insurgency through a catalogue of the hurricanes that have struck Grenada:

> Now, since Hurricane Ivan swoop down and *dékatché* (destroy) Grenada in September 2004, I'm thinking that Grenada's history for the half century from 1955 to 2005 might be titled, *From Janet to Ivan: Tout Moun ka Pléwé*, and this, of course, could also be the title of a calypso, the sung history of the land.
>
> *(Collins 2007, 1)*

The essay moves between reflection on the agency of external metereological forces and between metaphorisation of the idea of 'hurricane drama' as the social experience of revolution. Hurricane Janet is first described in terms of how it exposes class differences in land ownership on the island through its differentiated impact and briefly forges collective solidarity, and then used as a metaphor for the ferment of independence struggles expanding across the Caribbean:

> So much was happening in Grenada in the 1950s that it not surprising Janet decide to come and punctuate the story. Everything around was like hurricane touching it. [...] And while Janet doing she do, people getting used to the idea of other hurricane hurrying come over the Atlantic. And hurricane forming right inside Grenada self, hurricane coming back from other Caribbean country too, from Aruba, from Trinidad, from America, from England.
>
> *(Collins 2007, 4–5)*

This is suggestive of the ways in which, with their movements across space, hurricanes can symbolise and engender global political consciousness. Later in Collins's essay, the 1979 socialist revolution of the New Jewel Movement, led by Maurice Bishop against Gairy's government, is described as 'Other hurricane happening', a hurricane of the people (11). But euphoria of the storm gives way to lament at the failure of the revolution, riven by internal power struggles that culminated in the murder of Bishop, before it was crushed by the U.S. invasion, Operation Urgent Fury, in 1983:

> A calm will have to come right here, before we talk about serious storm. My heart can't take it – even now, all these years later, after revolution rise up and, under pressure, revolution fall down. In 1804, Haiti get cut off. [...] Haiti rehearse it for us and still we never know it. Is like with all we word *international*, we think is a country that exist of itself. Is One Caribbean, take it or leave it.
>
> *(Collins 2007, 11–12)*

In the previous passage, the hurricane signified a regional political collectivity extended across the archipelago during the independence struggle: 'hurricane coming back from other Caribbean country too, from Aruba, from Trinidad, from America, from England' (5). This form of politicised archipelagic consciousness is opposed to the kind of 'advanced weather consciousness' promoted by media weather channels that Andrew Ross criticises as driven by ideologies of mapping, discipline, and biopolitical control of both humans and storm-systems, which seek to contain and rationalise the complexity of nature (Ross 1991, 244).

Yet, even as she celebrates this consciousness, Collins links the failure of the Grenadan revolution both to the internal failures of power struggles within a vanguardist party-led revolution, and to the failure to forge an international collectivity across the Caribbean capable of contesting US imperialism and transnational capital. Collins returns throughout her work to the idea of the Haitian Revolution as prefiguring both the successes and failures of socialist struggles. In an interview, she responds to a question about why she continues to represent the 'failed revolution' (64) by invoking her student's description of the Haitian Revolution as an 'infinite rehearsal':

> All of the things that have happened in Haiti have happened in one way or the other in various Caribbean countries. The kind of treachery among leaders, the killings, the repression of the population ... the invasion, everything. So it's like an infinite rehearsal. I think of that little country Grenada—all of those lessons ever learned there—I think those have been huge lessons for a lot of people worldwide.
>
> *(quoted in Bishop and McLean 2005, 65, ellipsis in original)*

I would argue that this concept of rehearsal is not a fatalistic idea of tragic repetition, which assumes that history is doomed to a perpetual cycle of defeat, even if it is laden with what Collins calls the 'trauma' of the revolution's betrayal and the subsequent invasion (Bishop and McLean 2005, 65), but rather an imperative to detect the lessons within past failures in order to 'rehearse' different outcomes in the future, in anticipation of some final performance. Collins's essay *Tout Moun ka Plèwé* concludes by reiterating that new storms will come, using the hurricane as a metaphor for social possibilities yet undetected and dangers to be forestalled: 'What about other hurricanes around us, working and not always showing their intention?' (Collins 2007, 16).

This idea of recurrence appears throughout the storm-texts I have compared, expressing the 'marvellous correspondence' between moments of social transformation in discontinuous but symmetrical stages of history (Mazzotta 1999, 206). The spiral form of the tempest figures a revolutionary time that is not linear, but rather recurrent and periodic. All three authors confront and negotiate the limits of historical moments of revolution in the era of neoliberal capitalism (and in the case of Collins and Collen these are explicitly socialist revolutions) from the vantage point of socio-economic peripheries (in particular, plantation isles, where the ravages of capitalism are particularly salient) while attempting to recuperate the revolutionary praxes and forms of organisation forged during earlier conjunctures of peripheral insurrection. As such, they interrogate the limits of literature to reconfigure the imagination of the future through the excavation of past analogous moments, seeking to discover how social transformations were historically structured, and to evaluate both their successes and fault-lines. As Collins writes, '[s]ometimes the present jump out of the future and drive you back to the past for explanation' (2007, 9). This is world-literature as anamnesis or 'recollective fantasia', a poetic re-ordering of the past in order to make History − as political transformation and social emancipation − reappear as future possibility (Price 1999, 69).

These writers' explicit invocation of revolution as historical content is accompanied by a preoccupation with the temporality of revolution, as cycle and return, *corsi e ricorsi*, as periodicity rather than linear progress, crystallised in the symbolic imaginaries of the cyclone around which their aesthetics revolve. This recalls Timothy Brennan's description in *Borrowed Light* of 'history as Vico narrates it – that is, as punctuated, spiral, cyclical, accretive' (Brennan 2014, 4) and his advocacy of a 'historical logic predicated on continuity rather than rupture' (3), that approaches the history of left political organisation not in terms of breaks and perpetual crisis, but rather in order to tease out antecedents, returns, and homologies.

In *There is a Tide,* Collen uses the cyclone's revolutions to signify the millennial sense of historicity forestalled in the neoliberal present, in a moment when anti-capitalist struggles seem like 'a cyclone turning round and round uselessly' (Collen 1990, 243). Yet the cyclone also deploys the trope of turning in the sense of a cycle, of spiral periodicity, the return of the moment of historical opportunity when social conditions are ripe and revolution becomes possible again. Fatma calls this 'the moment of the sea' which 'comes of its own accord', encouraging her discouraged listener (243):

> Girl, when the pass in the reef is blocked … you don't panic. Keep your cool. Keep your eyes open. […] Patience, girl. Vigilance. That's the art. And then recognition. The moment of the sea is coming. Here comes the wave. See it approach, much higher than the others. […] And like a transporting force from inside the bowels of the earth, the wave, the very right wave, takes you over the coral reef ashore. A new beginning. […] With all the old experience in the boat.
>
> *(Collen 1990, 243–4)*

Rather than overemphasise the fleeting instance of spontaneity, the novel underscores the necessity of organisation over the long durée, of building left institutions and acquiring 'old experience', practicing the art of 'vigilance' and 'recognition' in order to seize the opportune time to act. The betrayal of the earlier general strike is experienced as a trauma, but Fatma and the other characters believe in the return of revolution, not its exceptionality:

> The wound of the defeat, and the memory of the love, is so strong, we cannot bear to remember the joy, the hope, the reality. […] But even if we do not speak easily about it, we all know, all who have ever been in such a revolution that it will come back, it will. But not on the cheap.
>
> *(Collen 1990, 210)*

In all four texts, tempests are used to invoke the sensoriums of revolutionary time, but are embedded in historicising narratives that attempt to move beyond accounts of revolution either as spontaneous rupture and messianic event, or as linear end, disaster, and failure, to a collectivised recollection of the continuity of struggle and the waxing and waning of the political energies, institutions, and environmental conditions that make insurrection possible.

Ecology and revolution

This leads to the second motivation of this chapter: to explore the ecology of revolution. Humans are powerful environment-making species, but they are also environments that are made and unmade by the activities of extra-human life and biospheric processes: from epidemics to climates, to bacterial microbiomes, to meteorological and geological forces. I am interested in the question of how to conceive the activity of extra-human nature in relation to human political agency in the making of more emancipatory environments, or what Jason W. Moore calls the *co-production* of nature in the web of life, attempting to move away from a dualist conception of humans *acting on* external nature towards a dialectical conception of humans acting *together with* the rest of nature. According to Moore, capitalism as a world-ecology emerged through the invention of 'Cheap Labor', which was dependent on the simultaneous invention of 'Cheap Nature', 'deploying the capacities of capital, empire, and science to appropriate the unpaid work/energy of global natures within reach of capitalist power' in order to render commodified labour-power less expensive (Moore 2016, 89). Moore's formulation of work/energy draws on the view of energy as the capacity to do work laid out in Richard White's *The Organic Machine*, which examines the historical remaking of the Columbia River in order to 'put the river to work':

> Work, in turn, is the product of a force acting on a body and the distance the body is moved in the direction of that force. Push a large rock and you are expending energy and doing work; the amount of each depends on how large the rock and how far you push it. The weight and flow of water produce the energy that allows rivers to do the work of moving rock and soil: the greater the volume of water in the river and the steeper the gradient of its bed, the greater its potential energy.
>
> *(White 1995, 6)*

Nature, for White, can be known through its labour, through the energy it absorbs and emits, through the way it rearranges the world (1995, 3). The formulation of 'nature's work/energy', whether geophysical or organic, is central to Moore's understanding of capitalism as a set of relations through which the '"capacity to do work" – by human and extra-human natures is transformed into value, understood as socially necessary labor-time' (Moore 2016, 89). The *appropriation* of extra-human nature's unpaid 'work' via noneconomic means outside the cash nexus, as in the work of rivers, plant photosynthesis, soil nutrients, or animal labour, is integral to the economic *exploitation* of human natures and commodified labour within the cash nexus because accumulation is dependent on the unpaid plunder of ecological surpluses.

The capitalist regime of 'Cheap Nature' denies nature's agency, conceiving of nature as a static, passive input, even as it simultaneously appropriates nature's energy and activity. This perpetual draining of the life and energy of ecosystems means that the capitalist logic of accumulation is also a logic of extinction, culminating in the contemporary era of ecological crisis which Justin McBrien calls 'the Necrocene':

> Capital was born from extinction, and from capital, extinction has flowed. Capital does not just rob the soil and worker, as Marx observes, it necrotizes the entire planet. Capital is the Sixth Extinction personified: it feasts on the dead, and in doing so, devours all life. The deep time of past cataclysm becomes the deep time of future catastrophe; the residue of life in hydrocarbons becomes the residue of capital in petrochemical plastics. Capitalism leaves in its wake the disappearance of species, languages, cultures, and peoples. [...] Extinction lies at the heart of capitalist accumulation.
>
> *(McBrien 2016, 116)*

But what then might be the agency of extra-human nature in environmental and social justice? What is the role of ecology in revolutionary thought, or what Murray Bookchin calls 'the ecology of freedom'? Is it possible to have a multi-species politics of liberation that refuses the logic of extinction and promotes instead an ecology of diversity alongside human/social individuation, which is ecological and post-capitalist but is neither anti-humanist nor post-humanist?

I think here of the problem raised by Donna Haraway's recent essay on the debate over Anthropocene vs. Capitalocene nomenclature, which is stirring in its advocacy of a multi-species ontology and its rejection of gendered versions of reproductive futurity, yet unfortunately concludes with a slogan that exhorts her readers to 'Make Kin Not Babies!' (Haraway 2015, 161). This slogan invokes the spectres of Malthusianism and anti-humanism, which attribute the problems of climate change and ecological crisis not to the systemic dynamics of capitalist exploitation and appropriation, but rather to unhistoricised conceptions of demography. The Anthropos, not the social, historical system of capitalism, which devalues human life as much as non-human nature, is posed as the main culprit, and an ethics of relation to other species, without any conception of the necessity for political struggle against material conditions, is posited as the solution. Increasingly dominant in many contemporary strains of ecological thought, including the subfield of postcolonial ecocriticism, is a post-humanist turn that poses anthropocentrism as the original ontological sin. This post-humanist turn is accompanied both by a paradoxically essentialist conception of the Anthropocene that dehistoricises the transhistorical shaping of environments, and by varieties of object-oriented ontology and new materialism that privilege the agency of objects and non-human natures while seeking to deconstruct the human subject.

If post-structuralist strains of postcolonial studies often seemed more scandalised by what Robert Spencer wittily dubs 'crimes against hybridity' (2017, 122) than by material conditions of exploitation and dehumanization, then post-humanist strains of ecological thought similarly seem more exercised by crimes of anthropocentrism, and devoted to overcoming binary conceptions of humans vs. nature. Yet, as Crystal Bartolovich reminds us, '[g]iven the flexibility of capitalism, its global logic is not in any respect undermined by descriptions that declare the divide between the binaries it materially enforces to be null. Only changing the conditions would accomplish that' (2015, 225). Furthermore, the revaluation of nature or the fore-grounding of natural agency does not require a corresponding *devaluation* of humanity. To the contrary, a revolutionary or reconstructive ecology would cele-brate ecological diversity and 'expand the environment' by 'enlarging the ecologi-cal situation as a whole', both for the human species and the species with which we are in co-relation (Bookchin 1999, 20). It would not deny humanity, but rather, as Bookchin put it, more fully 'humanize humanity' by enabling humans 'to fully realize their potentialities as members of the human community and the natural world' (24).

As Timothy Brennan notes in his stirring defence of the 'dissident humanism' invoked by anticolonial and socialist humanists:

> Whatever its intentions, post-humanism − to the humanist at least − gives alie-nation a philosophical and scientific respectability: to disembody human skill and intelligence, to de-realise human will and effort, to unthink the human. This is, importantly, not a sober observation but a desire. The human subject alienated from its powers of cognition, divorced from its body, descaled from its species, and deprived of its will, is the form of its sublime. It is a massive willed and historically determined effort to be done with will and history.
>
> *(Brennan 2017, 12)*

Such post-humanist strains of thought strip away or deny the importance of humans as political agents at the very moment when collective political action to end climate change and transform the capitalist production of nature is most urgent. Instead of green misanthropy, or a history of objects and external forces that denies the human, what would it mean to overturn the law of capitalist value by *revaluing* both human and extra-human natures, advocating a politics of liberation that is genuinely life-making, in which the necessity of human struggle and organization to the creation of a more emancipatory humanity-in-nature is foregrounded?

In a brilliant reading of postcolonial nature through the prism of Adorno's con-cept of the preponderant object, Bartolovich asks whether there is 'a role for the non-human in the struggles among "ideological forms" that Marx famously described as the sites "in which men become conscious of [...] conflict and fight it out" and whether the "non-human" can be more or other than merely a tool of, or means for, the human' (Bartolovich 2015, 226). She argues that the 'pre-ponderant' objects of the non-human world − rather than those mystified anthro-morphised commodities that Marx mocks as seeming to 'speak' − are 'formidably expressive' in their 'intransigence', that what non-human nature says, 'again and again, is "No!"' (227). This non-human negation 'carries with it the promise of an other or beyond to capitalism, the yet unknown realm of freedom, which cannot be produced in thought but only in active struggle with (rather than against) the material conditions that say "no" to capitalism' (227).

The literary texts I have discussed teem with commodities – the cash crops of plantation monoculture and imperial export, from opium in Ghosh, sugar in Collen, and cacao, nutmeg, and banana in Collins, to the commodities produced in export-processing zones in the clothing and electronics sweatshops of the Global South, as in the prison workshops of *Mutiny*. Yet, they also abound with representations of characters challenging the environments that have been organised around Cheap Labour and Cheap Nature, and of the resistance of extra-human nature to forms of capitalist organization and containment, as well as moments of profound demystification when commodities are rematerialised. A particularly striking episode occurs in *River of Smoke*, when the same typhoon that enables the Ibis mutiny smashes open the hold of another opium-carrier ship, the *Anahita*, en route to China, catapulting containers of opium into the bulkheads like cannonballs, and hurtling 'gobs of raw gum' like shrapnel (Ghosh 2011, 27). In an extended passage of grotesque realism, opium is transformed from a rationalised commodity of exchange back into a material slime, a dung-like sludge of vegetal mess and poppy 'trash', that coats the bodies of the ship captain and mate:

> Vico was covered in mud-brown sludge, from the crown of his jet-black hair to the toe of his boots. [...] His shirt, waistcoat and breeches were so thickly encrusted with opium that they seemed to have faded into his skin. By contrast his large, prominent eyes seemed almost maniacally bright against the matt darkness of his dripping face.
>
> *(Ghosh 2011, 30)*

As the storm rolls the ship, Bahram accidentally ingests the melted opium and is overcome by 'sudden nausea and weakness', beset by hallucinations, so that 'he had no thought for the losses he had suffered' (31). In the traders' bodies and affects, the material effects of the opium trade and of addiction are physiologically reincarnated in a forcible return of the repressed, and the value relation collapses: 'Each ball was worth a sizeable sum of silver – but neither Bahram nor Vico now had any regard for their value' (30). Opium in this passage 'speaks', not as commodity fetish, but as intransigent biophysical nature refusing value relations; together, the storm and the opium sludge refuse capitalism's radical simplification of nature and materialise extra-human externalities beyond human agency and instrumentalization.

This potential for demystification offers a repudiation of what Jacques Rancière memorably criticises as the tendency of the contemporary 'Marxism of the denunciation of the mythologies of the commodity' to overemphasise or fetishise the power of the spectacle, except here with a further emphasis on the activity of extra-human nature:

> Forty years ago, it was supposed to unmask the machineries of domination, in order to provide the anti-capitalist fighters with new weapons. It has turned to exactly the contrary: a form of nihilist knowledge of the reign of the

commodity and the spectacle, of the equivalence of anything with anything and of anything with its image.

(Rancière 2007, 3)

Crucially, in Ghosh's novel, the opium episode is directly preceded by the chapter describing Deeti's memory of the Ibis mutiny: the ideological demystification of the commodity and rematerialization of non-human nature are conjoined with the evocation of political collectivity and human agency as having real, practical, and transhistorical effects beyond the realm of discourse or ideology.

What is striking in all the uses of literary tempests that I have cited is not only how they are mobilised to depict the non-human world in terms of the negation of capitalist logic, but their emphasis on the material agency of biophysical nature in relation to human political agency. In Ghosh's tale of 'deliverance from the Ibis', the typhoon is described in classical terms as akin to the myth of watchful geese in Ancient Rome, as 'an instance when Fate had conspired with Nature' (Ghosh 2011, 13), but also in more immediate terms as a direct agent: 'then, in the same way that a parent leads a child's gaze towards something of interest, the storm had tipped back [Deeti's] chin' to observe the mutineers fleeing on a longboat (16). In Collins's essay, meteorological and geological forces, from hurricanes to volcanos, are described as authors: 'Nature is a prize-winning writer' (Collins 2007, 5); Janet 'decides' to 'punctuate and put in figure of speech to the story that developing in Grenada' (5), that of the independence struggle; the Atlantic ocean 'always have something to say in we story' (5). As Shalini Puri observes, in Collins's writing, 'the relationship between hurricane and political event' cannot be reduced to 'mere mirroring or mechanical correspondence' since '[n]ature and politics echo, amplify, compete with, or pass by one another in a series of delicate negotiations and translations. [...] The hurricane in Collins' work thus functions as a historical agent, a check on human agency, as well as lens, idiom and rhythm for understanding political events' (Puri 2014, 210). Collins's most dialectical conception of the co-production of socio-ecological relations occurs when she writes '[s]o thing changing, and naturally nature is part of the changing. How people going change and land stay the same?' (Collins 2007, 5). In this rhetorical chiasmus, non-human nature is imagined as an agent of social transformation, which helps make the very conception of revolt possible, while social transformation, in the form of the anticolonial movement, is also a transformation of the land itself. Nature inscribes human history; human history inscribes nature: the visions of justice and revolution which these texts offer through storm-events emphasise the active struggle of humans together with – rather than against – the material conditions of extra-human nature. The authorial figuration of nature is particularly interesting because it invokes the notion of a nature that can speak 'yes' to revolt, not merely offer its mutely eloquent 'no' as materialization of the limits to capital. The storms' activity must be conjoined with emancipatory human agency.

Guadeloupean theorist Daniel Maximin makes this point about the environmental history of resistance to slavery and colonialism in plantation isles, arguing that cataclysmic events such as hurricanes, earthquakes, and volcanos helped to engender in the oppressed a 'dream of revolt' through the ways in which 'the revolts of nature' destroy the physical structures of plantation and colonialism, from homes, to boats, to cities and ports (Maximin 2006, 93). He asserts that Caribbean geography and geology 'allied' with slaves and maroons, helping them to imagine the possibility of liberty, and literally enabling them to fight, to escape, and to achieve subsistence in maroon communities by rooting themselves in the ecologies around them and imitating a nature that says 'no' to the imperialist fantasy of total domination (91). Andreas Malm articulates a similar argument about what he calls 'maroon ecology' and 'partisan nature', those spaces of 'relative wilderness' which have offered refuge and freedom for subaltern practices and politics in direct contestation of capitalist oppression and slavery (Malm 2017). Outside of the Caribbean, Ghosh's *River of Smoke* evokes such a maroon ecology in the context of the Indian Ocean when it describes the *marron* communities who had inhabited the mountainous region of the Morne Brabant, where Deeti's Memory-Temple is located, whose 'inaccessibility had made it an attractive place of refuge for escaped slaves' and whose 'memory still saturated the landscape' so that 'when the wind was heard to howl upon the mountain, the sound was said to be the keening of the dead' (Ghosh 2011, 10).

Partisan nature should not be conceived as advocating a romantic view of wilderness, or solely proffering the imagination of nature's dissent as a refusal of capitalist appropriation, but rather as encompassing the extent to which the political content of social experience both shapes and is shaped by the material environment, and the way in which biophysical forces in conjunction with human struggle can reconfigure the horizon of what Rancière would call 'the perceptible':

> 'Politics [...] consists in transforming this space of "moving-along" into a space for the appearance of a subject: i.e., the people, the workers, the citizens: It consists in refiguring the space, of what there is to do there, what is to be seen or named therein. It is the established litigation of the perceptible.
>
> *(Rancière 2001, 11)*

Significantly, all the storm-texts I have compared repeatedly employ figures of tempests as prophecy and social anagnorisis that enable the constitution of dissenting political subjects: 'Janet made a lot of things possible', writes Collins (2007, 3). In *Mutiny*, the megacyclone changes the conditions of the possible, splintering the paralysed present to reveal the immanent seeds of transformation: 'What had seemed certain, isn't. It is in grave doubt instead. What had seemed unchangeable is changeable. It actually changes before our eyes. The previously immutable itself emits its own hints of change and seems to threaten to burst with impending transformations from within as from without' (Collen 2001, 323). In *River of Smoke,* Deeti heralds cyclonic winds as 'the power of change, of transformation' (Ghosh 2011, 18), while Neel, one of the mutineers, imagines the eye of the storm as a 'gigantic oculus, at the far end of a great, spinning telescope, examining everything it passed over, upending some things, and leaving others unscathed; looking for new possibilities, creating fresh beginnings, rewriting destinies and throwing together people who would never have met' (19). All of these literary imaginings of the conditions under which political possibility can be renewed are rooted in an ecological consciousness whose poetics foreground the inter-dependence of socio-ecological relations and the work/energy of nature's activity, insist on the rooting of social revolution in material nature, and revalue both human and extra-human nature as more than commodity, free gift, or cheap labour. Crucially, this shift in the conception of value does not remain solely at the level of ethics or ontology, but is explicitly linked in every text to organizational politics – to the active struggle of humans – emphasising the agency of extra-human nature not on its own or as a dualist opposite to human domination, but rather in the attempt to unleash new horizons of human emancipation.

Climate disaster and future storms

I have used the figure of the storm in this essay as an entry into the problem of figuring the ecology of revolution and the agency of humanity-in-nature because of its prevalence across so many world-literary texts, particularly those from the Caribbean and the Indian Ocean, whose environmental history is so indelibly punctuated by the rhythms of hurricane and cyclone. Yet, it is impossible to con-clude without a caveat about the future sustainability of storm-metaphorics to conjure utopian visions of revolution in an age of global climate change when (un) natural disasters are gaining in force and frequency. Collins's essay ends with a prescient question: 'How come hurricane didn't know where we was before, and hurricane know so good now?' (Collins 2007, 16). Hurricane Ivan seemed excep-tional because Grenada, along with Barbados, Trinidad and Tobago, is among the islands usually outside the hurricane belt and thus protected from the landfall of the worst storms. However, climate volatility is leading to an intensification of hurri-canes and other natural disasters across the globe. Indeed, the hurricane season of 2017 was unprecedented in the number of catastrophic storms, with Hurricanes Harvey, Irma, and Maria wreaking destruction across the Caribbean and the con-tinental United States, in many cases devastating regions previously protected or outside the hurricane belt.

Addressing the United Nations in the wake of Irma and Maria, the Prime Minister of Dominica Roosevelt Skerrit described the accelerated temporality of the storms as almost incomprehensible, when previous generations had never seen more than one Category 5 hurricane in their lifetime, and had now experienced two in two weeks, rendering the island nearly uninhabitable. Lamenting the basic injustice of climate change, in which the nations least culpable for carbon pollution were the most impacted by climate violence, he argued '[h]eat is the fuel that takes ordinary storms and super-charges them into a devastating force' (Skerrit cited in Grenoble 2017). Global warming is experienced unevenly not only because the southern hemisphere and tropics are warming faster than other regions of the world, but because of the conditions of uneven development and socio-economic inequality which render human populations and ecosystems in peripheries of the world-system more vulnerable to destruction in the wake of climate disasters. As Ashley Dawson warns, '[t]he inequalities of global capitalism are no longer simply characterized by uneven and combined development. As we inhabit an epoch of increasingly perilous climate chaos, global capitalism is characterized by uneven and combined disaster' (2017, n.p.). Nowhere has uneven disaster been so starkly visible than in the contrast between the disaster relief funds and emergency infrastructure provided to Houston by the US state after Hurricane Harvey and the abandonment of Puerto Rico after Hurricane Maria, using the Jones Act restrictions to prioritise debt obligations over human life, and blaming the islanders for the poverty and infrastructural underdevelopment caused by the neoliberal policies of the Puerto Rico Oversight, Management, and Economic Stability Act (PROMESA).

Even within Texas, the terror of climate violence was experienced unevenly, as Haitian novelist Edwidge Danticat recalls: 'For many undocumented Texans [Harvey] was not just a natural disaster but an immigration nightmare—many feared that they would be turned away from shelters, or even taken into custody' (Danticat 2017, n.p.). The age of climate violence heralds an age of mass migration of environmental refugees, dispossessed by catastrophic events, drought, floods, and rising sea levels, and subjected to increasingly racist and repressive state policies. As Christian Parenti warns, many countries have

> A surplus of repressive capacity, yet almost nothing in the way of disaster-oriented civil defense. [...] The rising waters of climate change threaten to erode not only beaches but also civil liberties. Mass migration and a racist backlash to it are already hallmarks of the early climate crisis. [...] Thus, as drought, neoliberalism, and militarism produce crises, warfare, and waves of refugees in the Global South, in the North they produce a reactive, opportunistic, authoritarian state hardening.
>
> *(Parenti 2017, n.p.)*

As the temporality and severity of climate disasters accelerates beyond the recognizable 'hurricane-time' of the past, when Category 5 hurricanes that experienced individually would take decades to recover from arrive in chains, new representational pressures will be placed on storm-metaphorics. The literary instrumentalization of storm-events with political intent could either be rendered less resonant, or reconfigured to reflect new imaginaries of climate justice in resistance to accelerating climate violence and the continued unravelling of the web of life in the age of the Capitalocene. Yet, without in any way seeking to downplay the real suffering unleashed by (un)natural disasters, I would still argue that the literary mediations I have explored in this chapter offer a powerful insight into not only the capability of world-literature to imagine revolution, but the ecology of revolution. Not only capitalism as world-system, but capitalism as world-ecology, demands transformation. To move beyond capitalism's production of Cheap Nature and uneven disasters, it is necessary to envision a form of emancipatory co-production that attempts to end both exploitation of humans and appropriation and devaluation of non-human natures, and that envisages transformation as the process through which human political struggle, together with the material activity and work/energy of the non-human world, seeks to promote the variety of life in all its forms.

Works cited

Bartolovich, Crystal. 2015. 'Postcolonial Nature? Or, "If Oil Could Speak, What Would it Say?', in Anna Bernard, Ziad Elmarsafy, and Stuart Murray, eds, *What Postcolonial Theory Doesn't Say*. 222–238. London: Routledge.

Bishop, Jacqueline and Dolace Nicole McLean. 2005. 'Working out Grenada: An Interview with Merle Collins'. *Calabash: A Journal of Caribbean Arts and Letters* 3(2): 53–65.

Bookchin, Murray. 1999. *The Murray Bookchin Reader*. Ed. Janet Biehl. London: Black Rose Books.

Bookchin, Murray. 2005. *The Ecology of Freedom: The Emergence and Dissolution of Hierarchy*. Oakland, CA: AK Press.

Brennan, Timothy. 2014. *Borrowed Light: Vico, Hegel and the Colonies*. Stanford, CA: Stanford University Press.

Brennan, Timothy. 2017. 'Introduction: Humanism's Other Story' in David Alderson and Robert Spencer, eds, *For Humanism: Explorations in Theory and Politics*. 1–16. London: Pluto Press.

Chase-Dunn, Christopher. 2017. 'Social Science and World Revolutions'. *Journal of World-Systems Research* 23(2): 733–752.

Collen, Lindsey. 1990. *There Is a Tide*. Port Louis, Mauritius: Lediskasyon pu Travayer.

Collen, Lindsey. 2001. *Mutiny*. London: Bloomsbury.

Collins, Merle 2007. '*Tout Moun ka Pléwé* (Everybody Bawling)'. *small axe* 22: 1–16.

Danticat, Edwidge. 2017. 'Daca, Hurricane Irma, and Young Americans' Dreams Deferred'. *The New Yorker* 6 September. Available at: https://www.newyorker.com/culture/cultural-comment/daca-hurricane-irma-and-young-americans-dreams-deferred (Accessed 7 March 2018).

Dawson, Ashley. 2017. 'The Global Calculus of Climate Disaster'. *Boston Review: A Political and Literary Forum* 6 September. Available at: https://bostonreview.net/science-nature/ashley-dawson-global-calculus-climate-disaster (Accessed 7 March 2018).

Ghosh, Amitav. 2004. *The Hungry Tide*. London: HarperCollins.

Ghosh, Amitav. 2008. *Sea of Poppies*. London: John Murray.

Ghosh, Amitav. 2011. *River of Smoke*. New York: Picador.

Grenoble, Ryan. 2017. 'His Country Destroyed by Hurricanes, Dominica PM Implores Climate Change Action'. *HuffPost* 25 September. Available at: https://www.huffingtonpost.com/entry/dominica-hurricane-climate-change-roosevelt-skerrit_us_59c916f0e4b01cc57ff3f094 (Accessed 7 March 2018).

Haraway, Donna. 2015. 'Anthropocene, Capitalocene, Plantationocene, Chthulucene: Making Kin'. *Environmental Humanities* 6: 159–165.

Jameson, Fredric. 2013. *The Antinomies of Realism*. London: Verso.

Khair, Tabish. 1999. 'Why Postcolonialism Hates Revolutions'. *Wasafiri* 15(30): 5–8.

Löwy, Michael. 1981. *The Politics of Combined and Uneven Development: The Theory of Permanent Revolution*. Chicago, IL: Haymarket Books.

Malm, Andreas. 2017. 'In Wildness is the Liberation of the World: On Maroon Ecology and Partisan Nature'. Isaac and Tamara Deutscher Prize Lecture, Historical Materialism London, SOAS University of London.

Maximin, Daniel. 2006. *Les fruits du cyclone: Une géopoétique de la Caraibe*. Paris: Éditions du Seuil.

Mazzotta, Giuseppe. 1999. *The New Map of the World: The Poetic Philosophy of Giambattista Vico*. Princeton, NJ: Princeton University Press.

McBrien, Justin. 2016. 'Accumulating Extinction: Planetary Catastrophism in the Necrocene' in Jason W. Moore, ed, *Anthropocene or Capitalocene? Nature, History and the Crisis of Capitalism*. 137–166. Oakland, CA: PM Press.

Moore, Jason W. 2016. 'The Rise of Cheap Nature' in Jason W. Moore, ed, *Anthropocene or Capitalocene? Nature, History and the Crisis of Capitalism*. 78–114. Oakland, CA: PM Press.

Parenti, Christian. 2017. 'If We Fail'. *Jacobin* 29 August. Available at: https://www.jacobinmag.com/2017/08/if-we-fail (Accessed 7 March 2018).

Price, David W. 1999. *History Made, History Imagined: Contemporary Literature, Poiesis, and the Past*. Urbana and Chicago, IL: University of Illinois Press.

Puri, Shalini. 2014. *The Grenada Revolution in the Caribbean Present: Operation Urgent Memory*. New York: Palgrave Macmillan.

Rancière, Jacques. 2001. 'Ten Theses on Politics'. *Theory & Event* 5(3): 1–19.

Rancière, Jacques. 2007. 'Misadventures of Universality'. Address at the Second Moscow Biennale of Contemporary Art. 1–9. Available at: http://2nd.moscowbiennale.ru/en/rancier_report_en/ (Accessed 28 February 2018).

Ross, Andrew. 1991. *Strange Weather: Culture, Science, and Technology in the Age of Limit*. London: Verso.

Spencer, Robert. 2017. 'Postcolonialism is a Humanism' in David Alderson and Robert Spencer, eds, *For Humanism: Explorations in Theory and Politics*. 120–162. London: Pluto Press.

White, Richard. 1995. *The Organic Machine: The Remaking of the Columbia River*. New York: Hill & Wang.

WReC. 2015. *Combined and Uneven Development: Towards a New Theory of World-Literature*. Warwick Research Collective. Liverpool, UK: Liverpool University Press.

10

NEGATIVE ENCHANTMENT

Mads Rosendahl Thomsen

The characteristically modern condition expressed by Max Weber's concept of 'disenchantment' – the lack of coherence or meaning in modern Western society – has become a staple of describing the spirit of the times in modernity. It has not gone uncontested, however. As Joshua Landy and Michael Saler (2009) suggest in their volume *The Re-Enchantment of the World: Secular Magic in a Rational Age*, contemporary culture seeks to fill a god-shaped void in various ways – predominantly as a positive exploration or presentation of alternative perspectives on being. In this chapter, I explore the engagement of literary works with traumatic events as a strategy for presenting forces that go beyond what can be explained by historical and political analysis. A sense of coherence stemming from trauma – what we might term 'negative enchantment' – is characteristic of a number of literary works that circulate broadly. I will also suggest that negative enchantment is important – crucial, in fact – for the international reception of certain works. International recognition has given these writers a political voice that is integral to their writings about traumatic episodes of recent history. After developing the basis of my thesis, I will turn to three contemporary examples of literature that connect trauma with enchantment: Roberto Bolaño's *2666*, Ben Okri's *Starbook*, and Mo Yan's *Shifu, You'll Do Anything for a Laugh*.

Disenchantment, re-enchantment

The disenchantment of the world is one of the central descriptions of the transformation of the nineteenth- and twentieth-century world view. It has given enchantment a bad name as being delusional, superstitious, naive. Weber's highly influential work still stands as a grand narrative of the modern world that humans inhabit and therefore, for some at least, provokes suspicion against the modernist tendency towards totality. The literary critic Georg Lukács supported this interpretation in his influential *Théorie des Romans*, in which he convincingly showed how the great novels of the nineteenth and early twentieth century are dominated by the individual's inability to come to terms with the world, and how the failed attempts to reclaim totality resulted in a negative romanticism that, while it produced great and moving works of literature, seemed a dead end in the project of gaining a new vision of the world. The hope for a new totality is disappointed again and again, although Lukács does not consider it impossible to achieve, somehow. He ends his work, written during the First World War, with some vague remarks on Dostoevsky, claiming that his works, by their capacity to become the *epos* of a new era, have transcended the novel:

> This world is the sphere of pure soul-reality in which man exists as man, neither as a social being nor as an isolated unique, pure and therefore abstract interiority. If ever this world should come into being as something natural and simply experienced, as the only true reality, a new complete totality could be built out of all its substances and relationships. It would be a world to which our divided reality would be a mere backdrop, a world which would have outstripped our dual world of social reality by as much as we have outstripped the world of nature. But art can never be the agent of such a transformation: the great epic is a form bound to the historical moment, and any attempt to depict the utopian as existent can only end in destroying the form, not in creating reality.
>
> *(Lukács 1971, 152)*

Later, Lukács would turn to Marxist philosophy and politics and renounce his earlier work in favour of what was (and to some still is) a man-made re-enchantment of the world, through a political vision that would bring an end to political struggles between the classes. But enchantment did not go away. In the age of postmodernism, interest in the sublime and in fictional worlds paved the way for a new interest in enchantment, and one that did not come laden with metaphysical requirements.

Enchantment comes in many forms, as Landy and Saler (2009) point out in their introduction to *The Re-Enchantment of the World*. They criticise two traditional ways of explaining disenchantment, and they add their own, less critical suggestion for understanding the role of disenchantment in the twentieth century: one that leaves room for a more complex understanding of the uses of enchantment (Landy and Saler 2009, 3). The binary approach to enchantment understands it as irrational superstition, something to be disposed of and replaced by rationality and enlightenment. A more complex notion of enchantment is the dialectical approach, which recognises the disenchantment that comes with modernity, but finds modernity itself to be enchanted, albeit in ways that are not fully apparent in the moment. Finally, the antinomial position posits that modernity paradoxically embraces a number of seeming contraries and that the question 'Enchantment or not?' is wrongly put. Landy and Saler go on to argue that it is the binary approach that has been dominant. They make the case for acknowledging an antinomial attitude to enchantment, one that takes into account how contemporary cultures could and should engage with enchantment on a number of levels (with echoes of, at a minimum, W. B. Yeats and Virginia Woolf):

> If the world is to be re-enchanted, it must accordingly be reimbued not only with *mystery* and *wonder* but also with *order*, perhaps even with *purpose*; there must be a hierarchy of *significance* attaching to objects and events encountered; individual lives, and moments within those lives, must be susceptible again to *redemption*; there must be a new intelligible locus for the *infinite*; there must be a way of carving out, within the fully profane world, a set of spaces which somehow possess the allure of the *sacred*, there must be everyday *miracles*, exceptional events which go against (and perhaps even alter) the accepted order of things; and there must be secular *epiphanies*, moments of being in which, for a brief instant, the centre appears to hold, and the promise is held out of a quasi-mystical union with something larger than oneself.
>
> *(Landy and Saler 2009, 2, emphasis in original)*

Landy and Saler's volume presents a number of phenomena that can be related to effects of enchantment – perhaps most importantly, the natural sciences, which in the nineteenth century provided a world view with little room for enchantment and at times displaying the hubris of reducing the universe to a collection of matter that would act mechanically until the end of time.

New understandings of physics emerged that would at once bring about more knowledge as well as showing how fixed categories held the potential for enchantment: time's relation to matter, as demonstrated in Einstein's theory of relativity, and the paradoxical uncertainties disclosed by Niels Bohr and others' work on quantum mechanics, are the two foremost examples of how science has enrolled itself in making ideas of enchantment relevant. It is also worth noting how the prolific evolutionary researcher and advocate Richard Dawkins uses the language of enchantment in the title of two of his books, *The Magic of Reality* and *The Greatest Show on Earth*. In this he follows up on Darwin's emphatic call at the end of *The Origin of Species* to see the grandeur in the complexity of nature evolved from a few principles. Beyond the natural sciences, Landy and Saler's collection of articles argues how fiction, architecture, and sports each in their way partake in creating the effects of enchantment. When the rhetoric of sports stars is so closely related to religious terms or other supernatural elements, it should be taken seriously as the fulfilment of a desire for enchantment rather than as an expression of false consciousness.

Enchantment still plays a significant role in literature. The global success of *Harry Potter*, *The Lord of the Rings*, and of magical realism in its many forms from Günter Grass and Gabriel García Márquez to Salman Rushdie and Haruki Murakami demonstrates that the enchanted is a significant factor in contemporary literary culture, if sometimes frowned upon. Fredric Jameson has expressed his disdain for literature that caters to enchantment:

> The formal result, for the novel, is strange and paradoxical, yet momentous: all successes grow to be alike, they lose their specificity and indeed their interest. Success sinks to the level of emergent mass culture – which is to say, fantasy and wish-fulfilment. Only the failures remain interesting, only the failures offer genuine literary raw material, both in their variety and in the quality of their experience.
>
> *(Jameson 2011, 17)*

Many works will have to be written off as uninteresting if Jameson is right. Yet there are plenty of interesting attempts to engage with enchantment. In her late autobiographical memoir 'A Sketch of the Past', Virginia Woolf writes about her struggles between a rational perspective of the world and her felt experience of it. She cannot comprehend the beauty and coherence of the world without making reference to some creator, mastermind, or artist who is responsible for all of this:

> It is only by putting it into words that I make it whole; this wholeness means that it has lost its power to hurt me; it gives me, perhaps because by doing so I take away the pain, a great delight to put the severed parts together. Perhaps this is the strongest pleasure known to me. It is the rapture I get when in writing I seem to be discovering what belongs to what; making a scene come right; making a character come together. From this I reach what I might call a philosophy; at any rate it is a constant idea of mine; that behind the cotton wool is hidden a pattern; that we – I mean all human beings – are connected with this; that the whole world is a work of art; that we are parts of the work of art.
>
> *(Woolf 2002, 85)*

But Woolf is also convinced that there is no such mind behind it all, least of all god. She goes on to say that this realisation shocked her. Rather, enchantment and the sense of coherence rely on the artist's ability to conjure them. In *The New Human in Literature*, I have argued that the desire to connect with a larger social fabric while retaining the sense of being an autonomous individual is a central element explaining Woolf's formal experiments in the inclusion of multiple voices, often underscored with explicit statements of how a sense of societal coherence is so important to her characters (Thomsen 2013, 96–8). The desire for enchantment and literary form go hand-in-hand in her work, as well as in that of numerous others.

The scandalous perspective: enchantment through the negative

Enchantment is used in literature almost exclusively in a positive way, even if naive; disenchantment is seen as a loss, even if it opens the eyes to a world that can be more as-it-is, less seen through the lens of mythical thought. The loss of absolutes – the loss of truths, of the hope for some higher power or principle – are all related to the narrative of disenchantment of the world. However, there are at least two kinds of negative enchantment that would be potentially problematic and scandalous.

The first, and perhaps most common, of these problematic varieties of enchantment would be to address both traumatic and supernatural events, or other modes of configuring enchantment. This could end up being disrespectful to memory, but it can also add a significant dimension to a work of literature, as with Kurt Vonnegut's use of this approach in *Slaughterhouse-Five*. Vonnegut's novel is a witness account of the bombardment of Dresden in the year 1945, and it could have been written without reference to the aliens of Tralfamadore. But the absurdity and the challenging ontology that these aliens bring to the story certainly adds to the work as a whole, as well as to the reader's understanding of the trauma.

The second rather problematic mode of negative enchantment – which could be more troubling – is to set the enchanting element within the presentation of the traumatic. Trauma too can convey a sense of coherence, of something being the closest we get to absolutes. Trauma creates identity, even if the sense that the negative reveals *principles* of violence, of hatred, of capitalism, is not a pleasing one. But there is no reason why revelations of coherence that come about as positive should not be matched by similarly structured revelations founded on the utmost discomfort.

In *Mapping World Literature*, I suggested that works about collective trauma, often involving mass killings, seem to occupy a special position in world literature. A number of traits could explain that to some degree. The importance of navigating social life in pursuit of love and power becomes secondary to the universally recognisable binary of life and death. The actions behind the Holocaust, the genocide in Rwanda, and other atrocities can be seen as the closest we get to absolute evil in a world without absolutes. Literary works have to navigate the representation of an incomprehensible loss of life while still presenting individuals as individuals, with all the respect that was otherwise taken from them. Such overwhelming loss is beyond comprehension, both to those inside the culture and to those outside it (Thomsen 2008, 110–13).

This insistence on the incomprehensible could of course be countered at certain levels, for example by claiming that such experiences are part of history and can be explained and accounted for, given access to the right sources. But this could be seen as insensitive to the wider cultural impact of such trauma. Our cultures insist on preserving the atrocities as something more than the sum of their parts, an indefinable and unrepresentable object that one must nevertheless work to find representations for. The interesting part, however, is not so much the presence of such a figure of negative enchantment in a literary work, but how it has been put to work. In what follows, I shall make the case for the importance of negative enchantment in the works of Roberto Bolaño, Ben Okri, and Mo Yan.

Bolaño, art, and violence

Robert Bolaño's status as the most prominent South American writer since the boom generation has grown steadily since his untimely death in 2003. Gabriel

García Márquez and Isabel Allende are two writers of an earlier generation with a very different status in literary criticism; both are authors who have attracted a large international readership and who offer a very explicit engagement in their work with magical, enchanting elements. On the surface, Bolaño's works constitute a significant break with these writers. His wry style and the absence of supernatural elements are clear markers of a different paradigm for literature. However, he uses many elements of enchantment that play in a different way to an antinomial conception of enchantment against a background of deeply disturbing themes.

The fascination with violence is evident throughout his work, not least in relation to the Pinochet dictatorship, which Bolaño experienced first-hand in his younger and formative years. What is also striking is the co-presence of violence and art – one of the secular means for getting closer to some kind of experience of enchantment. *Nazi Literature in the Americas* gives this connection away in its very title, and it portrays its aggrandising fictitious writers in a work that owes something to Jorge Luis Borges' idea of making portraits of non-existent authors. The connection between art and power is given a different twist in another early work, *Distant Star*, where fighter planes write poetry on the sky. In the large and complex *The Savage Detectives*, encounters between art and violence are also frequent, although the element of a decisive historical trauma is not central.

His main oeuvre, *2666*, revolves around two traumatic episodes unfolding in different settings of place and time: a wave of femicides in Ciudad Juárez, Mexico, in the 1990s, and the Holocaust in Europe during the Second World War. This huge novel begins seemingly innocently with the story of four European scholars who share a fascination with the mysterious German writer, Archimboldi. A candidate for the Nobel Prize in literature and a productive writer, Archimboldi is unknown to the public, and the four critics are willing to cross continents to uncover his real identity. Early on, the critics themselves commit acts of violence, taking their frustration out on a taxi driver, and from then on violence becomes more and more central in the novel. The depiction of the murders of women, often young and poor internal migrants in Mexico, is written in a language that at times resembles police reports and goes on for hundreds of pages. The final chapter reveals Archimboldi to be Hans Reiter, who was enlisted in the German army during the Second World War, served on the Eastern Front, and witnessed massacres of Jews and many other atrocities.

The juxtaposition of creative expression with violence on a scale so traumatic and unheard of can be interpreted in various ways. One reaction would be to question why Bolaño connects these two domains, rather than writing about these traumatic events without regard to the context of the will to produce art – particularly as, on the artistic side, he is not documenting actual events, whereas the femicides in Mexico and the Holocaust in Europe were real. In the context of memory studies, this is a divisive debate, whereby artistic liberty seems to have prevailed. This is also thanks to numerous works that show how there can be decorum with respect to victims within a context of fictive elements that frame the absurdity and evil behind the traumatic events (cf Schwarz 1999; Thomsen 2008). Another way to respond to

Bolaño's intertwining of art and evil is to see the artwork as a counterbalance to the evil of violence and abuse: even numbing and destructive violence cannot keep humans from finding new ways of expressing themselves and making the world more complex and, at times, beautiful. Still, the close connection between enchanting art and destructive violence is difficult to completely explain or come to terms with, if not as part of a discourse of some form of negative enchantment in which a condition of the fascination of the art is the backdrop to the horrors that humans have been capable of enacting.

On the level of the composition of the novel, Bolaño makes the connection between periphery and centre. The Holocaust, the most significant and defining crime of the twentieth century, is juxtaposed with a crime which, while horrendous, is very different in scale and occupies a much less prominent position in world history. No relation between the events is brought forward, but the connection between the violence of the Second World War and that of the drug cartels is suggested on another level as a sort of principle of how atrocities keep taking place.

Bolaño is not alone in playing with connections between seemingly unconnected events. In *The Brief Wondrous Life of Oscar Wao*, Junot Díaz employs an even more direct (and tongue-in-cheek) suggestion of a connection between central events in the US, such as the murder of John F. Kennedy, and in the Dominican Republic. Unlike Bolaño, though, Díaz suggests that spells – the *fukú* – can be real and can have powers that run through generations. Michel Foucault writes in *The Order of Things* of the 'madman' as someone who sees similarities where there are differences, whereas the poet 'is he who, beneath the named, constantly expected differences, rediscovers the buried kinships between things, their scattered resemblances' (Foucault 1970, 49). In Thomas Pynchon's *Gravity's Rainbow*, the phrase 'everything is connected' (1973, 703) is the quintessential formulation of a desire to find coherence, which again entails the potential for re-enchantment, if on the basis of very sombre themes. The desire for connections is seen as an almost existential need:

> If there is something comforting – religious, if you want – about paranoia, there is still also anti-paranoia, where nothing is connected to anything, a condition not many of us can bear for long.
>
> *(Pynchon 1973, 434)*

Can unlikely connections qualify as enchantment? If, following Northrop Frye, the difference between the romance and the novel is that the romance builds on archetypes whereas the novel uncovers the social realm – that the novel tends to be more realistic and historical – then playing with unlikely connections is certainly an element of romance (Frye 2000 304–5). Bolaño's fascination with unlikely connections goes beyond the violence of the past and the present. While the violence is obvious in *2666*, the importance of markets and capitalism is just as pronounced, in a way that could also be said to produce a sense of negative enchantment.

Bolaño's Santa Teresa is an emblem of how global streams of capital and interests transect a city whose autonomy has vanished at the hands of forces from outside. This is a powerful figure, and it is also important in, for example, Antonio Hardt and Michael Negri's *Empire*, which identifies capitalism as an almost mythical force and whose antidote depends on a vague but enchanted idea of the rise of the multitude (Hardt and Negri 2000, xv, *passim*).

Although ideas presented in a novel should not be taken at face value, it is telling that one of the minor figures in *2666* presents very directly a theory of suffering and coherence:

> And as far as coincidence is concerned, it's never a question of believing in it or not. The whole world is a coincidence. I had a friend who told me I was wrong to think that way. My friend said the world isn't a coincidence for someone travelling by rail, even if the train should cross foreign lands, places the traveller will never see again in his life. And it isn't a coincidence for the person who gets up at six in the morning, exhausted, to go to work; for the person who has no choice but to get up and pile more suffering on the suffering he's already accumulated. Suffering is accumulated, said my friend, that's a fact, and the greater the suffering, the smaller the coincidence.
>
> *(Bolaño 2008, 89–90)*

It is not a criticism of Bolaño that he deploys elements of romance – the hunt for the author, the disclosure of how all things are related – in a novel that is hardly romantic. Obviously his works should be criticised for what they are, with historical events juxtaposed with fictitious ones, and the form and style of the novel working together with the content. But just as interesting is to observe the success of Bolaño's novel and work as a whole, and what that tells us about the desire for connections of a certain kind, even if they are made against the background of some of the bleakest moments in history.

Okri, Africa, and magic

Ben Okri's 2007 *Starbook: A Magical Tale of Love and Regeneration* reads like a 400-page fable, on the one hand about Africa, on the other declaring its belief in universalism. The book contains very few proper names, referring instead to generic terms – the village, artists, princesses. There is no mistake, however, about the imagery, which is emblematic of the tragedy of the continent – the slave trade, which not only led to unimaginable suffering for those who were captured and sold, but also ripped societies apart.

Okri's book builds on the story of Africa as one marked by slavery, conflict, and exploitation. These become the unifying elements of this enormous continent, which in so many other ways cannot and should not be reduced to a single identity. Okri counters the underlying narrative with at least two significant elements. First, there is a persistent interest in creativity. While the violence, both among

Africans and of colonisers and slave traders, is certainly present, it is remarkable how many references there are to artists, to people who create masks and work creatively in order to bring something new into the world. One of the three parts is entitled 'The Master Artists', and the book meanders around the question of what creativity brings about and how it overcomes atrocities. In this way Okri is taking part in the creation of a counter-narrative to the stories of violence and superstition that are central to the most widely read novel from Africa, Chinua Achebe's *Things Fall Apart*, for all the other important qualities of that work.

The other element of the novel that counters the historical narrative of African trauma is the insistence on a particular mode of universalism. At the end of *Starbook* this is expressed not only in spatial terms, claiming that these stories are universal and not particular to Africa, but also in temporal terms, arguing that while there may be ups and downs, good times and bad times, it is all part of the same larger story. The short chapter 19 thus lists all kinds of atrocities, including genocides and world wars, yet insists on the beauty that still exists within the world. In the second-to-last chapter, which runs to only two sentences, this element of negativity and enchantment is evoked even more directly: 'The ways of time are indeed strange; and events not what we think they are. Time and oblivion alchemise all things, even the greatest suffering' (Okri 2007, 421). The last chapter then invokes how creativity will survive:

> All is not lost. Greater times are yet to be born. In the midst of the low tide of things, when all seems bleak, a gentle voice whispers in the air that the spirits of creativity wander the land, awaiting an invocation and the commanding force of masters to harness their powers again to noble tasks and luminous art unimagined.
>
> *(Okri 2007, 421)*

This insistence on universality despite the obvious historical trauma certainly engages in enchantment by shifting the focus away from the specific to the general, and from meaningless suffering to meaningful inclusion in a larger story. Okri is by no means insensitive to the historical events and individual suffering that belie the atrocities that his novel registers, but still his story can be read as a problematic relativising of actual events that instead favours a grand narrative of the universality of human experience. Okri is thus engaging not just in juxtaposing traumatic events with enchanted elements but also in integrating the traumatic events into his gesture of presenting a view of the world that blatantly – the subtitle is, after all, 'A Magical Tale of Love and Regeneration' – argues for seeing the world as enchanted.

Okri's early works, *The Famished Road* and the less well-known *Songs of Enchantment*, also seek to connect adversity with enchantment. Recently in 2017, Okri wrote about a very specific catastrophe when he responded to the Grenfell Tower fire in London with a long, partly rhyming poem which both is moving in its straightforward description of the suffering that took place, and engages with larger issues: 'Make sense of these figures if you will / For the spirit lives where truth cannot kill' (Okri 2017, n.p.). The poem ends with a call for change, as Okri sees Grenfell Tower as a symbol of much more widespread inequalities:

> In this age of austerity
> The poor die for others' prosperity.
> Nurseries and libraries fade from the land.
> A strange time is shaping on the strand.
> A sword of fate hangs over the deafness of power.
> See the tower, and let a new world-changing thought flower.
> *(Okri 2017, n.p.)*

The singular event is connected to the larger principle of the unequal distribution of wealth and opportunity in a world in which life and death are connected with the pursuit of wealth. Greater is the idea of fate and historical change invoked, again, as in *Starbook*, by the act of finding a sense of coherence in a world which confronts us with its darkest side. To cap off the relations between part and whole, as one also finds in Bolaño, Okri connects the specificity of Grenfell Tower with the hope for a universal change.

Okri can be criticised for doing what Fredric Jameson does not like – namely, offering fantasy and wish-fulfilment – but he does so in an interesting way. His particular blend of modes of enchantment rely both on traditional invocations of magic, and on a deep-rooted fascination with memory, culture, and creativity, which can be seen as modern sources of re-enchantment. This means that his work is also an attempt to bridge a gulf between myth-based and secular visions of the world, set against the backdrop of deep traumas.

Mo Yan, societal change, and the individual

When Mo Yan received the Nobel Prize for literature in 2013, he was criticised for not being critical enough of the People's Republic of China. Unlike a number of prolific contemporary Chinese-born writers, he is not a dissident, but a member of the communist party. It is also evident that criticism of Chairman Mao in his work is very subdued. But he takes on some of the traumatic events of recent Chinese history – the Great Leap Forward and the great famine of those years, and the Cultural Revolution when political suppression and terror turned millions of lives upside down for more than a decade. Corruption among officials and the consequences of the new free-market economy are also among the subjects on which Mo Yan draws in his very varied oeuvre, which ranges from works that are predominantly realistic to tales that draw heavily on inexplicable or magical phenomena.

The fable with supernatural elements is central to *Life and Death Are Wearing Me Out*. One of Mo Yan's most ambitious novels – it chronicles modern Chinese history – is told through the protagonist Ximen Nao's successive reincarnations in the form of five different animals before his rebirth as a human being once again.

The inventive allegorical potentials in this device are explored by Mo Yan to produce a sense of absurdity, but also to build a connection with something larger than the history of the past decades. Mo Yan is of course not alone in retelling historical events in a way that is at once irrational and enchanted. This can sometimes be controversial. In *Imagining the Holocaust*, Daniel R. Schwarz defends the allegory and the fable, which can be as effective as testimony, but can also risk being misunderstood or affecting readers so as to seem offensive and insensitive rather than providing a viewpoint that displays absurdity and tragedy (Schwarz 1999, 42).

A striking element of Mo Yan's stories is that the enchantment often highlights the individual and makes him or her stand out. This is particularly clear in the collection of short stories *Shifu, You'll do Anything for a Laugh*. The title novella is a ghost story. Here the uncanny serves as a symbolic wrench in the new capitalist machine, and as confirmation to the little man that there is more to the world than profit. In 'Love Story', set during the Cultural Revolution, the city girl He Liping masters martial arts in a way that leaves the villagers in awe of what she is capable of, yet they denounce her skills, which have no practical use. 'Iron Child' shifts from a very realist account of a child's life in a foster-home while his parents are working on a railroad project during the Great Leap Forward, to a story of two boys who find out that they can eat metal. 'Man and Beast' tells of the lonely survival during the Second World War of the narrator's grandfather, and his relationships with animals and with a Japanese woman who eventually gives birth to a 'furry baby' that owes its looks to an odd connection between man and animal (Mo Yan 2001, 81). 'Soaring' is the tragic story of a wife who thinks she is a bird and actually flies up into a tree before being shot down, justified by the rationale that she is no longer human but a bird. Each of these stories, like *Life and Death Are Wearing Me Out*, emphasises the extraordinary qualities of individuals. In the context of the collectivising projects of the People's Republic, this stands out as a very humane insistence on the possibility of resisting as an individual. Given the criticism Mo Yan has attracted for not distancing himself enough from the Chinese regime, and for his ways of writing with allegorical and magical elements, the question is whether this stance should be seen as a distracting sugar-coating of the traumas or as a strategy that enables him to write even more critically from inside China by means of these devices.

Conclusion

Traumatic events are important to literature. They chronicle the worst sides of humanity, as well as showing how people are ready to struggle, protest, fight, and endure the atrocities visited upon them. More controversially, the international reception and impact of works that deal with trauma can or should be seen in the light of how they can connect to readers in a different way from other works. The universal sense of life and death, the degree of evil injuring defenceless people, the sense of being in an exceptional state where the known is strange even to local people, and the challenge of representing overwhelming loss while respecting the individuality of the victims – all these aspects force writers to take their texts in new directions. They also give international readers something different to hold onto.

Not all texts that are composed on these premises engage with enchantment. The use of enchantment can in itself be viewed as problematic, but many writers have shown historically that it can also be carried out with decorum. A number of works do engage with what I have termed 'negative enchantment', where a chief element of the work is to connect enchantment with traumatic events. The two main strategies I have described here are the juxtaposition of trauma and enchantment, and the capture of a particular form of enchantment in what the traumatic events reveal. The first of these strategies is easy to identify, in particular in works that refer to supernatural phenomena. But the more secular types of enchantment, too, as presented by Landy and Saler (2009) – the fascination of art, literature, and sport – work to make the chronicles of traumatic events more complicated, or to portray them against a different, more optimistic background.

It can be more difficult to argue for the enchanting character of the traumatic events themselves. But as I have argued here, there is a remarkable emphasis on such coherence in Bolaño's and Okri's work – whether in the form of the unlikely connections in Bolaño's *2666*, which raise history and capitalism to a higher level, or the belief in universalism against the background of the exploitation of Africa, as conjured by Okri. Negative enchantment is seemingly an oxymoron; but, as is so often the case, it is in the exploration of paradoxes that literature's capacity to enable complex sense-making comes to the fore – even if we may not like the feelings awoken by our fascinations.

Works cited

Bolaño, Roberto. 2008. *2666*. Trans. Natasha Wimmer. New York: Farrar, Strauss and Giroux.

Díaz, Junot. 2007. *The Brief Wondrous Life of Oscar Wao*. New York: Riverhead.

Foucault, Michel. 1970. *The Order of Things: An Archaeology of the Human Sciences*. London: Routledge.

Frye, Northrop. 2000. *Anatomy of Criticism*. London: Penguin.

Hardt, Michael and Antonio Negri. 2000. *Empire*. Cambridge, MA: Harvard University Press.

Jameson, Fredric. 2011. 'Cosmic Neutrality'. *London Review of Books* 33(20): 17–18. Available at: https://www.lrb.co.uk/v33/n20/fredric-jameson/cosmic-neutrality (Accessed 13 August 2018).

Landy, Joshua and Michael Saler. 2009. *The Re-Enchantment of the World: Secular Magic in a Rational Age*. Stanford, CA: Stanford University Press.

Lukács, Georg. 1971. *The Theory of the Novel: A Historico-Philosophical Essay on the Forms of Great Epic Literature*. Trans. Anna Bostock. London: Merlin Press.

Mo Yan. 2001. *Shifu, You'll Do Anything for a Laugh*. Trans. Howard Goldblatt. New York: Arcade.

Mo Yan. 2006. *Life and Death are Wearing Me Out*. Trans. Howard Goldblatt. New York: Arcade.

Okri, Ben. 2007. *Starbook: A Magical Tale of Love and Regeneration*. London: Rider.

Okri, Ben. 2017. 'Grenfell Tower, June, 2017, A Poem.' *Financial Times* 23 July. Available at: https://www.ft.com/content/39022f72-5742-11e7-80b6-9bfa4c1f83d2 (Accessed 13 August 2018).

Pynchon, Thomas. 1973. *Gravity's Rainbow*. New York: Viking.

Schwarz, Daniel R. 1999. *Imagining the Holocaust*. New York: St Martin's Press.

Thomsen, Mads Rosendahl. 2008. *Mapping World Literature: International Canonization and Transnational Literatures*. London: Bloomsbury/Continuum.

Thomsen, Mads Rosendahl. 2013. *The New Human in Literature: Posthuman Visions of Changes in Body, Mind and Society after 1900*. London: Bloomsbury.

Woolf, Virginia. 2002. *Moments of Being*. London: Pimlico.

INDEX

For Product Safety Concerns and Information please contact our EU
representative GPSR@taylorandfrancis.com
Taylor & Francis Verlag GmbH, Kaufingerstraße 24, 80331 München, Germany

www.ingramcontent.com/pod-product-compliance
Lightning Source LLC
Chambersburg PA
CBHW071410100726
47908CB00004B/1123